'Truly remarkable reporting, opening a window into one of the planet's most important places, and the people who live out their lives amidst its riches. It will complicate your view of the world, which is usually a useful thing'
Bill McKibben, author of *The End of Nature*

'Bursting with wild clashes of human values and exposing profound greed, corruption, violence, courage, survival and the everyday contradictions within us all, this book offers us a new understanding of Western society's relationship to earth and to other cultures. A must-read, simultaneously heartbreaking and heart-filling'
Susan Southard, author of *Nagasaki*

'Alex Cuadros spent years culturally embedded with the Cinta Larga, and tells their tragic but exciting story. He achieves the remarkable feat of understanding and sympathising with both sides' attitudes, cultures and motives, with a vibrant cast of real people'
John Hemming, author of *The Conquest of the Incas* and co-founder of Survival International

'An unusually authentic and intimate account of a disappearing wilderness and its Indigenous people. Superbly written, it deserves widespread attention, and seems destined to become a modern classic of literary non-fiction'
Jon Lee Anderson, *New Yorker* staff writer and author of *Che Guevara*

WHEN
WE SOLD
GOD'S
EYE

WHEN WE SOLD GOD'S EYE

DIAMONDS, MURDER
AND A CLASH OF WORLDS
IN THE AMAZON

ALEX CUADROS

WEIDENFELD & NICOLSON

First published in the United States of America in 2024 by Grand Central Publishing,
a division of Hachette Book Group, Inc.
First published in Great Britain in 2024 by Weidenfeld & Nicolson,
an imprint of The Orion Publishing Group Ltd
Carmelite House, 50 Victoria Embankment
London EC4Y 0DZ

An Hachette UK Company

The authorised representative in the EEA is Hachette Ireland, 8 Castlecourt Centre,
Castleknock Road, Castleknock, Dublin 15, D15 XTP3, Republic of Ireland
(email: info@hbgi.ie)

10 9 8 7 6 5 4 3 2 1

ISBN (Hardback) 978 1 3996 2889 1
ISBN (Export Trade Paperback) 978 1 3996 2890 7
ISBN (Ebook) 978 1 3996 2892 1
ISBN (Audio) 978 1 3996 2893 8

Typeset by Input Data Services Ltd, Bridgwater, Somerset

Printed in Great Britain by Clays Ltd, Elcograf, S.p.A.

www.weidenfeldandnicolson.co.uk
www.orionbooks.co.uk

For my parents

CONTENTS

Prologue...1

PART ONE: THE TIME OF CONTACT

1. A New Kind of Yearning 7

2. The Indian Protection Service 20

3. What the Elders Couldn't Explain.....................33

4. Raul's Men..41

5. Idealists...52

6. The Feast...57

7. Gravedigger...67

8. Revenge and Forgiveness..................................74

9. A Kidnapping...87

10. Into the World...95

PART TWO: THE TIME OF HARDWOOD

11. Chiefs.. 101

12. Poor People 115

13. Encounters with the Bureaucracy 124

14. Unity and Betrayal 131

15. "Who Wants to Be Civilized?"........................ 146

PART THREE: THE TIME OF DIAMONDS

16. Old Luca 155

17. The Stream of the Blackflies 163

18. A Small Operation... 172

19. The Rush 183

20. Losing Control 195

21. Negotiations 206

22. Bodies.. 218

23. Investigations 230

24. The Crazy One.. 240

25. April 7 257

Epilogue.. 268

Acknowledgments 283

Notes on Sources 285

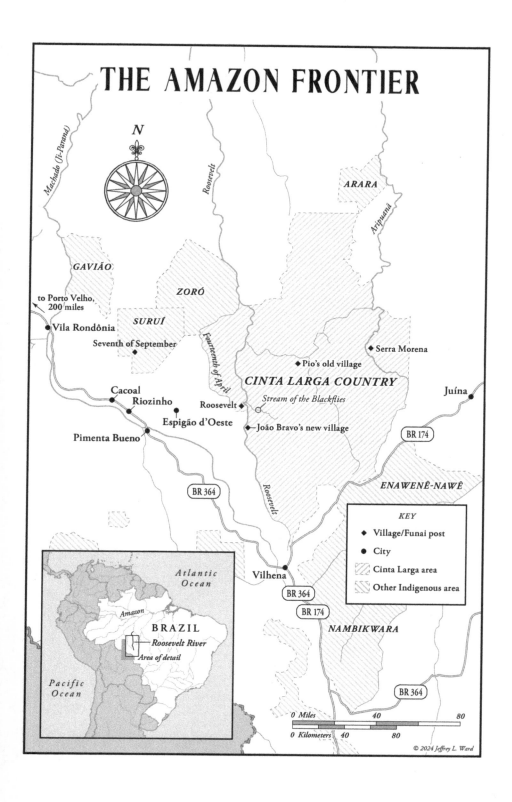

THE AMAZON FRONTIER

N

Machado (Ji-Paraná)

Roosevelt

ARARA

Aripuanã

GAVIÃO

ZORÓ

to Porto Velho,
200 miles

● Vila Rondônia

SURUÍ

◆ Seventh of September

Fourteenth of April

◆ Serra Morena

◆ Pio's old village

CINTA LARGA COUNTRY

Stream of the Blackflies

Juína ●

● Cacoal
Riozinho ◆

◆ Roosevelt

Espigão d'Oeste

◆ João Bravo's new village

● Pimenta Bueno

BR 174

BR 364

Roosevelt

ENAWENÊ-NAWÊ

*Atlantic
Ocean*

Amazon

BRAZIL

Roosevelt River

Area of detail

*Pacific
Ocean*

Vilhena ●

KEY

◆ Village/Funai post

● City

▨ Cinta Larga area

▨ Other Indigenous area

BR 364

BR 174

NAMBIKWARA

0 Miles   40   80

0 Kilometers   40   80

BR 364

© 2024 Jeffrey L. Ward

PROLOGUE

NOVEMBER 9, 2023—VILHENA, BRAZIL

Nacoça Pio Cinta Larga limped across the courtroom, using one hand to steady himself on a table. In the air-conditioned chill and fluorescent glare, his crown of black and brown feathers shuddered with each step, a lonely reminder of the rainforest beyond the white-painted walls. A Brazilian flag hung limply in one corner, the national motto, "Order and Progress," concealed in its folds. "The prosecution says that, on April 7, 2004, around 11 a.m. in the Gully of Tranquility, you, sir, together with other members of your tribe, took the lives of several prospectors," Judge Rafael Slomp began.

Pale even for a white man, Slomp wore a pink button-up beneath his robes. His goatee was immaculately trimmed, his tone bland, emotionless, entirely mismatched to the crimes he was describing. He listed twenty-nine victims, twelve never identified: "a massacre." Hands tied, they'd been unable to defend themselves, he said, an aggravating factor. "The prosecution also alleges a base motive," he went on. "That the Indigenous people who committed these acts wanted to keep anyone else from mining diamonds on their lands." Greed, in other words.

Pio looked back at Slomp through wire-rimmed glasses, his right eyelid half-drooped, half-hiding a prosthetic eye. When he thought back to the first time he saw a diamond, he shook his head with dis-belief. It was probably 1972, not that he had any notion of dates back then. His people had never known calendars or clocks. Nor did they consider any stone precious. There was no such thing as money, no such thing as a market or even trade, really. As Pio put it, "When we wanted something, nuts or honey or fruit, we would go look for it in the forest."

Back then the forest was still whole, with giant mahogany and cherrywood and pink-flowered *ipê* forming a ceiling so dense, only the odd stab of light reached the ground. The canopy petered out at the Roosevelt, which Pio had always known as the River of Rapids, though there was a calm eddy by the bank where he liked to bathe. That day he tromped through the tangle of riverside bush to find a raft made of two tree trunks split by fire, with an awning of dried palm fronds. A white man rotated a metal wheel on the deck. The man must have heard of the Cinta Larga, notorious cannibals. Yet while Pio carried a bow and a bundle of arrows, he hardly cut an intimidating figure. Not quite adolescent, he wore nothing but flip-flops and overlarge underwear, the waistband rolled down to hug his narrow hips. "Hey, kid," the man said. "Turn this for me. I'm going to roll a cigarette and take a piss."

Another Cinta Larga might have been more cautious. By now they all knew about the white men's guns, about their poison. But the con-traption piqued Pio's curiosity. A tube poked into the water, faintly tugging this way and that, interrupting the ripples of sky on the river's surface. Taking the man's place, he listened to the metallic creak, a new note in the forest racket of birdsong and shrieking monkeys. He had no idea he was pumping air to a diver. He was, in his own words, "a proper Indian—raw, raw, raw." When blackflies started stinging his legs, he let go to swat at them.

The man was on his way back when he saw the wheel sitting idle.

He broke into a run, shouting something Pio couldn't understand, finally grabbing it and cranking furiously. Eventually a kind of huge copper egg emerged from the water—an old-fashioned diver's helmet, with little portholes on the front and sides. Then a humanoid body with a loose-hanging, jet-black skin—a rubber diving dress.

At first Pio thought the diver might be a *pawô*. He'd grown up hearing about these beings who whistled from the trees, shapeshifters who tricked you into following them. Everyone knew you shouldn't go outside alone if you woke in the dark to urinate. A *pawô* might lead you around all night and safely return you home, but it also might strangle you to death, or if you were a woman, have its way with you. No sense trying to kill it. People told of a *pawô* who appeared one night lounging on the crossbeam of a longhouse. A man shot three arrows into it and dragged the corpse outside. In the morning he saw blood on his arrowheads, so he knew it hadn't been a dream. But the *pawô*'s body had disappeared.

When the diver removed his helmet, Pio could see he was just a man. He watched as the man emptied a sack of muddy gravel into a sieve. His partner tossed away a few large rocks and briefly submerged the sieve, lifting and whirling to rinse the sand out. Then he delicately combed through the fisheye-size stones that remained. When he found nothing of interest, the process repeated. Pio didn't understand the point of any of this, but when the men invited him to help, he was, again, too intrigued to resist. He even camped with them for a few days, studying their methods. Finally the moment came when he noticed an offbeat glint in the gravel. It was a crystal of carbon, stained by traces of boron—a blue diamond—one of the priciest of precious stones.

Judge Slomp looked at Pio over an open laptop. Seated in an expensive-looking office chair, he almost seemed to be presiding over a conference room. All of the lawyers, too, were white, in suits and ties.

Following the script, Slomp continued, "I would like to know, sir, if this accusation against you is true or false."

Pio sat with his hands on his jeans. He could hardly deny the part about the diamonds; the Federal Police had tapped his phones. They knew he was involved in the Stream of the Blackflies, an operation said to be worth $20 million a month, frequented by smugglers from Antwerp, Tel Aviv, and New York City's Diamond District. In the press, Pio had been labeled a "diamond baron," rumored to own three mansions and a fleet of imported trucks with white chauffeurs. Some of this, he conceded, was true, at least for a time. But he would always insist he'd tried to *stop* the massacre. With the unshakable calm that had always been his quality, he responded simply, "False."

As for the question of greed, Pio would be left to ponder: Was it greedy to desire the things he'd been taught to desire by white men standing in for fathers?

PART 1

THE TIME OF CONTACT

1960s–1970s

CHAPTER 1

A NEW KIND OF YEARNING

Pio could never forget the first time he saw a white person. He thought of that time as "when we were still wild." He was perhaps six years old, accompanying his father on a trip to an uncle's village. In those days, footpaths were marked only by the occasional broken twig or twisted leaf. Already Pio knew how to tread lightly with bare feet. Left to roam unsupervised, he'd learned about the inch-long bullet ants that hauled nectar down from the treetops, whose sting could leave you writhing in pain for a whole day. One kind of wasp made its nest close to the ground, under banana leaves; another attacked from above by swarming into your hair. You also had to watch out for poisonous caterpillars, pit vipers that curled around low-hanging branches, electric thunderfish and twenty-foot anacondas lurking in waterways. Jaguars mostly avoided adults but would eagerly pounce on a child. The forest's very architecture was a risk, as old trees—some wider than a person is tall, with winglike buttress roots that offered perfect hiding places—occasionally keeled over.

Of course, the forest also provided sustenance. Journeys to other villages were never just about reaching your destination. If Pio and his father spotted a beehive, they'd stop to knock it down and shovel honey into their mouths with rolled-up leaves. Each variety of bee made honey with a distinct flavor, one citrusy, another licorice-like. They would also stop to gather fruits scarcely known outside the Amazon—*dēdêna, madéa, ingá, oykap, bixâma*—as well as cacao, so sweet on its own that the Cinta Larga never thought to turn it into chocolate. There were also the berries that stained your hands purple, which outsiders knew as *açaí*; peach palm, with its soft, edible pulp; and *pasáp*, a tree whose green fronds could be woven into backpacks. Not to mention *pasáp*'s little coconuts with larva burrowed inside, which also tasted of coconut. Even in the dry season, hydration could be found in a thick woody vine that released fresh water like a faucet when sliced open.

Like every Cinta Larga boy, Pio carried a child-size bow and practiced shooting lizards and little birds with featherless arrows. He dreamed of becoming a great hunter like his father, Mankalu, but he was small even for his age. Full-size bows were six and a half feet tall, taller than Mankalu himself, and you needed muscles like his to pull the string taut. Most of all, though, you needed skill. To take down a wild pig, you had to know exactly where to strike—under its left foreleg, piercing the heart—before the whole pack of fast-moving beasts, with their long, sharp incisors, could charge you. Even a monkey could be dangerous. If your first shot didn't kill it outright, the monkey might pull the arrow from its own body and throw it back at you like a spear. Men died this way. Your bow had to feel like an extension of your body. Mankalu once took down a black panther; had he missed, he wouldn't have lived to hunt again.

A hunter's skills went beyond archery. When you needed the element of surprise, you'd construct a kind of miniature house in the forest, to become invisible to your prey. To bait a hawk, you could hang a dead snake from a vine. You also had to identify footprints in the muck of the forest floor, to single out the voice of your quarry amid the chatter of *pykpykkyp* and *keiketkyp* and *xulipkyp* birds, to whistle and wail in perfect imitation of its call. The more you could embody your prey, the better you were at hunting it.

Mankalu, like any good hunter, also knew his herbs. One plant gave off the cloying musk of a wild pig: chew it up, spit it on your hands, and rub it all over your body to disguise yourself. Another plant, a stimulant consumed as a tea, sharpened your vision to spot camouflaged birds. Others were thought to work through a kind of magical symbolism. There was a leaf that resembled the foot of a tapir, a long-snouted mammal that could weigh as much as four hundred pounds—a lumbering feast of delicious, dark meat. If you made a tea from this leaf and drank until you vomited, tapirs (the thinking went) wouldn't run from you. There were also herbs to induce dreaming, as certain dreams portended successful hunts. If a hunter dreamed about crossing a river, it was a sign he'd encounter a tapir—perhaps because these beasts like to cool themselves in shallow water. If the hunter dreamed of sex with a woman, his catch would be female; if he dreamed of sex with a man, it would be male. If he dreamed about picking parasitic larva from his feet, he'd encounter a harpy eagle, because (according to Cinta Larga dream logic) this recalled the majestic raptor's talons.

Pio's uncle lived a few days' walk away, but that was nothing for a Cinta Larga. People took every excuse to visit far-flung relatives, whether for a grand Feast of the Pig or to trade news of marriages. In Western terms, their territory stretched perhaps eighty miles from east to west, 130 miles from north to south, but even without maps they held all of it in their heads, guiding themselves by the waterways, the direction of the sun, and when it shone through a clearing at night, the Milky Way, which they called the Right Way. In the absence of any form of writing, waterways also served as markers for important events, great hunts and battles, though they often had different names depending on what part of the territory you lived in.

For Pio, the journey was a rare chance to learn, almost by osmosis, how to be a man like his father. Mankalu wasn't very affectionate. Unlike other adults, he never joked around. "If my father was in a dark hut," Pio recalled, "you would think nobody was inside, because he wasn't the type to have a conversation." Pio didn't admire him any less: "Back when we lived in the forest, someone who knew how to make a well-crafted arrow, using the hairs of a wild pig—that was like a diploma for us. And my father had a doctorate in arrow-making." The shaft was a light bamboo, stabilized in flight by multihued feathers. The arrowhead was a harder bamboo, traditionally sharpened with the tooth of the agouti, a long-legged rodent. Each man left a signature in the form of geometric designs, instantly recognizable to others, when he stitched the two pieces together. Different sizes and shapes were used to target different animals; always the artistry was key. Mankalu, though, never taught his methods. Pio was left to figure it out on his own, and his own arrows always came out "ugly." Observing a cousin whose father made beautiful arrows for him, he'd think, *I want that, too!*

Reaching the so-called Roaring River, Mankalu led his son across a footbridge of lashed-together branches, using a vine as a handrail. They announced themselves with the trilling of panpipes, and Pio's uncle rushed to string up hammocks for the customary exchange of greetings in improvised song: *"He has traveled here and all is well…"* These visits, like the journeys themselves, were never hurried. One morning Pio and his uncle were crouched on the riverbank, drinking water from cupped hands, when they heard a thundering crack like an enormous branch breaking. And then another, and another. Upriver, just visible in the distance, some kind of craft was crossing under the footbridge. Because the Cinta Larga never developed the canoe, boats were alien to them—and this boat was loud, propelled by an outboard motor. Pio ran back to his uncle's village, looking for his father, but couldn't find him. Terrified as he was, though, he wanted to know about the outsiders. Returning to the riverbank, he hid himself in the foliage to watch as they floated by.

* * *

Pio had heard about the outsiders. At the time the Cinta Larga didn't think of them as "white people" but as *mokopey*, roughly "those who cover themselves," a reference to their clothes. This was another alien concept, though Pio's people did adorn themselves. They got their Portuguese name thanks to the *cinta larga*, or wide belt, traditionally worn by men. Made from the inner bark of the towering *wabép* tree, it was tied so tight with string that your flesh pushed over the edge with each breath. But it was meant for protection in battle, not against the elements, much less for modesty. Men felt naked only if they lacked their penis-sheath of straw, and among women the concept of nudity didn't exist at all. "Men would look and see who had a large vulva, who had a small one," chief João Bravo would recall. "I'm not lying. We weren't ashamed."

Lacking the language for Western clothing, the Cinta Larga called it a "skin." Some speculated the outsiders weren't even human: with their freakish height and hairy faces, perhaps a new species of monkey? Others said they must be *pawoy*, those mythical shapeshifters. Whatever their nature, the outsiders were known to be dangerous. They'd been spotted roaming the forest, searching for the trees that bled milky-white. First they made a diagonal gash in the bark, leaving a cup to collect the liquid. Later they dried this substance over a fire, molding it into a bar as thick black smoke rose into the canopy. Indigenous people had collected latex for thousands of years, using it to make balls for ritual sport in what is now Mexico. The Cinta Larga knew of the stuff from their neighbors to the east, the Enawenê-Nawê, whose women wore tight rubber rings to swell their calves, a mark of beauty. At the time, though, they couldn't imagine what these outsiders were doing with it—that it could be traded for valuable paper and transformed into all manner of goods.

The Cinta Larga would always maintain that, when meeting a stranger, they came in peace—at least at first—cautiously offering the greeting *pa ikinin pa mã*: "Let's have a look at one another." In response, the rubber tappers simply opened fire. In one encounter, a Cinta Larga warrior took a bullet to the knee, leaving him unable to retreat, and when his comrades went back to rescue him, they found his body cut to pieces and thrown on a grill. For years afterward, they believed that the clothes-wearers devoured their enemies. Only later would they revise this impression: the outsiders planned to feed the corpse to their dogs.

There was a girl from another village, Mabeuíti, who would come to be known as Maria Beleza—Maria the Beauty. Her grandparents used to have premonitions. Someday, they told her, you will live among the outsiders, you will speak their language, and you will even cover yourself like they do. They failed to foresee more imminent dangers. One day when the men were off hunting, Maria and the other children were taking turns on a rope swing, launching themselves into the river, when suddenly Maria heard that same branch-breaking crack, deafeningly close. She saw the outsiders with their strange second skin, hair peeking from every gap. The sound repeated in rapid fire, and the children toppled over. Maria played dead while the outsiders went after the women with machetes. They set fire to the longhouse before disappearing back into the trees.

When Maria tried to lift herself, she felt she couldn't move. The next thing she knew, she was waking up, and realized she'd fainted. Seven of her friends had been killed. Her grandmother had also been killed, along with several other adults. Little wonder that the Cinta Larga came up with another word for the outsiders: *dayap*, an onomatopoeia for a gunshot.

When the boat passed by Pio's hiding place on the riverbank, he couldn't help feeling fascinated by the sight of the weapons pointed right over his head. He figured the outsiders had noticed the footbridge and fired to scare off any Indians. But it didn't work. When Pio's father returned to the village, Pio and his uncle told him what they'd seen, and Mankalu plunged into the forest right away.

*   *   *

More than a great hunter, Pio's father was a great warrior. His full name was Mankalueey Akat, literally "killer of the Mankalu," a neighboring Indigenous group he was said to have wiped out in battle. Not that you could say it to his face. It was taboo to utter someone's name in their presence. In later years, no one could quite explain why, but back then, anyway, you hardly needed names. The Cinta Larga numbered between one and two thousand, scattered among a couple dozen villages. Lacking numbers above twenty, they had no way to count their population, but they could easily rattle off the intricate family connections, whose grandfather wedded whose granddaughter, how many children they had, who was widowed and remarried, the various overlapping webs of in-laws and brotherhood. Among the Cinta Larga themselves, there was no such thing as a stranger: family was society.

In those days they didn't actually think of themselves as a unified tribe. Sometimes they used generic words like *panderey*, which simply means "us" or "our people." Other times they described themselves as *matpetamãy*, "experts with the bow." But they lacked a name for their group as a whole. They had no central authority, no chief. They were merely a smattering of bloodlines who spoke the same language, traded wives, and saw one another as human.

The way Pio's elders told it, their three main lineages descended from a divine mingling with the plant world. Ngurá, the Creator, had grown lonely without a family, walking by himself in the forest. He found a beautiful rock, and made the rock his wife, and a son emerged like a bird hatching from an egg. His son produced a grandson, also named Ngurá, who would bring human beings into existence, though not without some false starts. First he tried copulating with a hole in the ground, but nothing happened. Eventually he found a *kaban* tree, whose flowers eject stamens that resemble shooting stars. Like the agouti, that long-legged rodent, Ngurá made a hole in the shell of the *kaban*'s sweet, white fruit. But instead of eating the fruit, he made love to it, and five days later a son was born—the first member of the Kaban lineage. Ngurá did the same with the yellow nut of the *kakin* vine, creating the Kakin lineage, and then once more with the pod of the Brazil nut tree, *maam*—which was Pio's lineage.

Remarkably, for such a small group, the Cinta Larga divided themselves even further based on whether they lived closer to the headwaters (making them *paabit*), near the middle (*paabir*), or farther downstream (*paaepit*). But war, if nothing else, united them. To the south they fought the Nambikwara, with their ash-stained bodies. To the north they fought the Zoró, with their arrowheads that whistled. To the west their rivals were the tattoo-faced Suruí; to the east, not only the Enawenê-Nawê but the Rikbaktsa, who covered their crotches with straw. In border areas where prized resources grew—particular varieties of bamboo or thatch, say—chance encounters inevitably sparked conflict. There was no diplomacy, no trade. "The Cinta Larga never had any friends," another man of Pio's generation, Roberto Carlos, would explain.

Being a man was synonymous with being a warrior. Every boy trained for it. João Bravo's father taught him to zigzag by shooting arrows at him; the arrows lacked the usual sharp point but could still break your skin. In war, the Cinta Larga made no effort to be sporting. Though they didn't shy from spontaneous skirmishes, ambush was the preferred form of engagement. Sometimes they sneaked into enemy territory and hid in the trees until dark. One by one, they'd tiptoe into their enemies' longhouse and take up positions by hammocks, holding three-foot clubs of heavy black wood. Then, when someone gave the signal, they would beat their sleeping enemies to death. It was a risky maneuver, but in Roberto's words, "We were never afraid. We all knew we were going to die one day."

Foreign women could be integrated into Cinta Larga society; Mankalu himself had married a Zoró girl captured by an ally. The men, though, were never spared. "When an enemy group killed one of ours, we would kill *all* of theirs," another of Pio's cohorts, Oita Matina, would recall. "The Arara—there are hardly any Arara left anymore, thanks to us. The Zoró were terrified of us. And the Suruí? When the Suruí showed up, we were monsters....The Cinta Larga were the wildest Indians of all." After a raid, they'd burn the village to the ground.

If the Cinta Larga believed the clothes-wearers to be cannibals, it was partly because they, too, consumed their enemies' bodies. Though taboo within their own group, it was actually how they divided the world into "us" and "them." Other groups were scarcely considered human. Before battle, Mankalu and his fellow warriors would sing songs in which their enemies were monkeys or tapirs: defenseless prey. Afterward, as João Bravo would describe it: "The bodies are cut into pieces and put on a grill to be cooked, including the decapitated head....The warriors shave their heads and paint themselves with red *urucum*"—a shrub whose spiny seed pods yield a red dye—"to look like the king vulture. Once everything is ready, the banquet begins with the warriors imitating the sounds and movements of the king vulture eating its carrion."

Not everyone partook in the ritual. Eating human flesh was believed to cause seizures in children, and new parents had to steer clear to avoid harming their babies. The warriors, though, ate everything, even breaking the bones to suck the marrow. The anthropologist João Dal Poz later asked people why they did it. He heard a simple answer: *Zokópa té*—because they were angry. And what did it taste like? Some compared it to the dark, delicious meat of the tapir. White men's flesh, on the other hand, was far too salty.

* * *

Ordinarily Mankalu would have organized a feast to summon other villages for a battle. With the intruders already headed downriver, he had no time for this. But he knew he'd find a willing companion for war in João Bravo, who'd lost his wife, Maria Beleza's grandmother, in the massacre. João saw the interlopers as a kind of hybrid entity, "*pawô*-people with evil hearts." Not that he was afraid to go after them. On the contrary, he was bound by the tradition of *wepíka*, which translates roughly as "revenge," only with a sense of obligation, as with a debt that must be zeroed out. Over the years he would become, as he sometimes bragged, a prolific killer of white men.

Yet there was another, possibly even more compelling reason to go after the outsiders. Some years earlier, in the southern reaches of their territory, a group of warriors was campaigning against the Nambkiwara when they came upon a wide swath of flattened vegetation that stretched as far as the eye could see in either direction. In the middle, tall wooden posts poked up at regular intervals, linked crown to crown with a kind of heavy string—a telegraph line. The stations were manned by what the government called "civilized" Nambikwara, but because they wore clothes, the Cinta Larga saw them only as *mokopey*, indistinguishable from rubber tappers.

In one encounter, Nambikwara workers were at the station known as Vilhena when, as a government report described it, "to everyone's surprise, a group of approximately twenty Indians, including one female, showed up walking calmly along the trail of the telegraph line." At first the meeting was friendly. The two groups embraced and attempted to make conversation, even without a common language. Then, amid the confused, excited babble, a gun accidentally went off, and "in a fraction of a second everything changed....An arrow [came] like a lightning bolt, mortally wounding the citizen known as Parazão, who fell almost lifeless to the ground, receiving immediately afterward five more arrows." Another worker was struck in the arm; a woman took an arrow to the eye. One of the warriors was about to fire an arrow at the worker's son, until one of the Nambikwara cut his bowstring with a knife. The report made no mention of Cinta Larga casualties, but one warrior was shot in the face. Somehow he survived and made it back home, where he earned the nickname "eye of *pawô*."

The battle marked the start of a long war. Another report detailed the aftermath of a Cinta Larga victory: "The house that [the Nambikwara] had built was burned down, and the posts of the telegraph line were knocked over with machetes belonging to the guards." For a Westerner, it would be easy to gloss over the detail about the machetes. But for the Cinta Larga, it was nothing less than a paradigm shift. According to lore, it was in these battles that they first discovered *ndabe*—metal tools.

The first time he saw a steel axe put to use, Pio's friend Tataré gaped with wonder as two men chopped down a towering Brazil nut tree in perhaps forty minutes, allowing them to collect the pods that fell naturally just once a year. Suddenly, the most arduous of tasks—clearing fields, building huts—required a fraction of the labor. Machetes proved stronger and more durable than sticks for digging up earth to plant crops. Knives sliced almost magically through meat or hard vines. Metal pots were lighter, more durable, and quicker to heat and cool than the traditional ones of clay. On top of all that, a long, sharp blade was deadlier than a wooden club in a sneak attack on a sleeping enemy.

The warriors made other curious discoveries. After one battle, they returned with the head and tail of "a different kind of tapir"—a mule—which they presented to their wives. They also plundered the stiff, strong telegraph wire, which could be used to craft arrowheads with internal stitching, making them more stable in midair. Women, meanwhile, used the wire to punch holes in beads, and incorporated metal nuts and washers into their necklaces. People spoke of a new kind of yearning: *ndabe-kala*—the desire for metal tools.

The Cinta Larga were far from alone in assimilating Western goods even before they knew the Western world. In New Guinea in 1951, an Australian patrol officer became the first white person to meet the Baruya people but found they'd already acquired steel axes and machetes by trading salt with other, less isolated groups. Similarly, when missionaries reached the Yanomami, on the border between Brazil and Venezuela, around the same time, they noticed plots of bananas and plantains, crops imported to South America by Europeans. The Cinta Larga, for their part, raised chickens, another foreign species. The practice began when they pillaged some from an enemy village; how these enemies got chickens to begin with, no one knows.

When Mankalu returned from his assault on the interlopers, he brought stories of a bloody clash. Even with the element of surprise, he and his fellow warriors had been forced to retreat by those fearsome weapons. But it wouldn't be his last attempt to plunder *ndabe*. Just about every dry season, Pio would watch as his father set off with a war party carrying whole baskets full of arrows. Weeks or even months later, they would return with baskets empty, the odd blade glinting from their belts of bark.

The problem was that a blade never lasted long. In the world of the Cinta Larga, nobody "owned" these tools. When you finished using one, you simply dropped it on the ground for somebody else to pick up later. Shared among a whole village, an axe head could wane to half its original size. People might try sharpening it with a rock, but they lacked proper whetstones or honing rods. Because of this, they saw these objects like bamboo or straw, natural resources to be used up only for the forest to replenish later. And so Mankalu set off on another campaign, and another.

CHAPTER 2

THE INDIAN PROTECTION SERVICE

Apoena Meirelles was only twenty the first time he made contact with a so-called *silvícola*, a "jungle-dweller," someone still unfamiliar with Western society. It was July 16, 1969, the same day that NASA's Apollo 11 took off for the moon. As part of Operation Cinta Larga, he'd already spent ten months dealing with eye-licker wasps, mosquitoes that thickened into clouds at dawn and dusk, bouts of malaria, fungal infections—all the difficulties that made outsiders think of the Amazon as a "green hell." Not to mention the boredom of days-long downpours, though you could never really relax. Alcohol was forbidden. It was too risky to hunt, so the only meat came in tins. Payroll almost always came late, and when it did, a few workers would quit to try their luck as prospectors, leaving everyone else to pick up the slack. Apoena also complained that, "after two months in the bush, we young men suffer horribly for lack of a woman."

Just to reach the camp was an undertaking. First Apoena flew from the coastal metropolis of Rio de Janeiro to the boomtown of Porto Velho, smack in the middle of the South American continent. Then he drove three hundred miles down the BR-364, which clung to the telegraph line that the Cinta Larga liked to raid—the first highway ever to penetrate the southern reaches of the Amazon. Built in 1960, it remained unpaved, a ribbon of blood-brown dirt in an endless dark green canopy. At the height of the rainy season, December to March, truck ruts deepened into mud-logged ravines, stranding vehicles for days or even weeks. Now, in the dry season, the ruts hardened, and passengers were thrown violently up and down, side to side, without cease. Bumping along in a government truck, Apoena would see a cloud of orange dust on the horizon, expanding as it approached, and then as it passed, a bus full of tired faces peering back through dust-pasted windows. Or an old flatbed with men, women, and children huddled together in the searing sun—settlers who'd heard the propaganda about a "land without people for people without land," and hoped to eke out a living on the frontier.

In those days of political upheaval, Apoena fancied himself a left-wing radical—and with his wiry frame, long, curly hair, and wispy beard, he looked the part. In Rio he'd been arrested twice for marching against the military dictatorship. He knew how wrong the government propaganda was. Even before the first Portuguese ships landed on Brazil's shore in 1500, as many as twenty million people already lived in the rainforest. Humans are thought to have arrived in South America some ten thousand years ago, spreading first along the Andes Mountains and then, five thousand years ago, into the Amazon Basin. Some societies grew shockingly large, though they left few obvious traces: mounds of pottery shards, elaborate roadways since reclaimed by jungle, peach-palm orchards woven into the forest itself. Often settlement was so dense that it left behind "black earth," a rich soil formed by the centuries-long accumulation of ash, ceramics, and human feces.

As a kid, Apoena had been taught to venerate the Brazilian pioneers known as *bandeirantes*, or flag-bearers, who made their name in the 1600s. Many others tried and failed to penetrate the rainforest on foot, but the *bandeirantes* raked through in boats, raiding villages and killing the inhabitants as if they were "boar or deer," in one observer's words. They enslaved hundreds of thousands of the people they called Indians. Jesuit missionaries tried to save the Indians—or at least their souls—but only hastened their extermination, as the survivors were gathered into settlements where previously unknown diseases flourished. Their children went on to mix with European colonists and African slaves, gradually coming to think of themselves simply as "Brazilian." By the 1960s, of the two hundred thousand Indigenous people left in Brazil, almost all of them had some degree of contact with national society. But a few didn't.

The Amazon is the world's largest rainforest, nearly as large as the contiguous United States, nurtured by a labyrinth of one thousand rivers. Some are born at 21,000 feet, with seasonal melts from the Sajama ice cap in Bolivia. Others are born in the dark rock of Peru's Apacheta cliff, where glacial seepage sprays white from its pores. Most are just tributaries of tributaries, headwaters for much larger rivers—the Caquetá, the Madre de Dios, the Iriri, the Tapajós—any of which, on its own, would already be among the largest rivers in the world. Wide and placid, these waterways are easy to navigate. But there are also rivers born in Brazil's high plains and savannas, strangled into whitewater gorges that no *bandeirante* could hope to overcome. It was on their banks that the Tupi people, during a long-ago expansion to the Atlantic coast, left behind a branch known as the Tupi-Mondé, who in turn splintered into the Cinta Larga, the Suruí, the Zoró, and a few other small groups.

A thousand miles from Brazil's populous coast, this region stayed mostly undisturbed until 1907, when a young military officer named Cândido Rondon was tasked with building the telegraph line. Rondon, a great hero of Apoena's, was nothing like the reactionary generals now in charge of Brazil. Nor did he fit the usual profile of Western explorers. For one thing, he was himself of largely Indigenous descent. Even more remarkable, he dedicated his life to the Enlightenment principle of universal human rights at a time when most Brazilians agreed with Theodore Roosevelt: "I don't go so far as to think that the only good Indians are the dead Indians, but…nine out of every ten are." Entering the lands of so-called *indios bravos*—"wild Indians"—Rondon often came under arrow fire. But he insisted his men never respond in kind: "Die if you must, but never kill." Instead he offered gifts: mirrors, colorful beads, and—most appealing of all—metal tools. Always respectful of "our brothers from the jungle," he made friends with groups considered irredeemably hostile, like the Nambikwara, whom he persuaded to man the telegraph stations.

Rondon's best-known expedition set off in 1913, and among its members was none other than Roosevelt himself, who'd come to Brazil for adventure after losing his run for a third term as president. The goal was to descend an uncharted waterway Rondon called the River of Doubt, because he didn't know where it emptied. Just to reach its source took two months, first by steamboat up the Paraguay River, then up one of its tributaries, and finally by muleback for four hundred miles through swamp, scrub, savanna, and jungle. The river started out placid, a dark mirror of the sky, meandering to the point of seeming directionless. Roosevelt calmly watched the butterflies, the blue-and-gold macaws, and the many palms, "towering and slender, their stems a stately colonnade, their fronds an arched fretwork against the sky." But the men soon came upon the first of the rocky gorges where the water churned furious-white. They had no choice but to spend two and a half days lugging their heavy wooden dugouts, laden with supplies, through forest Rondon described as "monstrously fecund."

"We were bitten by huge horse-flies, the size of bumblebees,"

Roosevelt wrote. "More serious annoyance was caused by the pium and boroshuda flies during the hours of daylight, and by the polvora, the sand-flies, after dark....The boroshudas [blackflies] were the worst pests; they brought the blood at once, and left marks that lasted for weeks." Approaching the next rapids, a canoe capsized; one man drowned, and Roosevelt's son Kermit barely swam to safety. Another man was shot to death in a dispute over rations. Roosevelt himself was nearly killed by a leg infection, and also got dysentery and malaria.

"Through sheets of blinding rain, we left our camp of misfortune for another camp where misfortune also awaited us," Roosevelt wrote. That day, Rondon took his dog Lobo into the forest to hunt. Hearing what sounded like the howl of a spider monkey, the dog rushed into the trees, and Rondon heard yelps of pain followed by human voices—"brief exclamations, energetic and repeated in unison." Lobo came running back, wounded by two arrows. To scare off the attackers, Rondon fired his shotgun into the air. Still hearing the voices, he fired again. But he couldn't risk a confrontation, so he retreated back to camp. Returning later with a few other men, he found Lobo dead. The arrows featured a serrated bamboo point unlike any Rondon had seen—confirmation, in his mind, that this group was still unknown to the West. He laid out axe heads and colorful beads as gifts.

Though the people never revealed themselves, they allowed the outsiders to continue in peace. Rondon renamed the river for his American guest.

*   *   *

At the time of Apoena's journey, the Wyoming-size territory of Rondônia, named in Rondon's honor, was still almost entirely covered by rainforest. But that was changing fast. On either side of Highway 364, trunks lay scattered like a game of pickup sticks. It was

September, the height of the dry season, when settlers took advantage of the weather to clear fields with fire. Not only was this method cheap; the ash also served as fertilizer for coffee, corn, and grass for grazing cattle. It was all part of a national project, a belated echo of Manifest Destiny, which had sent American settlers westward—to finally conquer the Amazon with highways and agriculture. Just in the past decade, Rondônia's population had doubled, nearing 120,000. Many were blond and blue-eyed, from Brazil's South, intensely populated by German immigrants.

Halfway to his destination, Apoena passed through the settlement of Vila Rondônia, which had sprouted from a telegraph station. The journalist Lilian Newlands described the "haze of dust and torpor" of the dry season, when the sun beat down so relentlessly that zinc roofs would swell and break in the heat. Many observers compared the region to the American Wild West. "Everyone went around visibly armed," wrote Newlands. There was, wrote another, "always the feeling that someone would fire a bullet from behind some corner....You breathed death; all people recalled was deaths—violent, brutal deaths. Ranchers who had shot Indians to death, Indians who had killed some backwoodsmen..."

Of course, permanent settlement was only part of the Amazon's allure. Brazil's original pioneers, the *bandeirantes*, were driven by a desire for precious metals and stones. Spaniards searched for the mythical city of El Dorado—literally the Golden One, a reference to an Indigenous chief rumored to cover his skin with gold dust. In Rondônia, people spoke of a similar place, Urucumacuá, said to hold enough gold to pay off Brazil's foreign debt. But they had better luck finding diamonds. In the late 1940s, a prospector known as Amiguinho (Little Friend) turned up sixty-four carats of gem-grade stones in the bed of the Machado River, which ran through Vila Rondônia.

Even as the rest of Brazil industrialized, the Amazon remained a place where fortune-seekers faced cannibalism—a source of morbid fascination since the first European arrivals to South America, and one that, more than anything else, marked Indians as "savages." When it came to the Cinta Larga, the first case was documented in July 1952, when a group of prospectors were attacked near the Roosevelt. One was killed, and the survivors claimed to have seen the victorious warriors—described as "Vulture Indians" because they painted their skin black and shaved their heads—devouring the corpse.

For the government, the raids on the telegraph line, the backbone of Highway 364, posed an even bigger problem. "The victim's body had the flesh cut from its bones," one official wrote after an attack. "The head was removed from the body and impaled on a stick...[and] both arms and one leg were never found....The attacking tribe belongs to the so-called WIDE BELTS....The government believes they are jungle-dwellers in a primitive state of barbarity." A local congressman, adding a flourish of his own, declared that the Cinta Larga "are great appreciators of human flesh, and they eat it roasted with honey."

Operation Cinta Larga was meant to put a stop to all this. Apoena's father, Francisco "Chico" Meirelles, was actually in charge. As a young man, Chico himself had been arrested for his activities in the Brazilian Communist Party. But as the son of a senator, he was allowed to join Rondon's Indian Protection Service (Serviço de Proteção ao Índio, or SPI), which sent him to remote jungles where he was unlikely to cause trouble. Like Rondon, he trained as a *sertanista*, a kind of backwoodsman with the wit, sensitivity, and courage to "pacify" hostile groups. And he became a national hero. Most famously, in the 1940s, he established the first peaceful relations with the Xavante people, bringing his family along even after two priests and his own mentor had perished in previous attempts. The Xavante called his wife Tipizari—"owner of the pots and pans," for her prodigious gift-giving. Already raising two young daughters, she gave birth to their son in a boat, while trying to reach a government outpost. He was named Apoena after a Xavante headman who was among the first to warm to them.

To scope out his latest mission, Chico had flown over the area north of Highway 364 and identified twenty-one packed-dirt clearings in the otherwise pristine canopy, each with as many as three longhouses, which he termed "cities of straw." The Brazilian press, breathlessly following his exploits, called it the largest Amazonian tribe that didn't yet know "civilization." Though no one yet distinguished between the Cinta Larga and other Tupi-Mondé groups, their total population was thought to be five thousand, spread across five million acres of rainforest. The military regime declared the whole area off-limits to outsiders so that Chico could work his magic.

Chico, despite his radical past, took care not to antagonize the settler class. Though they hardly cared about protecting the Indians, they did want the region "pacified"—and the SPI was perennially short on funds. Visiting ranchers and rubber tycoons, Chico spoke sympathetically of the "great sums" they'd lost to Indian raids, and persuaded them to pay for supplies and a few dozen laborers. He'd hoped to hire more, to amass a contingent large enough to ward off attacks, but people doubted his crew would survive. Chico already had a bad leg from a horse-riding accident, making him an attractive target.

Despite Apoena's young age, he was unusually qualified for an operation like this one. He'd grown up speaking Xavante as well as Portuguese and was only five when his father first took him on a major expedition, to the jungles of Amazonas state. He'd started working for the SPI at fifteen, informally at first, since he was a minor.

Apoena, for his part, idolized his father. But he'd grown disillusioned with the service. At sixteen he'd met a left-wing SPI agent named

Antônio Cotrim, and the two spent their days talking philosophy—and when they had time off, all night boozing at nightclubs. Reading opposition newspapers and Gorky's revolutionary parable *Mother*, Apoena came to see the SPI as a well-intentioned piece of an unjust system. Its purpose was only nominally to protect the Indians; what the government really wanted was to make their lands safe for development. In the Xavante language, *apoena* means "he who sees far." But Apoena's namesake had failed to predict what would come of his truce with the white men. Many Xavante died of disease. Many others were forced to abandon their lands to make way for cattle. Once-proud warriors ended up performing manual labor for miserable wages, sometimes earning nothing more than a meal.

The story was similar with just about every other group the SPI had contacted—the Kaingang, the Xokleng, the Nambikwara. Frustrated, Apoena quit and moved to Rio. His aim, adolescently grandiose, was to change the system itself. (Marching with Rio's students, he also learned to dance samba.) Then he was arrested, and arrested again, and his well-connected father had to bail him out. Apoena planned to go into exile in Chile, where the socialist Salvador Allende would soon become president. His father proposed a very different kind of escape: Operation Cinta Larga. Chico knew all too well what had become of the Xavante and so many other groups. Yet he also believed that no one could stop the advance of the Amazon frontier—and that, if he didn't act, many Indigenous lives would be lost along the way. "A bad deal is better than a good fight," he said.

Ultimately, what persuaded Apoena had nothing to do with political ideals. "You're my only son," Chico told him, "and I have no one else to count on to continue my work."

*   *   *

By the time Apoena arrived in Rondônia, Chico had already established their base of operations. Setting out on foot from Highway 364, he'd followed an old logging road and then an overgrown footpath used by rubber tappers before hacking a trail suitable for pack mules through forest that showed few signs of human habitation. For a Cinta Larga, this would have been a minor journey, but for Chico and his crew, it took thirty-seven days to travel seventy miles. On September 7, Brazil's Independence Day, they came upon a few old *tapiris*, shelters consisting of four stakes topped with palm fronds, of the sort that Indigenous people built for hunting trips. Naming the site for the auspicious date, Chico decided that it would be their main "attraction post."

Chico was following a tried-and-true formula from Rondon. The first phase was known as "flirtation." One of the *tapiris* showed signs of recent use: fresh ash from a campfire, strings for hanging hammocks. After laying out an assortment of machetes, knives, axes, and aluminum pots, Chico and his men cut a footpath back to camp, an invitation to visit. At night, Indigenous interpreters shouted into the forest to announce their peaceful intentions, in case the Cinta Larga spoke a similar language. Then Chico's white laborers played the guitar and the tambourine and sang and danced, hoping to send the message that they meant no harm, as he who comes silently comes to make war.

For months the Indians didn't allow themselves to be seen, but took the gifts. Sometimes they communicated their desire for a specific tool by leaving, say, two pieces of straw and two loops of string arranged like open scissors. They also left offerings of their own: arrows, baskets, headdresses of spotted-jaguar skin. "It looks like they're up for civilization," Chico said.

In December, as the rains started in earnest, with heavy sheets falling for hours at a time, Chico put Apoena in charge so he could attend his daughter's wedding. He cautioned his son not to rush the delicate dance of contact. After so many clashes, the Indians clearly remained wary. One, spotted gathering gifts, ran off when an interpreter called out to him. "This is a big responsibility, because my name is at stake," Chico told Apoena.

It was an unusually sensitive mission. Previously obscure, the Cinta Larga had recently become known to the rest of Brazil—and the world—for a horrific atrocity committed against them. The Massacre of the Eleventh Parallel was named for the latitude of a village by the Aripuanã River. In 1963, gunmen shot down half a dozen people there with automatic weapons. A woman and her five-year-old child were left standing; the woman was hung upside down and hacked in two with a machete. Then the child was shot in the head with a revolver. This was everyday stuff as far as the Amazon went. It would have gone unreported, like the massacre at Maria Beleza's village, except that one of the gunmen told a priest—whether out of guilt or anger that he wasn't paid his fifteen-dollar fee, it was never clear.

In cosmopolitan Rio de Janeiro, it was hard for middle-class readers to believe such horrors were possible. In the United States and Europe, even harder. But there was more. The military regime had been investigating the Indian Protection Service to tar the civilians who used to run it. Some SPI agents were exposed as Kurtzian figures who forced newly contacted groups to clear fields and grow crops, selling the product for their own profit and leaving little to eat for the Indigenous people themselves. A few agents colluded with local politicians and judges to sell Indigenous lands outright. Others trafficked Indigenous girls to brothels, earning the SPI an alternate name: Serviço de Prostituição de Índias, the Indian Prostitution Service.

Hoping to control the damage, the government dissolved the SPI and replaced it with the National Foundation of the Indian (Fundação

Nacional do Índio, or Funai). That didn't stop the United Nations from announcing an investigation of its own. London's *Sunday Times Magazine* emblazoned the word GENOCIDE on its cover, and the accompanying article dedicated three whole pages to reports of attacks on the Cinta Larga, including rumors that their villages were targeted with dynamite dropped from planes. This was never substantiated, but the massacres were all too real. Chico told a reporter, "I've never worked on a front like this one, where the Indians are so persecuted."

Making matters worse, local authorities were encouraging the invasions; one mayor even built a landing strip inside the area declared off-limits to outsiders. Settlers liked to say they had their own "constitution," whose only article, No. 44, referenced the caliber of a Winchester rifle. Rondônia's own governor told Chico, "We have no problems with Indians in my territory. If necessary, we can drop some *bombinhas* on them." In Portuguese, *bombinhas* can mean "little bombs" or "fireworks"—a troubling ambiguity, given the rumors of dynamite attacks.

At the Seventh of September camp, Apoena threw himself into his newfound leadership role, overseeing the construction of two large wooden buildings on stilts, clearing fields, and planting manioc, corn, and rice. At first, when he gave an order, the men would laugh at him. To win them over, he denied himself the privileges of expedition chief, eating half rations of canned food when provisions ran short. Usually a dozen men went to leave gifts at the lean-to, for strength in numbers—but Apoena would go alone to demonstrate his courage.

Apoena seemed equally motivated by his ideals as by his idealistic self-image. "To be a *sertanista* consists in a human being's devotion to the Indigenous cause, giving the maximum of oneself for others, and spending the majority of one's time by oneself," he wrote. He also scribbled this in one of his books: "What good are vanities, money, ambition, if all that will survive in the end is our life's work?"

Apoena's efforts finally paid off when, at the height of the dry season of 1969, he saw an Indian in the trees and ran after him. Alone in the half-light of the rainforest, the young man allowed Apoena to approach. Apoena was trembling with fear, but he noticed that the young man was trembling, too. Suddenly both burst into laughter. They embraced. From then on, people from the young man's village visited the Seventh of September post almost daily to exchange gifts. Apoena even learned the young man's name: Nauara. A headline in the *Estado de S. Paulo* newspaper blared: THE CINTA LARGA HAVE BEEN PACIFIED.

By now Chico had returned to share in his son's glory. Past experience led him to believe that Nauara had already passed word of their exchanges to the rest of the tribe, even after an interpreter, having once been their prisoner, identified Nauara's group as the Suruí. They, too, slung belts around their waists, but of dyed cotton rather than tree bark. Far from being a mere Cinta Larga clan, as Chico imagined, they were a separate people with their own language, not to mention mortal enemies.

CHAPTER 3

WHAT THE ELDERS COULDN'T EXPLAIN

According to his government ID card, Pio was born on January 28, 1959. But this date was made up by Brazilian bureaucrats. Pio was actually born in the dry season, which runs from June to August—when giant cicadas howl from the trees, and plunging water levels reveal the caimans in their riverbed lairs. A group of people from his village were camped out by a stream shrunk to stagnant pools. The men were beating the surface of the water with the *dakáptapóa* vine, which releases a substance that asphyxiates fish, causing them to bob to the surface, to be collected and cooked on a fire. That's when Pio's mother went into labor, walking alone into the trees to give birth.

It wasn't unusual for a mother to give birth alone, though a more experienced woman often helped, cutting the umbilical cord with a bamboo razor. Another woman might rub the baby's body with hands warmed over a fire. Otherwise, in those early days, it was as if the baby was still part of its mother's body, never apart. Year after year, though, Pio's mother had given birth only for her child to die mysteriously a couple of weeks later. No matter that she always followed the correct dietary restrictions, drinking only the fermented juice of the manioc root for the first five days and then eating only the wolf fish. No matter that she always bathed herself and her child in water infused with the correct herbs. People whispered that someone was poisoning her. True or not, she'd given up on trying, so she left her newborn son on the forest floor.

When Pio's mother returned empty-handed, his sister went to investigate, and found Pio covered with ants. She took over his care, even sleeping in the same hammock back at their village. Whenever he cried, she'd bring him to another new mother to breastfeed, until he was weaned with honey-sweetened fruit. Eventually his sister got married and moved away, leaving him with his grandmother in another village. He was four or five when his grandmother moved back to his father's village. By then his mother had died; he never learned how.

Pio's village was actually just a single structure, albeit a vast one, oblong in shape, with a soaring roof of dried palm fronds that curved all the way to the ground. Inside it stayed dim and cool even in the noonday sun, dry even in a downpour. Eight families shared this long-house, each with their own vague area where hammocks of stringy rainforest cotton hung from rafters that doubled as storage for what few belongings they possessed: arrows, cooking pots, jewelry. "There were no chairs, no tables," Pio would explain. "When you wanted to sit down, you sat wherever you wanted, on your own legs."

Women had a particular way of sitting, sticking one leg straight out ahead of them, tucking the other underneath their bottom, perfectly comfortable. They were typically plumper than the men, less muscular, but no less fit, as they would carry a baby in a sling even when collecting heavy loads of root vegetables. They sang as they worked, always narrating: *"Let's go find firewood because the hunt is for us..."* Back at the longhouse, they carved necklace beads from off-white armadillo armor and dark brown *xikába* fruit shells. They loved to decorate their children with their handiwork. The name Nacoça Pio is actually a Brazilianized version of the term *nakósapíap*, a kind of necklace worn diagonally across the chest. Pio's grandmother draped so many on him that it became his nickname. With the taboo on uttering someone's real name, in later years Pio wouldn't even remember his.

Just about every morning, at least one of the men in Pio's village went off to hunt, usually on his own. Pio spent most of his time practicing, taking aim at little birds. Otherwise it was make-believe, with one boy in the role of hunter, another his prey. Hunting wasn't only a necessity; it was a calling. The Cinta Larga word for "to hunt" literally means "into the forest," because what else would you want to do there? Sitting in the village clearing in the evening, men could spend hours talking about their forays to catch different varieties of wild pig, curassows (birds with black plumage and a bright red wattle), or Amazonian deer. There were few animals they eschewed: bats and most snakes. But they did eat boa constrictors.

When the hunter returned with his kill, he'd proudly heave a basket onto the ground, and his wife would lay the meat on a bamboo grill. A hunter's spoils were considered his to dispose of, and every man was expected to provide for his own immediate family. But in Pio's words, "There was no such thing as running out of money and going hungry." If a hunter brought back more than his family could eat, he was supposed to give away the rest. One myth told of a group of men who killed a drove of pigs but didn't share a single piece with an unsuccessful hunter; the men were themselves turned into pigs. If monkey was on hand, and honored guests were visiting, they would be served the brain, a prized delicacy. Otherwise, any excess meat was offered first to the village headman—in this case, Pio's father, Mankalu.

Pio was still just a boy when a previously unknown creature flew over his village, its shiny undercarriage gliding just above the treetops. It was orders of magnitude larger than any bird anyone had ever seen, and much louder. "Giant hawk that purrs like a jaguar," some called it; only later would they realize it was an airplane. Most of the men simply gawked, but Pio's father took off in pursuit, running into the forest with his bow and a handful of arrows.

In Cinta Larga terms, Mankalu was *zapiway*, "the owner of the house." A Westerner might have called him a "chief," but this implied authority he didn't possess, as no Cinta Larga man could impose his will on any other. Nor was Mankalu an idle landlord. The position wasn't hereditary. If people lost faith in a headman's leadership, they could move to another village or follow an upstart in founding a new one. The first *zapiway*, as everyone knew, was Alia—the Sloth. Ngoyan—Thunder—used to hoard all the world's corn for himself. Before people even knew what corn was, Alia discovered Ngoyan's lover with some chewed-up cobs, and went to ask Ngoyan for some. Ngoyan gave him only cooked kernels, to keep him from cultivating it. But Alia came back with a grasshopper who furtively cut down a cob that hung from Ngoyan's rafters, allowing Alia to hide a raw kernel in one of his long sloth-nails. Back home, Alia planted it. As soon as a few little cobs sprouted, people wanted to eat them, but Alia insisted they wait. A couple of years later they had corn in abundance, the kernels fat and juicy, some yellow, some red, some black.

Men were always eager to hunt, but found agricultural work tedious. As *zapiway*, it was Mankalu who rallied them to plant corn, peanuts, and a variety of tubers: yams, sweet potatoes, manioc. Clearing the field was a task that used to take many men many days. For countless generations, they'd fashioned axes of stone, and had to strip the bark to weaken trees before ever so laboriously hacking them down. Now, of course, they possessed a few metal axes, which made the job easier. At the height of the dry season, they set fire to the fallen trunks—much like the settlers on Highway 364, though really the settlers had learned this from Indigenous people.

Mankalu also directed an even more monumental task: moving the entire village when the roof began to break down, the rafters became termite-infested, the soils became exhausted, and nearby game grew scarce, every five years or so. First they had to scout a new location, preferably in a patch of forest where the vegetation was already thin, perhaps because it was the site of a long-abandoned village. Once they'd made a fresh clearing and transferred their crops, everyone would pick up and move, setting up camp while they built the new longhouse. Gathering dozens of strong, straight branches, they would lash them into an expansive three-dimensional grid, and overlay a thick dome of fresh thatching from *açaí* palm trees. The whole process could take two years. Even for this vital purpose, though, people didn't work without cease. They avoided the hottest hours of the day, when the tropical sun beat down hardest, and leaped at any excuse to take a break and gossip. After laboring for several days in a row, they also liked to rest for a few days. There was no real need to do more. Game was abundant, and they lacked the means to accumulate much beyond some ears of corn. People almost always felt free for visits, expeditions, adventures—like chasing the mysterious bird.

When Mankalu finally returned, the other men asked if he'd caught it. "It perched on a tree by the river, and I tried to shoot it," he said. "But I missed."

A boy named Pichuvy poked fun at Pio, saying, "Your father is a liar!" Still, no one could deny Mankalu's courage. When it came to facing the unknown, he was courageous to a fault.

* * *

In those days, the dry season wasn't quite as hot as it is now. Sometimes, when an Antarctic front blew in, it got downright cold. In the longhouse at night, Pio stayed warm by keeping a fire beside his hammock, waking now and then to stir the coals. On the coldest nights, the elders would wake all the children before dawn. Pio and the other kids would run shivering and plunge into a nearby stream, which was normally cool and refreshing but now felt warm. They were supposed to absorb the water's force before the dragonflies woke and began sipping it away for themselves. Sometimes an adult would yank their arms upward to help them grow. Just the same, Pio remained small.

Back at the village, the children would gather around a fire as the elders told stories about the origins of things. First came Ngurá, the Creator. When there was nothing else but the hot sun, Ngurá made the forest rise from the earth. He also made the waterways, such as Ndiga Xi, the Stream of the Blackflies, as well as the river it emptied into, which Pio knew as I Sere Berá, the River of Rapids (and which Westerners now called the Roosevelt). At the time, the Cinta Larga had no way of knowing that these tributaries fed a much larger river, the Amazon, which in turn flowed into an unthinkable expanse of water, the ocean. Surrounded by enemies, they could hardly cross on foot. Because of all the rapids, it was just as perilous to travel by water— which may explain why the Cinta Larga never developed the canoe.

After Ngurá spawned the three main lineages, Maam, Kaban, and Kakin, he continued to spread his seed far and wide. He also impregnated animals: stinging wasps, little long-whiskered fish. In those days, animals were a kind of people who spoke a language the Cinta Larga could understand. One legend told of Nekópetáy, the mother of all jaguars, who would ask you to groom her for fleas; she was irrepressibly flatulent, and if you laughed, she'd eat you. The elders also told stories about a boy raised by a tapir, a girl who fell in love with a frog, a feast thrown by an anteater. Unlike in Western societies, the line between nature and human culture was never clearly drawn. The few who called themselves *wãwã*, or shaman, straddled more than one category. To become one, you had to encounter a jaguar and resist the urge to flee *or* attack. The jaguar might approach you, its tail undulating. Then it would stand and pull its own skin up from feet to head, revealing itself to be a man—a shaman himself—who would bestow you with the power to cure. A shaman could heal a scorpion bite by blowing smoke in someone's ear. But he possessed darker powers, too. Whenever there was an unexplained death, the cause was often assumed to be sorcery.

But Pio's elders were increasingly at a loss to explain what was happening in their little universe of forest. Like the giant bird. Or the telegraph line. Or the rubber tappers with their metal tools. It was the dry season when, for the first time, the sky filled with smoke so thick, the sun faded to a pale disk, and you could stare straight at it without hurting your eyes. People started coughing; their snot turned black. Pio asked where the smoke came from, and the elders spoke of a conflagration Ngurá once sent to punish people for killing too many of their kin. They still couldn't imagine that human beings, even the clothes-wearers with their alien technologies, could generate smoke on this scale.

Some actually came to believe that the Suruí had come up with a way to make their own metal tools. Pio's friend Tataré had lost his brother, and nearly his father, in an ambush by Suruí warriors. When his grandfather led a revenge attack on a Suruí village, the warriors looted a shockingly large cache of machetes, axes, and knives. They had no idea that Apoena and his father were distributing them at the Seventh of September post, deep in enemy territory.

And then came the discovery that would turn Cinta Larga society on its head. The boy who would come to be known as Roberto Carlos was slightly older than Pio, from a village on the Stream of the Blackflies. One day he and a cousin followed the stream to its mouth in the Roosevelt and climbed a tree to perch in the overhanging branches. Whenever a *mulípkabe* surfaced to eat fallen leaves with its squarish, humanlike teeth, they pulled their bows taut and released an arrow—the standard way to fish, in the absence of hook and line. They were walking home with their catch when they spied a small craft on the water, emitting the deep, loud belching of an outboard motor.

"Look at the people," Roberto's cousin said.

On the deck, a hairy-faced man rotated a metal wheel. A diver wore a rubber suit and copper helmet. It was the same scene Pio would later witness, on this same stretch of the Roosevelt: prospectors.

"What kind of people are these?" Roberto wondered.

"I think they're *mokopey*," his cousin replied—clothes-wearers. "Shall we go and speak to them?"

"We shouldn't talk to them alone," Roberto said. He knew to be cautious: his own father had fought at the telegraph line, only to be shot dead by rubber tappers. Instead the boys ran home to tell the others.

In those days, the Cinta Larga lacked a word for what these outsiders were looking for. But they happened to live in one of the world's oldest areas of continental crust, which occasionally appeared in the form of dark granite boulders that littered the forest—and also contained less obvious minerals. Once, when Roberto himself was a little boy, playing in the dirt of the longhouse, he'd stumbled upon a crystal as big as the tip of a man's thumb. He liked the way it looked, so he washed it in the stream and showed it to his parents, who were duly impressed, but not overly so. Eventually, in the way of kids and toys, he lost track of it. Only many years later would he realize he'd been playing with a diamond that weighed thirty or forty carats, potentially worth hundreds of thousands of dollars.

On another occasion, a group of women were digging clay from a stream bed to fire cooking pots when they found a clearish round stone so large, they said it looked like Ngurá *inhakíp*—"God's eye." It would have been worth an almost unimaginable sum. But they had no use for it, so they tossed it back in the water.

CHAPTER 4

RAUL'S MEN

Pio was around nine when Oita Matina showed up at his village with news: the divers on the Roosevelt were freely giving away metal tools. Oita, like Roberto, hailed from the Stream of the Black-flies, but closer to its headwaters. Perhaps seventeen, he was wiry, lacking the sturdy build of most Cinta Larga men. But he already bore the piercing below his lower lip, a long spike of hardened tree resin, that marked adulthood for men and women alike. That meant he'd undergone the rites of passage that awaited Pio: clutching a branch crawling with wasplike *ataptavei* ants and holding back his screams as they stung him, climbing a towering *maam* tree to retrieve its unripe pods, being left in the middle of the forest, far from any footpath, to see if he could make his way home on his own. (The trick was to navigate by the treetops.)

Oita came from a large family, and in a world where family was literally society, this implied a certain prestige. His grandfather had four wives, fifteen sons, and probably as many daughters. Oita's father, a shaman, had succeeded him as *zapiway*—"a great leader," Oita would boast. According to Roberto, though, Oita's father fought constantly with his own brothers, and Oita inherited this difficulty in getting along with people—even, or perhaps especially, those closest to him. As a kid he didn't even believe his own father was a shaman, until one day his father summoned a drove of wild pigs to their village. The animals arrived the next day, practically offering themselves up to be killed and eaten.

When Oita was in a good mood, he had an infectious laugh, high-pitched and rapid-fire, that gradually took control of his whole body before taking control of yours. He loved to make jokes; in later years he'd claim to be fishing for sharks, just to startle outsiders. But he was also quick to misinterpret others' jokes. He'd descend into dark moods and make empty threats, an almost unbelievably reckless impulse. In those days, *akwésotá*—literally "bad talk," saying nasty things to someone's face—was nearly equivalent to physical violence, inviting a proportional response. It was not unlike eighteenth-century Europe with its culture of honor and dueling, except that just uttering a man's name in his presence could drive him to murder. Though he became renowned as a killer of white men, João Bravo, Mankalu's companion in arms, didn't hesitate to spill his own people's blood. As he himself would recall, "Any little thing I heard, I would kill the guy." For all the Cinta Larga might romanticize their past, some acknowledged that life could be precarious. "In those days," recalled Roberto, "if you even looked at someone the wrong way, he'd kill you....It was really ugly."

Oita's friends never took his threats too seriously. If a Cinta Larga planned to kill someone, he never tipped his hand in advance. Instead he laughed, bided his time. When his target was least suspecting it, looking the other way, he might swing a club or a machete down on his head. Or simply poison his food.

Thanks to the logic of *wepíka*, that debt-like obligation to vengeance, a homicide rarely went unanswered, and bloody feuds could last a generation or more. It was much safer to gossip behind someone's back, probably the favorite Cinta Larga pastime after hunting. People loved to whisper about Oita. When he was around eight, his father was shot to death by rubber tappers. Five days later, Oita's mother married one of her late husband's brothers, Maria Beleza's father. While this was simply the way things were done, Oita felt it was too fast, revealing that his mother never really liked his father. He moved out of their village and became, in his own words, a "castoff": "I stayed at other people's houses—a little bit in one place, a little bit in another…an uncle's, a cousin's, a brother's…and that's how I lived." In his telling, he learned completely on his own how to hunt, how to shoot an arrow, how to become a man like his father. "Nobody liked me," he said.

Oita's loner instinct might seem to clash with his people's love of the collective, the sharing of surplus meat and custom of living all in one house. At the same time, though, they placed great value in self-sufficiency. While the *zapiway* oversaw the village crops, each man was expected to plant his own. Eating from someone else's field, while not exactly stealing, was considered shameful. This was also why young boys like Pio were encouraged to roam freely, to become independent from early on. Even as toddlers they were allowed to play with sharp blades, to play with fire, learning the hard way how to avoid cutting or burning themselves. This extended into old age. In the fields, elderly women would silently pass a basket around to see who might carry her vegetables. If there were no volunteers, she'd just as silently do it herself, making do with a lighter load.

Oita was always wandering, always searching, hoping to somehow find the admiration, the recognition, he would never again get from his father. Now he'd found something to set himself apart. Arriving at Pio's village, he carried a bucket filled with tiny, uniform objects that were unnaturally heavy and perfectly cylindrical: proof he'd met the interlopers. "Take a look at the *mokopey*'s arrows," he said, and Pio and the other kids marveled at what they would later learn were shotgun primers, the brass capsules of gunpowder that ignite the shell when the trigger is pulled. Oita threw a few into the fire; the deafening pops briefly terrified his audience.

*   *   *

The idea of a friendly clothes-wearer seemed absurd on its face. But Oita wasn't the only one to have met them. He'd arrived at his village one day in the midst of a heated discussion about the divers on the Roosevelt. Some men said simply, "Let's go down there and kill them." They already knew what horrors the outsiders were capable of. If they attacked now, they would have the element of surprise. Oita, too, wanted *wepíka*—revenge for the death of his father. But he just scoffed and said, without a hint of self-awareness, "I don't believe you'll kill them. Anyone who talks about it isn't going to do it."

According to tradition, big decisions called for consensus, and consensus could be reached only through long, baroque discussions. People would sit in a rough circle, looking at the ground, fidgeting, sometimes yawning loudly though they weren't remotely bored. Women were expected to stay quiet, but any man could make his case at length, uninterrupted. A discussion could take hours, sometimes days, with breaks to sleep and eat. This time, there were also those who said, "Let's not go looking for a fight. Let them be the first to attack." And in the end, this position prevailed. It was testament to that other Cinta Larga tradition, approaching strangers with a friendly *pa ikinin pa mã*: "Let's have a look at one another."

In Oita's telling, it was he who led the approach. "I'm going to talk to them," he told the others. "If they shoot me, you can kill them." Anyone who knew Oita knew never to assume his stories were true—he was always making himself out as the improbable hero. But his version was strikingly similar to that of a prospector named João Bento, who encountered the Cinta Larga at a spot known as Raul's Beach. As *O Globo* reported in March 1969, "It was around noon on Sunday… when the prospectors, who were already getting ready for lunch, heard a shout from the opposite bank of the river. Surprised, they made out an Indian man with one hand flat across his chest, making signs that he wanted to cross the river. At first, João Bento and his companions thought it was a trap, as the jungle-dwellers are experts in such things." Still, two decided to paddle over in a canoe while the others, guns at the ready, covered them.

They needn't have worried: "The Indian received them with a smile, embracing and kissing them. Then…he began to grind his teeth like a *queixada* (jungle pig). He was calling to the other [Indians], who began to draw closer and whistle, imitating the *macuco* bird." From the trees there emerged eight men, two adolescent boys, and two women, one of them perhaps eighteen, with a newborn baby in her arms. João Bento described them as people "of medium stature, muscular, with light skin and attractive faces"; other observers would remark on the men's pageboy haircuts. It took three trips to ferry them all to the prospectors' camp.

In later years, the Cinta Larga would always describe the food as the strangest part of these encounters. "That first time was difficult," Oita would say, laughing. Eating was at the center of village life, but they'd never known spices or salt. Instead, the first question asked of a hunter was "So, is it fat?" Everyone knew the time to hunt monkeys was when they were well fed on ripe fruit; women would boil the meat until the fat floated to the top, to dip starchy root vegetables into. The Cinta Larga did prize variety—but the Brazilian staples of rice and heavily seasoned beans looked, and smelled, absolutely foreign. "Don't eat that, son," Roberto's mother warned. "It could be poison." Others demanded their hosts consume some first to prove it was safe. Still, all they agreed to sample was a mixture of water, *farinha*—a flour made from manioc, a tuber well known to the Cinta Larga—and sugar.

What happened next depends on whom you ask. When the prospectors attempted to communicate, Oita imagined they were saying, "Here, take these gifts." The Cinta Larga were all too happy to receive their cooking knives, invaluable *ndabe* that warriors often risked their lives for. One of Oita's brothers also came away with a prospector's dog. Though they'd never seen such a creature, the Cinta Larga traditionally kept pets—monkeys, macaws, even sloths—whenever they captured a baby animal while hunting.

In João Bento's description, he and his companions simply stood by as the Indians, completely on their own initiative, carted off the camp's cooking utensils, smiling all the while.

* * *

Raul's Beach was named for one of Rondônia's most successful prospectors, Raul Moreda. Better known as Raul the Spaniard, he'd initially left Spain for Cuba, where he would claim to have met Che Guevara, even though the Argentine revolutionary had yet to set foot there. This kind of mythmaking was common among prospectors. Many were essentially drifters, fleeing criminal records or child support payments or simply hoping to reinvent themselves. They followed word of mouth from one site to another—so much so that, in Brazilian prospecting slang, the Portuguese word for "gossip" (*fofoca*) was synonymous with a mine. Raul, for his part, had come to Brazil in 1954, declaring his profession as "carpenter," though he was more of an adventurer. According to one fellow prospector, he was searching for precious metals and stones on the northern edge of the Amazon when he heard about the diamonds in Rondônia, a thousand miles south.

Ever since colonial days, when gold was the heart of the Brazilian economy, prospectors had followed the adage "Wherever water flows downstream, prospectors go upstream." And it had served them well. Panning for gold in the early 1700s, they stumbled upon precious stones, and Brazil became the world's main producer of diamonds for the next hundred and fifty years.

In those days, no one knew for sure where diamonds came from, because they only ever turned up in waterways, alluvial plains, and river deltas, amid sediment flushed from elsewhere. Then, in 1869, an eighty-three-carat stone turned up in South Africa, and prospectors finally dug into the host rock. Dubbed kimberlite (after Britain's Earl of Kimberley), it was soft and yellow near the surface, hard and bluish deeper down, and it contained more diamonds than anyone had thought possible in one concentrated area. For geologists, it was also a kind of portal into Earth's distant past. Diamonds, they came to understand, took shape in the unfathomable heat and pressure of the mantle, a hundred miles down, as carbon atoms were squeezed into densely repeating structures over a billion, two billion, possibly even three billion years. First the carbon crystallized into graphite. Then the "diamond cubic" lattice, the tightest configuration of atoms in the known universe. These little stones floated around in molten rock until some two hundred million years ago, when a small but violent eruption brought them to the surface, leaving a column of magma that cooled into a carrot shape—the kimberlite.

The discovery led to the first major open-pit diamond mine, South Africa's Big Hole, which in turn gave rise to De Beers, the international diamond cartel. Conditions in the Amazon, though, were far less favorable. Saturated by heavy rains for months on end, the silt would collapse before prospectors dug even a fraction as deep. Instead, well into the twentieth century, they kept on working like they always had, combing waterways with a sieve.

Raul brought a new kind of professionalism to Rondônia's prospecting world. Whenever he found a promising site, he and his men would clear an area of trees for a packed-dirt landing strip where a single-engine plane could ferry in supplies. For Brazilians on the Amazon frontier, far from the modern cities of the coast, even this rickety little craft was a novelty. When it took off from Vila Rondônia, kids would run after the plane to feel the powerful downwash, unbothered by the reddish dust it kicked up.

Raul was thirty-eight when he married another recent arrival, fifteen-year-old Maria Graça, who cleaned and weighed his hauls. In her recollection, he brought back diamonds by the literal pound; he kept them in thirty-ounce bottles of Presidente cognac. Most were merely industrial-quality—small, irregular, marred by internal flaws, which made them suitable as drill bits but not for a rich person's wedding ring. Maria also learned to identify the occasional gem, though. Some were champagne-colored, some blue, some greenish like an emerald, some the purest white. (Raul once had a ring made for her; prone to drunken rages, he later took it back.)

One observer called Raul "a first class adventurer of the old [Wild] West kind" who repeatedly "escaped...death, snake bites, arrows of wild Indians." When he made his first foray into Cinta Larga country, in the late 1960s, it was via a tributary east of the Roosevelt River, where people were less willing to give him the benefit of the doubt. Raul and his men began to feel they were being followed. They heard bird calls they recognized as an Indian signal to attack. And then came the arrows. Raul lost one man to a buttock wound that got infected. A well-to-do Italian, along for kicks, was later killed outright. Still, given the disparity of arms, the fights were hardly fair. In one skirmish, Raul's men shot and killed ten Cinta Larga.

"But my husband was a very intelligent guy," Maria would recall.

"He wanted to show the Indians that the region was his, and he wasn't going to leave—that he respected them, but he had work to do there." When he established himself on the Roosevelt, it was he who started handing out gifts—just like the great Cândido Rondon, founder of the Indian Protection Service, though Raul almost certainly didn't know that.

* * *

In the Cinta Larga conception, it wasn't the white men who "pacified" them but they who "pacified" the white men. As word of Oita's encounter spread, people from other villages followed. Sometimes they brought gifts of their own: necklaces, yams, sweet potatoes, corn. Sometimes they sang and danced, following protocol for visits to friendly villages. Their dance wasn't hard to learn: two rows facing each other, taking a few steps forward and then a few steps back. When the prospectors failed to join in, the Cinta Larga started pinching them, gently pushing them, giggling. The prospectors got the hint and started dancing, too. The Cinta Larga always left laden with tools—so many that the prospectors started hiding them, so as not to lose everything at once.

In these exchanges, sugar proved almost as popular as *ndabe*. The Cinta Larga had never had such ready access to sweets, because they didn't cultivate bees. Now the prospectors gave them whole sacks full of sugar—though once a Cinta Larga scooped a handful of fine white grains into his mouth without realizing it was salt, and thought he'd been poisoned. Another man, thinking a container of cooking oil was honey, poured the stuff down his throat. Despite such mix-ups, the mood was unfailingly jolly.

Oita, Roberto Carlos, and a few other adolescent boys became the most assiduous visitors. Hanging out with the prospectors, they even started picking up Portuguese, though not without some hiccups. The

Cinta Larga name taboo was so ingrained that, when asked theirs, the boys misunderstood the question and gave answers like *oy tamina*, which means "I am a man." This was the origin of the name Oita Matina, though he himself would later claim it meant "strong warrior man, hard to kill." The prospectors, in any case, came to call him Maloqueiro, which roughly translates as Rapscallion. Confusingly, Roberto was known at first by a similar name, Oitamina. His long flowing hair reminded the prospectors of the Brazilian crooner Roberto Carlos, so they started calling him that instead. Other kids just got Portuguese names like Manoel and Antônio. In time, they'd use these names even when speaking among themselves.

Sometimes the boys watched as the outsiders sieved through the gravel from the riverbed. Noticing their interest, the prospectors asked them to help. The Cinta Larga never saw the gifts they received as "payment." The concept of wage labor was completely unknown to them. As Oita later remembered it, chuckling to himself, "I didn't know what a diamond was. I didn't know what money was. I didn't understand anything." He just liked feeling welcome, useful, having spent so many years as a "castoff." Also, it was fun. Though the boys couldn't understand much of what was said, the outsiders were always laughing, telling highly embellished stories about fortunes won in the mud and lost in brothels, about run-ins with *bandidos* and police. Prospectors in Rondônia were an eclectic bunch: "adventurers, madmen, and starvelings," in the words of the anthropologist Claude Lévi-Strauss. One was an Evangelical who would preach to his fellow fortune-seekers, pointing to his Bible as he declared, "This teaches the way of life and salvation." Then he'd pull out his .38 pistol and say, "This is the way to death and hell." These men would never be found working a nine-to-five in an industrial mine. Closer to gamblers, they relied on intuition, not the expertise of geologists. "You might earn nothing for six months, but then you find a ten-carat stone or a kilo of gold," one would recall. "You go back to your tent for a little *cachaça*"—sugarcane liquor— "knowing that you're set for the next two years."

The prospectors had nicknames of their own: Grumpy, Jumpy, Little One, Brains. Many were simply called by the name of their home state: Maranhão, Ceará. If two men hailed from the same place, they also got adjectives: the fat one, the Black one. The boys had no way of knowing, of course, where Maranhão or Ceará might be. But they did pick up on the way the outsiders talked about skin color. The Cinta Larga already distinguished themselves this way, to some extent. The Kakin and Kaban lineages were said to be lighter-skinned; some even had reddish hair. The Maam—Oita and Pio's lineage—were said to be darker in complexion, with one subgroup considered "black." Still, the first time they met an Afro-Brazilian with very dark skin, they tried to scrub the blackness off, thinking it must be body paint.

The prospectors themselves, whether of African, European, or Indigenous descent, or some typically Brazilian mix of the three, usually classified themselves as "white" as a simple matter of opposition to the people they called "Indians." By the same token, they scarcely distinguished between the Cinta Larga and other Indigenous groups— Indians, all of them. As the boys absorbed these concepts, their view of the world, and their place in it, started to shift.

But there was nothing like seeing a new reality with your own eyes. When a prospector named Justino invited the boys to a place he called "the city," Oita and Roberto didn't hesitate. A kid called Manoel came along, too. They had little reason to suspect that anything might go wrong. As Roberto would remember it, Justino seemed like a "100 percent decent guy."

CHAPTER 5

IDEALISTS

A group of prospectors showed up at the Seventh of September camp to complain about Indians carrying off their tools. Even with mule trains bringing fresh supplies, they couldn't keep up. Never mind that these men weren't allowed to be there, inside the area declared off-limits by the military regime. Chico Meirelles, back in charge for a while, received them well. Concerned about the potential for violent misunderstanding, he decided to set up an attraction post in Raul the Spaniard's area, some fifty miles east, on the Roosevelt River.

While preparing for this new expedition, he and his son hosted a series of journalists, documentary filmmakers, and foreign researchers. Apoena, who'd learned to pilot during his time away from the Indian Protection Service, sometimes flew the visitors in to a newly built landing strip on a single-motor plane. Most of the journalists came and went without making an impression, eager to report on what they thought of as Stone Age people, just as eager to leave once they saw these people up close. "I must say, in all honesty: I was afraid," one wrote. "I sensed a tension in the air, that I was being observed, investigated, analyzed, smelled...I [felt like] the proverbial colonist in the cauldron, surrounded by hungry savages."

Possidônio Bastos, a twenty-four-year-old reporter from *O Globo* newspaper, stood out. He was thrilled by what he observed. The Suruí now visited almost daily to receive machetes and axes. They would hang out and chat in a language made up of gestures, with a bit of their own native tongue and the odd Portuguese word thrown in. Unlike the other visitors, Possidônio immediately felt comfortable with them. One photo shows him sitting with his arm around a Suruí kid as two others crowd around him, one speaking into his microphone.

Possidônio was there to witness the first visit by Suruí women, an important sign of trust. Though it was still too soon to visit one of their villages, he and Apoena spent the night at a Suruí camp. Apoena felt an immediate bond with Possidônio, intuiting a "volcanic strength" in the face of adversity. He also picked up on a rare sensitivity: Possidônio was the type to bring a record of the Spanish guitar composition *Concierto de Aranjuez* to the jungle. Even the Suruí noticed their connection, calling Possidônio "Apon-Karmen," brother of Apoena.

Possidônio listened hungrily as his hosts argued about the "Indian problem." Chico was adamant that the only way to save the Indians was by assimilating them. The gifts he handed out were not only friendship offerings but propaganda for the world he wanted them to join—propaganda that was all the more effective because Chico himself fervently believed in it. Going back to the earliest efforts by Cândido Rondon, protecting the Indians was only the first step. The original name for the SPI was the Service for the Protection of Indians and Localization of National Workers, because the ultimate goal was to bring them into the Brazilian economy, to make them productive citizens. For all his enlightened humanism, Rondon shared the view of social Darwinists that Indigenous people belonged to a primitive stage of human evolution, the endpoint being some version of Western civilization.

The irony was that this lofty self-image held even as the great European nations plunged into the First World War, in which violence was mechanized, chemical weapons were deployed en masse, and tens of millions died in disease-ridden trenches. The feeling of superiority only deepened after the Second World War, with its concentration camps and its atom bombs. Yes, the West could put a man on the moon. But its vision of progress was one in which the world's largest rainforest, a miraculous system that overflowed with life-giving water, tens of thousands of species of flora and fauna, natural resources that scientists didn't even fully understand or know about yet—a system that sustained twenty million Indigenous people for hundreds, if not thousands, of years—should be cleared to make way for highways and cattle ranches. It never occurred to men like Chico—or Rondon, or Americans such as Theodore Roosevelt—that there might be more than one way of living a meaningful life. Based on his own conversations with newly contacted Indigenous people, Chico himself truly believed they wanted "to live like us." To go against this, he maintained, would amount to "blatant racial discrimination."

At the time Apoena chafed at this view. "You know [the Indians] are naive," he told his father. "They have no idea that, once they've been civilized, they'll be little more than slaves to white people"—like the Xavante, Chico's first professional success. "It's better to leave them as they are."

As far as Chico was concerned, this was "nonsense" that only a young person, with little experience of the world, could swallow. Assimilation, he insisted, was the only way to keep the Indians from being wiped out. "Isolation or resistance to progress will lead inevitably to the marginalization and, consequently, the destruction of the jungle-dweller," he argued—referring to Indigenous people by their official classification as something akin to forest creatures.

Father and son went in endless circles like this. The debates spanned countless nights in the rainforest and even made their way into newspaper reports. Apoena was already gaining a reputation as a troublemaker. Unlike his father, he didn't hesitate to lash out against the settler class. At one point, he publicly advocated arming Indians with guns to defend themselves, earning criticisms that he was "rash," "suicidal," or simply "naive" himself.

Within the government, Apoena was viewed with suspicion. The military regime was so paranoid about communist infiltration that intelligence agents kept tabs on him even in the Amazon. One of their reports cited "strong suspicions" that guerrillas were being trained inside the official Cinta Larga reserve—sheer fantasy. Another described Apoena as "an individual with a marked subversive tendency" who was "almost always discontented with the current Administration." Yet another cited his "explosive temperament," adding that, "during his alcoholic excesses, he was arrested a few times [in Porto Velho], and the prestige enjoyed by his father got him out of jail." Apoena, for his part, always bristled at the official hierarchy, frequently doing whatever he pleased, spending government money, even when authorization was denied. As he put it in his diary: "Fuck all bureaucrats."

Even intelligence reports, though, hinted at his allure. One dossier opened with a photo of him in the jungle, staring with his dark eyes intensely into the camera, an unlit cigarette sticking from the side of his mouth. His uncompromising idealism attracted young men and women alike. When he fell in love with his first wife, the anthropologist Denise Maldi, he wondered in his diary: "Perhaps with her I will achieve more for the Indians?"

Possidônio was drawn in, too. One night, as he and his hosts tried to tune the radio to Brazil's World Cup match against England, he blurted out, "I'm not going back to Brasília"—the city where he lived. "I'm going to stay here to help you both. Will you have me?"

"If you can handle it," Chico replied. "It's a tough job, kid."

Eventually they managed to tune in to the BBC. They celebrated Brazil's victory—and Possidônio's career change—with a bottle of Cinzano vermouth, poured into tin mugs.

Possidônio did return to Brasília, but only briefly. He'd barely finished writing his articles about the trip when he put in his resignation. Announcing his plan to join Funai, he left a note for his colleagues: "Interpret my decision how you please: escape (possible), vanity (not an unreasonable hypothesis), selfishness, or egocentrism....But my romantic, adventurous temperament has led me to a different kind of struggle. A struggle to help the Indians, who are so exploited and misunderstood....If necessary (maybe it will be pointless) I will give my life for them."

CHAPTER 6

THE FEAST

A week had passed since Oita, Roberto Carlos, and Manoel joined the two prospectors on a journey beyond the borders of their territory. Certain the boys had been killed, their families started organizing a reprisal. Messengers traveled along the Stream of the Blackflies, summoning people to a feast at Roberto's village. Pio and his father lived too far away, but so many others came that not all could fit in the longhouse, and many sat in the surrounding trees.

Maria Beleza, the girl who survived the massacre, was around ten years old, too young to be anything but a spectator at the feast. In any case, women played only a secondary role. Their main responsibility was to make *i*, a Cinta Larga staple. First they dug up large quantities of manioc, carrying the heavy loads by a strap slung around their foreheads. They cooked and ground the roots into a kind of tapioca; then they chewed up sweet potato and spit it into the pot. The saliva helped the mixture to ferment, but never for more than a few days, so that it didn't become too alcoholic. The quantities had to be large, as guests were expected to drink so much they vomited, only to fill their bellies with it once again, ideally multiple times. Hundreds of gallons were stored in the hollowed-out trunks of *abolup* trees.

Men did have tasks of their own. To sweeten the *i*, it was they who knocked down the wild beehives. To prepare the music, they gathered a variety of bamboo whose thick green stalks could be made into pipes. They also captured wild pigs and fattened them to be ritually killed with bow and arrow. Still, Maria would insist, "It was harder to be a girl." After the death of Oita's father, it was her father who'd married Oita's mother. If Oita was around, and she was too lazy to gather firewood, her father would tell him to discipline her, and Oita would fire blunt arrows at her feet. "How it hurt!" she would recall, her face twisting with the memory.

Oita's younger sister Alzira had it worse. She was only three when her mother's brother took her to his village "to raise me to be his wife," in her words. In principle, there was nothing unusual about this. Among the Cinta Larga, as among some other South American groups, the ideal marriage was between a girl and her maternal uncle. Girls were often married off before puberty, though there was no expectation of sexual activity until after their first menstruation, when man and wife would both be painted with black *wesuáá* dye, zigzags, stripes, and dots marking the change.

Adolescent boys, similarly, were paired up with old widows—or even with one of their own father's other wives—who initiated them into sex without the impetus to have children. (This was probably the case with João Bravo, who was still a young man when he was married to Maria Beleza's grandmother.) There was no sense of shame in any of this. Boys and girls both learned about sex by stumbling upon the frank conversations of women, who answered any questions openly, with laughter and illustrative gestures.

Romance wasn't unheard-of; adolescent girls sang angsty songs with drawn-out vowels: "*I want a lover / I want a lover / I want a lover to marry...*" Like in most other societies throughout human history, however, marriage wasn't a romantic enterprise so much as a glue between families, villages, lineages. Courtship usually meant showering your future in-laws with gifts. Then, when a father "gave" away his daughter (along with her hammock), the groom would pay a bride-price of arrows and necklaces. But that was just a down payment: he'd spend his whole life amortizing the debt, bringing them choice pieces of meat and helping to tend their crops. In time, the father's sons could expect to receive a bride from the groom's village, further strengthening the relationship. It was the same reciprocal logic that powered *wepíka*, the obligation to exact revenge. And it helped to explain a curious paradox: parents actually preferred female children. A man who fathered many daughters was said to have big testicles.

The problem for Alzira was her uncle's first wife, who refused to give Alzira food. Unless an aunt brought some from another village, she often went hungry. Not allowed the usual fire by her hammock, she'd shiver all night. On journeys through the forest, the woman would even abandon her "to be eaten by jaguars," Alzira would recall.

Jealousy was a powerful force in Cinta Larga life. According to legend, menstruation was the Moon's revenge for being forbidden from sleeping with his sister; possessive, he wanted to stop her from having sex all the time. Maria's grandfather had always taught her not to even look at another woman's husband, lest the woman poison her. True to what she'd learned, when a man once ordered her to dig up some manioc, she didn't meet his eyes. "Look at me when I'm talking to you," the man said, but Maria merely replied, "I have ears to hear you with." He threatened to kill her; still she didn't return his gaze. Enraged, he brought a steel axe down on her shoulder, leaving a wide, bleeding gash. The scar would remain visible into old age; the man suffered no punishment.

There were a few exceptions to the rule of female subservience.

Maria would always remember her grandmother as a kind of female *zapiway*, responsible for leading the village women: "I never saw her hunt but she knew how to use a bow and arrow. She knew how to kill fish with poison. She was like a man, she did everything." In later years the Cinta Larga would disagree as to whether this figure existed. Anthropologists never identified it at all. For Maria, though, it was an important reference, proof that women, too, could be powerful.

For boys like Oita, it was different. In adolescence they were almost expected to exhibit, in the words of the anthropologist Carmen Junqueira, "a certain petulance or even aggressiveness…in contrast to the feminine serenity." The divide carried through to the smallest of things. Only men carried the special sticks that could be rubbed together to make fire. When a woman traveled unaccompanied to another village, and had to camp along the way, she was allowed only an ember. If it went out, she could expect a cold, damp, dark night.

At the feast, Maria watched as the women played their usual supporting role. Having spent hours chewing roots for the ceremonial *i*, they waited as men and boys drank the first round. It was men who played the pipes, blowing into the bamboo stalks to produce a constant, deep, percolating warble. It was men who sang the songs, their voices rising and falling, some high-pitched, others guttural, in a kind of call-and-response: "*When the pig runs with an arrow sticking from it, the bamboo smacks the trees / Let's kill the pig / Let's take the path…/ My wife will stay at home.*" Dancing, women lined up behind the men, their arms around the men's waists, always facing a mirrored row of marching men and all-but-hidden women. At the time, though, Maria couldn't imagine another way—and the truth was that everyone, not just men, loved these celebrations. "It was the most beautiful thing," Maria would recall. "Everyone dressed up…" Women attached bright red and blue and yellow feathers to their necklaces; everyone painted their bodies with red and black patterns. Some men wore headdresses of white harpy eagle feathers, so light and fluffy that they bounced with every little movement. Others wore crowns of golden straw that hung nearly to the ground, and golden straw across their chests, and golden straw around their necks and ankles. When men from other villages showed up, they laid their finest arrow at the *zapiway*'s feet, apologizing for its ugliness even when the craftsmanship was obvious. Each arrow spoke to his prestige, but the *zapiway*, in turn, scarcely acknowledged it.

Feasts were one of the main purposes of Cinta Larga life. It took months to plant all that manioc, gather all that bamboo, capture all those animals, and craft all those arrows. Yet it was a form of investment entirely at odds with the Western way of settlers. Rather than building up resources, capital, some kind of lasting empire, and continuously expanding, a *zapiway* used it all up in a single, magnificent, redistributive flash.

* * *

Maria could never forget the moment that Oita, Roberto, and Manoel showed up at the feast with the two prospectors. The boys were wearing clothes, and Maria was so terrified by the sight of them—using the same "second skin" as the men who killed her grandmother—she ran and hid under some straw. (When Manoel found Maria's hiding place, he spoke what he claimed was the outsiders' language, which sounded like gibberish to her, and was just as terrifying.) It was almost certainly the first time Westerners had come in peace to a Cinta Larga village. Many guests weren't at all pleased, not only because of the atrocities committed by other clothes-wearers. Usually prospectors were generous with gifts, but these two hadn't even brought their own hammocks. To placate their people, Oita and the other boys promised that the white men would bring tools later—and in the end, this argument won the day. There was no more need to prepare for war; the feast became a celebration of the boys' safe return.

Amid the festivities, people asked the boys what they'd seen, but the boys lacked the words. How to explain Highway 364, which was to a footpath what a tree trunk was to a vine? How to explain the settlement of Pimenta Bueno, tiny by Western standards, but with more houses than any Cinta Larga had ever seen in one place? Then there was the "house that moves," which emitted black smoke—a bus. The prospectors, Justino and Didi, also took them to a smaller outpost, Riozinho, where the boys played in the Little River it was named for. Still repulsed by the outsiders' food, they barely ate for days. As for how they ended up back here, the prospectors had asked the boys to return the favor. Roberto would remember hearing the first coughs along the way.

A feast could go for days, if not weeks. At night, guests slept under little lean-tos outside; in the morning, the festivities resumed. The captured pigs were set loose one by one in the village clearing. Ironically apologizing for their incompetent archery (their aim was flawless), men shot them with so many arrows that they resembled porcupines. Like in previous encounters, the prospectors were invited to dance. To their Western ears the music must have sounded discordant, almost menacing: a trancelike tune with no discernible melody, the tension constant, never resolving. But it was also infectious, and so they gamely joined a row of men, taking three paces forward, three paces back, as women clutched their waists from behind. Arrows were stashed on the rafters; wide belts of bark hung overhead. With so many people packed into the longhouse, the air became thick with sweat. Some draped the white men with necklaces as a show of goodwill.

It seems the prospectors got carried away by the good feeling, and the lightly alcoholic *i*, and the sight of so many naked Indian women.

At some point Justino or Didi, or possibly both, began sidling up to Cinta Larga girls. One gave Maria a candy and grabbed her hand, even though she'd yet to reach puberty. Maria's mother gestured for the prospector to let go, saying the girl had to sleep. But he either didn't understand or didn't want to. You didn't need an anthropologist to tell you this was a dangerous breach of local norms (as it would be anywhere).

Maria's mother began to cry. One of Maria's brothers grabbed a club and made it clear the prospector would die unless he released her. At last the prospector relented. Still fearing she could be carried off, Maria's brother took her that very night to seek refuge at João Bravo's village, a hundred miles east.

The mood souring, the two white men wisely decided to leave—but not, according to Cinta Larga lore, before slipping some obscure substance into the *i*.

* * *

The Cinta Larga knew their poisons. The forest was full of them. One could be extracted from the inner bark of a certain tree and applied to a victim's eyes to cause temporary blindness. Another was so lethal, you had to wrap leaves around your fingers and toes just to handle the bush. Very carefully, you would secure the bush with your feet and bleed it with a thorn, collecting the liquid in a section of bamboo. A few drops in your victim's meal, and he or she would promptly seize up and die. Given the intimacy needed to taint someone's food, this was the preferred form of homicide among those you knew best, the people in your own village: family. Little wonder that poison, even more than sorcery, was the usual explanation for mysterious deaths.

The Cinta Larga would always maintain that, in the old days, no one got sick. Prior to contact, Indigenous groups in Rondônia were barely in contact with one another, much less the wider world, and had neither the dense cities nor the herds of domesticated animals from which most viruses sprang. So isolated were they, even malaria—thought to have arrived in South America on European slave ships—was unheard-of. What they *were* used to was parasites. Indigenous Amazonians actually developed a genetic resistance to the so-called kissing bugs that cause Chagas disease, which can otherwise be life-threatening.

After the two prospectors went on their way, the revelers kept on. In the words of Pio's friend Pichuvy, "The Indians drank and drank and drank until they finished." Soon, though, the coughing spread. People's heads grew hot. "They began to feel pain, to vomit a lot," Pichuvy would recall. Some took to hammocks inside the longhouse. Others, believing the village had somehow been cursed, fled for their homes, where the sickness spread.

The same conditions that had long prevented homegrown viruses also made the Cinta Larga unusually vulnerable to imported diseases. It was the same story every time Westerners came into contact with Indigenous people anywhere. In the 1600s, an outbreak of smallpox essentially wiped out the Omagua people of the Upper Amazon; in the 1700s, another outbreak may have killed nine out of ten Hopi in North America—just two of hundreds, possibly thousands, of groups to suffer this fate. According to some estimates, more than a hundred million people lived in the Americas in 1492, and all but ten million were killed by smallpox, influenza, whooping cough, cholera, measles, malaria, typhoid, even the common cold. It was a story that was supposed to have ended centuries ago, playing out again in the age of modern medicine.

Back at his family's village, Oita became delirious. He saw a light that was like the moon but wasn't the moon, and heard a voice that said, "You can sleep. Don't be afraid, you're not going to die. You can sleep." When he woke up, he realized almost his entire sprawling family had perished. Two babies were somehow still alive, one suckling its mother's breast, even though its mother was dead.

Word of the sickness traveled fast. Sometimes just to receive the news seemed to invite it into your home. Even innocent messengers came under suspicion. One kid, sent to warn another village, was killed by its wary inhabitants. No one would ever discover what caused the outbreak to begin with. Given the short incubation, it may have been influenza. In later, documented cases of flu among the Cinta Larga, the illness developed quickly into pneumonia, causing shortness of breath, chest pain, and death at shocking rates; in one village, at least 45 percent of the population died in a single outbreak. Tuberculosis was similarly deadly. According to one report, an outbreak among their neighbors the Suruí "reached all age groups, death occurring within two months after the appearance of a hoarse cough, which filled the forest in the evening."

The feast entered Cinta Larga history as an epochal event, forever dividing their "before" from their "after." As the story passed from person to person, memories mingled with rumors, suppositions, suggestions. As proof of the white men's treachery, many would recite the phrase "Those who didn't drink [the *i*] didn't die." Others, though only small children at the time, would remember the sickness starting when airplanes sprayed some kind of gas or dropped bombs—possibly conflating their own memories with apocryphal press reports. They also magnified the scale, claiming that as many as fifteen thousand had died—an impossible figure, given that their entire population was maybe a tenth that number, but one that accurately reflected the sense of loss. By the 1980s, the Cinta Larga population would fall below four hundred. It was mass death on a scale that few societies have ever experienced, including those considered victims of genocide.

Over time the feast also blurred with other atrocities. Many came to refer to it as part of the Massacre of the Eleventh Parallel, carried out by gunmen six years earlier—as if they had suffered a single, coordinated ethnic cleansing, rather than a messy process of violent expansion, broadly encouraged by a negligent state. According to the logic of *wepíka*, these events could never be separate. Instead there was an inescapable accounting: which side, white or Cinta Larga, had taken more from the other?

Justino, in their oral tradition, came to be known as Pamapat, a word that means "great death." But Roberto, for one, believed he "had no malice." The next time he saw the prospector, Justino had no idea about the tragedy. He felt touched by the welcome he'd received: no one had ever thrown a party for him. In fact, he wanted to visit the village again. "But I told him what had happened," Roberto would recall. "I told him there was nobody left alive, just bodies....I think he felt really bad about it, too."

Roberto himself had spent five days too weak to lift himself from his hammock. When at last he felt well enough to move, he made a discovery just like Oita's: everyone else was dead. In the Amazonian heat, their bodies were already starting to rot. He wanted at least to bury his mother, but he lacked the strength. He could only drag himself out of the longhouse, hoping to find someone else left alive.

CHAPTER 7

GRAVEDIGGER

When the rains arrived, rhythms shifted. For prospectors, it was a mixed blessing. The rivers became fuller, less turbulent, easier to navigate. But planes couldn't land on washed-out airstrips, so Raul the Spaniard holed up in Vila Rondônia to build houses and furniture for newly arrived settlers. Loggers, likewise, had to pause their labors, as they relied on their own narrow dirt roads, and trucks laden with hardwood inevitably got stuck in the mud. For the same reason, the flow of migrants on Highway 364 dwindled to a near halt.

The Cinta Larga knew the rains were coming when the cicadas stopped howling in the trees and the cherry-like *abía* fruit ripened. That first outbreak of disease didn't necessarily reach other villages, two, three, four days' walk from the Stream of the Blackflies. At Pio's village, life didn't change at all. When *mamóri* ants emerged from their anthills and took flight, Pio helped collect them to be fried on a hot pan. This was also the time when the *maam* tree released its heavy pods, which crashed down from a height of a hundred and fifty feet. Pio joined the trips to break them open, revealing two dozen nutshells arrayed like orange segments, with delicious Brazil nuts inside.

Pio's life hardly changed even after Tataré showed up with a few other family members. Tataré was one of the few of their generation who would remember his real name. In later years he would become a kind of guardian of Cinta Larga lore, saving stories and myths that others forgot. He always listened intently to his elders, even as many died off. Tataré's father had already survived a Suruí ambush but was no match for the poison at the fateful feast. Nor was Tataré's grandfather. Tataré himself went twenty days without eating before he found some relatives—an aunt, an uncle, and a grandmother—all of whom now hoped to join Mankalu's village. Far from turning them away, Pio's father offered them a place in his longhouse to hang hammocks.

When the downpours began in earnest, the sky dark with low-hanging clouds, the Cinta Larga traditionally put their feasts, war parties, and even most visits on hold. Women harvested corn to make a different variety of *i*, which people drank as they munched on *maam-dik*, a toasted Brazil nut crumble. Now and then the sun came out, and the time was right for catching armadillos; finding a burrow, you would light a fire in the hole and blow smoke inside until the armadillo was forced to emerge. Mankalu and the other men spent the rest of their time crafting arrows. For all you tried to retrieve those that went astray after a hunt or a battle, you could never have enough. After one bloody clash, Raul the Spaniard found two hundred littered on the ground.

Despite the horrific stories from Tataré's family, Mankalu wanted to make his own trip to acquire tools from the prospectors. Having missed the initial rush, he'd fallen behind other headmen, and he was still more concerned with internal feuds and intrigues—most often born of disputes over women, like in Ancient Greek city-states. Going back to 1492, Indigenous leaders had often seen Western settlers as bit players amid their conflicts, sometimes even forming alliances with white men against other Indigenous groups, as the Iroquois did in North America. João Bravo, who had once fought the clothes-wearers alongside Mankalu, was also spared the initial wave of disease. But he became convinced that other headmen were after his tools, and began preemptively raiding their villages.

Once the rains had petered out, Mankalu embarked on his first expedition to the outsiders' camp on the Roosevelt. Pio, ever desperate for his father's affection, leaped at the opportunity to join him. One of his brothers and several other young men came along, too. When, after a two-day journey, they arrived, Pio stared with amazement. A sandy spit of land, almost an island, stuck out into the river. Atop it was a house unlike any Pio knew, perfectly rectangular rather than the familiar oval shape, with vertical walls and a pitched roof of palm fronds instead of the usual dome. Strangest of all, the whole structure was raised on stilts. A few men in clothes emerged. Pio had gotten a glimpse of the interlopers near his uncle's village, but not up close, and now he gaped at their strange adornments—floppy hats, rubber boots. One appeared to be sucking smoke from a burning twig—a cigarette, he realized later.

After sending a canoe over to retrieve Mankalu's group, the white men brought out aluminum pots of rice and beans. It was the first salty food Pio had ever eaten, and when he took a taste, it felt like his mouth was burning. Overwhelmed, he stayed quiet as his father explained what he wanted. The white men didn't understand even the most basic of Cinta Larga words, but hardly needed to. They handed over the desired machetes and axes, as well as some clothes, which Mankalu saw no use for but took anyway. Satisfied for now, he led Pio and the others back home.

*　*　*

Pio and his father had no way of knowing the camp had changed hands. In December 1969, Chico and Apoena had received fresh news from the prospectors. After months of friendly exchanges, the Cinta Larga had apparently invited Didi to return to their village. When he failed to come back, a few others went looking for him, but they found the longhouse abandoned, the decaying corpses of two Indian women inside. Spooked, the prospectors had fled for town, in such a hurry that they left much of their equipment behind.

Chico saw an opportunity: to repurpose the prospectors' camp as his second attraction post, to reach the groups in Raul the Spaniard's area, on the Roosevelt River. The journey would take two weeks on rain-muddled mule paths, but even before they arrived, they should have sensed that something was off. At one point Chico and Apoena ran into four Indians and gave them some tools, receiving wide belts of bark in return. Despite the goodwill at the Seventh of September post, however, these Indians didn't smile. One was wearing a shirt that Chico suspected was Didi's, but when asked about the missing prospector, the Indian said nothing. Little did Chico know, Didi was already dead, struck in the back as revenge for the suspected poisoning.

At the abandoned camp, Chico installed ten workers with a two-way radio, christening it Posto Roosevelt. Ideally he would have left a much larger contingent, led by a trained *indigenista* like himself. But at sixty-one, his health was poor, and he was soon assigned to Funai's office in Porto Velho. Apoena couldn't stay behind either. Whatever his left-wing tendencies, he was good at his job, and Funai asked him to be the director of the Aripuaná Indigenous Park, as the Cinta Larga reserve was known.

Even after the feast, groups like Mankalu's continued to come for gifts. In January 1970, the workers radioed, "Emergency call. The Indians took our sugar, *farinha*, and rice. We're eating nuts. Situation is difficult; we need medicine urgently." Another dispatch followed: "They rifled through everything, opened our suitcases, embraced us, took our clothing and also some papers." Even when fresh provisions arrived by mule train, the workers complained that "the food was contaminated with impurities, third-class materials, *farinha* mixed with pork hairs, shards of glass, matchsticks, etc." Many quit. For one whole month the only agent on duty was Pedro, a young, Portuguese-speaking Arara who'd escaped from a rubber plantation as a child.

Pedro was there when Oita, the one white men called Rapscallion, showed up. After the feast, Oita had awoken at his village to find that his brother was still alive. Looking for other survivors, they ran into Roberto Carlos, the boy with the long flowing hair, who was doing the same. Across three villages on the Stream of the Blackflies, just eight people, almost all kids, were left to rebuild their lives. As much as Oita felt like a loner, it was different to face actual solitude. For a Cinta Larga, your family was your world—an individual existence simply wasn't an option. To start a new family, though, they needed wives, and there was only one small girl in their group.

Chico and Apoena Meirelles, and Cândido Rondon before them, believed that attraction posts worked by luring primitive people with new technologies. But the attraction also came from a vacuum, after the destruction of the society that once flourished there, which left survivors desperate, adrift, drawn by any new source of gravity, any suggestion of life. It was this force that brought Oita back to the camp on the Roosevelt. (Roberto, like Maria Beleza, sought refuge at João Bravo's village, to the east.)

Oita had every reason to hate white men, prospectors in particular. But he'd always have a soft spot for the ones who'd welcomed him at Raul's camp, and he took a liking to a Funai worker known as Sapecado, who used to work for Raul himself. Oita started joining him on side adventures, even as it became clear that Sapecado was as much a *bandido* as a prospector. Panning for gold once, he was said to have murdered his fellow workers by giving them poisoned watermelon, just to take their haul. Oita would later deny he ever went around with Sapecado at all, but Tataré heard him brag about shaking a vine to distract a rubber tapper so that Sapecado could swoop in for the kill. "Sapecado was Oita's teacher," recalled Roberto. "Oita learned to shoot from him."

Oita took to spending the night at Posto Roosevelt, though he always returned to the forest to hunt and look for survivors with his brother. Sometimes, when Pedro Arara was left on his own, subsisting on little more than squash from the garden, Oita and his brother would share freshly caught game with him. By now they'd learned enough Portuguese to taunt him, saying, "Funai abandoned you. Let's go back to the forest."

But Pedro demurred. Having grown up among white people, he didn't feel at home in the forest anymore. And he didn't want to lose his job.

"Ah, you're afraid we're going to kill you," Oita told him. "We won't kill you. You're an Indian, too."

* * *

It was the dry season of 1971 when Mankalu made his second trip to the camp on the Roosevelt, again bringing his two sons with him, as well as Tataré. Pio, as always, relished these opportunities to spend time with his father. "You have to learn how to hunt," Mankalu would tell him. "You have to get so good at hunting that you can take down a harpy eagle"—the large, proud birds whose white under-feathers were highly prized in headdresses. "And you have to learn how to plant crops. If you don't know how to do these things, how are you going to have your own family, have children, have a wife?"

At first the visit seemed unremarkable. Oita was elsewhere. Once again, the white men happily handed over their axes and machetes. On the way back, though, Pio's father began to cough. His brother, too. Back in their longhouse, red rashes broke out on their faces and necks and spread across their bodies. Their lips split open, their mouths filled with white spots. Their eyelids swelled up; they couldn't bear seeing light.

The sickness soon spread to the rest of the village. Based on the symptoms, Pio would come to believe it was measles, which had plagued Brazil's contact efforts since the earliest days of Rondon's SPI. Even when a measles vaccine became available, Funai did little better. Antônio Cotrim, the agent who'd so influenced Apoena as a teenager, quit around this time, explaining, "I don't want to be the Indians' gravedigger."

Strangely, the outbreak hardly affected Pio at all. He watched as everyone else grew feverish and weak. Suspecting the sickness came from inside the longhouse, many fled into the forest. Even Mankalu fled, despite his courage. Pio and his brother followed close behind, until his brother fell to the ground. Pio tried to drag him, but he was too small for his brother's helpless weight. He resorted to pulling his brother's hair, but the hair came out in his hand, so he left him there.

In the forest, Mankalu built a lean-to where they could wait out the disease. But he soon realized he wasn't going to make it either. "I want to die in my house," he said to Pio. Mankalu had barely begun teaching his son how to be a man, but now it was Pio who helped *him*—the hunter who'd faced down jaguars, the warrior who'd battled gun-wielding white men—make his way back. Once inside their hut, beneath rafters he'd lashed together with his own hands, Mankalu dropped into his hammock, unable to move again.

Pio stayed by his side until, three days later, his father's skin went cold. Many others would remember the sight of parents and grandparents lying motionless in faintly swinging hammocks. Some would remember fleeing, trying to save themselves, and hearing the cries of babies left behind. There are even stories of jaguars devouring helpless victims. According to tradition, the dead were supposed to be buried right there in the longhouse. Roberto Carlos was far from the only one who'd been too weak to fulfill this duty. But Pio, small as he was, took it upon himself to bury his father. He used a knife to dig a shallow pit below his father's hammock and cut the strings. The body slumped into the grave; Pio covered it with dirt.

CHAPTER 8

REVENGE AND FORGIVENESS

After quitting his job at *O Globo*, Possidônio Bastos entered Funai's official *indigenismo* course. His instructors, perhaps detecting his left-wing sensibilities, deemed him "temperamental," and he failed to receive a certificate. But his mind was already made up: he wanted to join Apoena. He gave up his apartment in Brasília, said goodbye to his girlfriend, and flew to Rondônia. Delighted to see his friend, and unconcerned about credentials, Apoena initially hired Possidônio as a rank-and-file worker at the Seventh of September post. What the reporter lacked in experience, he made up for with enthusiasm. After just a few months on the job, Apoena sent him to take charge of Posto Roosevelt.

There was no question the camp needed enlightened leadership. Sapecado, the former prospector, continued to pan for diamonds on the side. Most of the other workers were settlers who'd failed to make it elsewhere on the frontier. Some, Possidônio discovered, were trading clothes for sex with Cinta Larga girls, described by one worker as "chubby, beautiful…like a rancher's wife." He banned them from handing out gifts when he wasn't around.

Oita continued to visit, and while he still spent time with Sapecado, he also took a shine to Possidônio. "The first time he met me, he gave me three chocolates," Oita later said. "He gave me a recorder and told me, 'Speak into this microphone, son.' I didn't want to. I wanted to break it to see who was talking in there, but he wouldn't let me. He knew how to calm me down, and he'd hide the recorder so I couldn't smash it to pieces." This boy who was always looking for approval seemed at last to have found it. Possidônio was also there when Oita's mother, his sister Alzira, and a few other relatives showed up. "My relatives cried a lot," Oita would recall. "My mother thought I was dead. Possidônio watched it all and cried, too." Oita's mother wanted to take him to a Cinta Larga village. But in Oita's recollection, Possidônio said, "No, he's my friend. Even if you tie him up, I won't let him go."

Roberto Carlos, the boy with the long flowing hair, also arrived around this time. Sucked in by the same vacuum as Oita, he became one of the first permanent Cinta Larga residents, stringing up his hammock next to Possidônio's. Apoena had tasked Possidônio with transforming the camp into a permanent base, erecting five shacks with local wood and preparing the fields for rice and beans, corn and squash. Just as they had with the prospectors, the boys were all too happy to lend a hand. They had little way to grasp the larger purpose: to construct a model village where future waves of Cinta Larga could become agricultural workers, leaving behind lives as hunters to enter Brazilian society. Even Apoena, despite his youthful idealism, had come to support this plan. He was warming to his father's pragmatism. Initially, after one prospector was authorized to pan for diamonds nearby, he'd objected, calling it "incoherent" with the "defense of our Indians." Faced with the need for an airstrip at Posto Roosevelt, however, he swallowed his pride and sought the assistance of Raul the Spaniard. Roberto and Oita helped in the endeavor, too, flattening the earth with a heavy wooden stomping tool.

Despite Rondon's timeless dictum, "Die if you must, but never kill," most Funai agents slept with a shotgun by their side. Even if they didn't intend to use it, displaying the weapon prevented nighttime sneak attacks. Possidônio, though, didn't feel the need. In a letter to a colleague back in the *Globo* newsroom, he wrote, "Indians, like children, are good. But you must never shout at them or get angry with their chiefs. They receive the white man well as long as, obviously, the white man is well-intentioned with them....Tell everyone it's easy to live with Indians. They're much more docile than traffic cops."

What Possidônio didn't realize was that, no matter how friendly Oita and Roberto might seem, some Cinta Larga visited not just to receive gifts but to scope the camp out for an attack. Much like Apoena and Chico failed to distinguish between Cinta Larga and Suruí, plenty of Cinta Larga saw all white men as one and the same. Even after killing Didi, they wanted revenge for the feast.

* * *

Pio wasn't the only one to survive the outbreak at his village. Tataré eventually recovered, too. Emerging from the longhouse, he found Pio perched at the edge of a stream, bow and arrow in hand, trying to shoot fish as they darted by, without much success. Not a single adult was left to take care of them. Tataré's grandmother had perished; his aunt and uncle had fled in panic. Pio's stepmother was still breathing, but she was barely past puberty herself, and remained too weak to rise from her hammock.

A few other kids had survived, and after several days without food, they were hungry. They dug up some manioc from the village fields, which kept them from starving, but their bodies yearned for meat. One of the kids wasted away to little more than skin and bone; whenever he tried to walk, he fell down.

Up until that point, hunting had been a game for Pio, a way to dream at becoming a man like his father. Now, for the first time, he actually needed to procure sustenance. He hid by the stream, waiting for little birds to come and bathe so he could try to shoot them, wondering, *Where should I go now? What should I do with my life?* There was a slightly older boy in their group, but he was just as hopeless at hunting. Left without anyone to turn to, Pio discovered that he could remain calm in the face of extremity, and take the initiative when others failed to. There was a kind of rat that made its nest in the yam bushes of the village gardens. Pio had grown up hearing the myth of Popóa—the Owl—who brought a rat to his mother to cook; she refused, but Pio couldn't afford to be so picky. With his child-size arrows, he finally managed to kill one.

Pio, as the hunter, had the right to decide how his catch would be divvied up. Meager as it was, he invited everyone else to eat with him, and rallied the boys to pursue even the most pathetic of animals. Sometimes they hunted lizards, sometimes frogs. Later Pio would learn they were far from the only kids to go through this. One little boy survived by foraging for berries and insects, becoming an expert at climbing trees. When at last he found refuge in another village, he came to be known as Fruit.

Pio was small for his age, but hunger made him brave. Walking through the forest one day, he came upon a burrow that gave off the distinctive musk of a wild pig, and found a mother tending her young. Pio's arrows were far too small to kill her, so he raised his arms and shouted, making as much noise as he could. The animals scattered. Running after the piglets, he managed to grab hold of one, and he swung it by the feet as hard as he could against a tree trunk. He killed three this way before the mother charged him. He clambered up a tree to avoid her long canines. Eventually she gave up—and that night, the kids ate their fill.

A month after the outbreak, Pio's stepmother started to feel better. The kids were still hungry most of the time, but she took to making *i*, their manioc beer, and this provided some comfort. One day she said she wanted to make *maamdík*, the toasted Brazil nut crumble, so they all went to collect some fallen *maam* pods. The journey took a day and a half each way, and when they got back to Pio's village, they sensed that someone else had been there. Inside the longhouse, once their eyes had adjusted to the dark, they noticed a strange artifact on the crossbeam where men normally stashed their arrows. It was a long, dark metal tube seated in smooth wood—a shotgun.

"What is that?" Pio asked.

"That's the white man's weapon," his stepmother said. "Be careful. It could explode and kill us."

Pio had already seen the "white man's arrow," the shotgun primers that Oita had once shown off, but never anything like this. Terrifying as it was, Pio couldn't help feeling curious. Like when he'd spotted the interlopers with his uncle—like he would again and again—he couldn't resist the temptation to get to know the white man's things, the white man's world. He took the shotgun down and held it in his hands. "How do you use it?" he wondered aloud.

"See that hole?" his stepmother said. "You blow there and it shoots."

Lucky for them, the gun wasn't loaded. The kids were still examining it when the two straw hatches of the longhouse entrance parted, and a bar of sunlight penetrated the dark. It was Pichuvy, the boy who'd joked that Pio's father was a liar. He was from the Kakin lineage, but their families were close.

"You're here!" Pichuvy said. "What happened?"

Pio told him about the poison, about the deaths. It was no shock to Pichuvy, whose own father and grandfather had attended the feast with the prospectors. His grandfather had succumbed to the sickness, but his father was still around, and they'd joined up with a handful of other survivors, including some able young men. The group was camped at a stream a couple of hours away, beating the water with the *dakáptapóa* vine. They'd already collected dozens of fish. "Come, let's eat!" Pichuvy said.

Pio and Tataré and the other kids arrived to find Oita at the stream. It was he who'd left the shotgun in Pio's longhouse. He still hunted with bow and arrow—and he'd just taken down two full-size pigs. It was more meat than the kids had seen in months. *Now the misery is over!* Pio thought.

They all spent several nights camped by the stream. Pio's step-mother wanted to go to João Bravo's village, to seek refuge with her late husband's ally. She asked Pio to go with her. Tataré would join her there, like many others. But Pio had already decided to follow Oita and the other men wherever they went—even when they said they were going to the very same place where his father had caught the disease.

* * *

Pio found a kind of happiness at Posto Roosevelt. Roberto Carlos, seeing how small he was, took Pio under his wing, helping him get a handle on their new reality. At first Pio couldn't stomach even the smell of the food, and ate only *farinha* mixed with sugar. Little by little he got used to the rice and heavily seasoned beans. Possidônio also gave him clothes, but they were far too large for him, so he wore a billowing T-shirt that was almost like a dress. Oita, for his part, preferred actual dresses, far more comfortable than shirts and pants. He and Roberto already spoke some Portuguese; now Pio learned by trial and error. Possidônio would ask him to fetch a *martelo*—a hammer—and Pio would go off and grab a random tool, bringing back one after the other until he got it right.

One day Pio heard a deep buzz coming from the sky. He felt the vibrations of the propeller slicing through the air even before the little plane could be seen descending from the clouds. *What kind of animal is that?* Pio wondered. Then he saw a person inside and more or less figured it out. What mystified him was when the pilot leaped out of the cockpit and asked for a glass of ice water—probably a joke, since there was no electricity.

The bush planes brought supplies as well as cash, which Possidônio redistributed to the workers—including his Cinta Larga helpers. "This money is for buying shirts, shoes," he told them. "Funai is paying you for your work. The government is paying you." Of course, it was impossible to convey what all this meant, even more hopeless than explaining ice water. "Roberto, what is this?" Pio asked. Roberto had no clue either. At one point Pio tried tearing up the tough little pieces of paper, but Roberto told him, "Save this stuff. It might be useful for something."

Outsiders always remarked on Pio's endless curiosity, his eagerness to meet new people. At one point a game hunter came to the post, and Pio led him into the forest to track down a jaguar. As thanks, he gave Pio a towel, though Pio (once again) couldn't imagine what on earth it was for.

One day in November 1971, a strange group of Cinta Larga men showed up. They'd come on previous occasions, but always refused to socialize with the white men. Perhaps sensing that trouble was brewing, Sapecado, the prospector-cum-*bandido*, chose that moment to quit. Almost all the other workers followed, leaving Possidônio with no other staff but the radio operator and an Indigenous cook, Maria, Pedro Arara's mother. Nothing seemed off to Possidônio, though. When the strange group decided to leave, he ran after them, insisting all were welcome there.

That night, the visitors told Maria to prepare some *i*. They sang and danced. Possidônio actually recorded it, perhaps feeling safe because his new friend Oita joined in. After he went to sleep, some of the men sneaked into the storeroom and gaped at all the supplies, wondering, *How could someone accumulate so many things and refuse to share them?* Then they grabbed the radio and threw it in the river. They killed the mules with bow and arrow. Pio was far too young to be included in any plan, but Roberto could see what was coming. Pleading with the men not to kill anyone, he persuaded them only to spare Maria. Though barely adolescent, he was sleeping with her, and now declared her to be his wife. "If you want to kill her, you'll have to kill me," he said.

When Possidônio woke in the morning, he went to the river to wash his face. The men were waiting for him there, carrying bows and arrows, machetes, and a shotgun taken from the storeroom. Trying to appear unthreatening, they smiled and said in their rudimentary Portuguese, "How are you, how are you?" Oita's own story of this episode would go back and forth over the years. Sometimes he'd chuckle and say he joined the ambush. Other times he'd insist he tried to stand in the way. While he had no special connection to the radio operator, he felt an intense bond with Possidônio, this white man who was so affectionate with him. But in this version, his own brother, finally seeing his chance to get even, had joined up with the strange new group. "If you don't let me kill them," he told Oita, "I'll kill you, too."

Possidônio didn't try to escape. Slowly the men approached, surrounding him. The radio operator, realizing what was happening, ran and jumped into the river. The current carried him away; he'd never be seen again.

When Pio realized what had happened, he wondered, *What am I going to do now? Where am I going to go?* But there was no time for despair. Fearing that other white people would come to take their own revenge, he and Roberto saw little choice but to follow Oita and the rest of the men back into the forest, bringing Maria Arara with them. The warriors looted two rifles, two revolvers, and half a dozen shotguns. Most of the ammunition remained in the storehouse, and when they set fire to it, the shells and bullets exploded. Following tradition, they left nothing standing.

*　　*　　*

Apoena arrived with a small crew to find Posto Roosevelt in ruins. He discovered Possidônio's rotting corpse a mile and a half downriver, caught in some low-hanging branches. Machete blows had left his face unrecognizable. His shoulder was riddled with shotgun pellets. Two arrows protruded; Apoena pulled them out.

Having seen Possidônio's ease among the Suruí at the Seventh of September post, even Chico was shocked. "This could have happened to me, to Apoena, or to any one of us, given the great trust we had built," he wrote.

Chico saw the razing as a clear sign the Cinta Larga didn't want anyone there. At the very least, he felt it prudent to wait before rebuilding. But Apoena ordered his crew to put up tents amid the ashes. The government sent a half-dozen police officers to guard them, but Apoena insisted they carry only the most innocuous of weapons, rusty old muskets from the First World War. He did take some precautions, ordering everyone to be up before dawn with fireworks ready to be fired straight at any attackers. "The Indians have already seen guns, and they won't be scared off by shots in the air," he explained. Taking Rondon's dictum to a new level, he added, "I must make clear that anyone who gives in to his cowardice, and fires his gun at an Indian, will be killed."

During the day, Apoena and his crew searched for the radio operator's body. They also strung a cord between two trees and hung up knives, axes, and machetes as gifts, along with the two arrows that Apoena had retrieved: a peace offering. This was a critical moment in any contact effort: weathering an attack and showing they didn't want revenge. For weeks, the gifts remained untouched, but at night the camp would hear the calls of the *nambu*, the *mutum*, the *jacu*—birds that aren't nocturnal—interspersed with the high-pitched whistle of monkeys. Spooked, a police sergeant said, "Who ever heard a monkey whistle at night? If arrows start to rain down on us, you can bet we won't end up on a skewer. We'll be shooting back."

As usual, Apoena was brave to the point of recklessness. At one point he plunged into the forest alone, ignoring the sergeant's pleas. A few minutes later, no fewer than eight shotgun blasts came, one grazing his shoulder. He ran back to camp, where the cops set off fireworks.

* * *

Pio and Roberto didn't stay long in the forest. Maria Arara cried every night, insisting that they return; Roberto, meanwhile, was having nightmares. He became convinced that a notorious warrior, Amissut—Ugly Nose—was coming for them. In a fresh outbreak of disease downriver, Amissut's son had died, and Amissut interpreted this as the clothes-wearers' revenge for the deaths of Possidônio and the radio operator. Blaming that strange Cinta Larga group for starting the feud, he exacted his own revenge, killing Oita's brother when he was hunting alone. It was the logic of *wepika*, become a hall of mirrors.

Even as a teenager, Roberto stood out for combining Cinta Larga boldness with a peculiar sensitivity. "Shall we go give ourselves up to the white men?" he asked Pio. "Better to be killed by them than by our own people."

When Pio and Roberto returned to the Roosevelt post, it was teeming with activity. Seeing Roberto carrying three firearms, the cops steeled themselves for battle, but Maria shouted in Portuguese that they came in peace, and a canoe was sent across. Roberto tried to make it clear he'd opposed the attack, saying he'd taken the weapons to make sure they didn't fall into the wrong hands. He even offered his help in retaliating, miming the shooting of a gun.

Apoena only asked Roberto to convey a message: he bore no grudge. He wanted the attackers to know that Funai, unlike other outsiders, hadn't come to invade their land but to help them. It took a few months, but the warriors finally agreed to return Possidônio's recorder, notebook, and revolver as a show of goodwill. What really won them over was when one showed up with an infection, and was successfully treated with a newfangled medicine. Some even moved to the attraction post; Oita and Pichuvy came back, too.

Apoena would never feel comfortable at Posto Roosevelt. He couldn't help imagining how his friend had died, and felt responsible. "He was very abrupt and gruff, much more than at any other place we visited," one reporter noted. Denise Maldi, Apoena's anthropologist wife, admitted that she "never liked" Posto Roosevelt, that it "seemed to conceal a sinister air." Still, she attributed Possidônio's death to "incomprehension," lamenting that "it wasn't yet possible for these peoples to know who their heroes were." And indeed, it's worth wondering if Oita might have turned out differently with Possidônio, rather than an outlaw like Sapecado, as his "teacher."

The Cinta Larga, for their part, remained obviously suspicious: "The whole time those eyes, men, women, children, staring, following every movement," as the reporter described it. Chico sometimes flew in with supplies. Once, when he offered Pichuvy food, Pichuvy demanded he eat it first to prove it wasn't poison. Chico didn't understand, so Pichuvy grabbed a spoonful and shoved it in Chico's mouth.

Pichuvy couldn't stop wondering when the white men were going to kill him. He worried about the radio the outsiders used to summon their friends. He said to Pio, "Let's throw the radio in the river," as Oita's group had done before killing Possidônio. But Pio refused.

"My grandfather died because of the white man's disease," Pichuvy told Pio. "Your father is dead, your brother is dead—why are we living with these white men?" Pichuvy even claimed he would have joined the attack himself, if he were older. "Let's kill these white men," he said.

Pichuvy also argued with Roberto. "Is the white man your father?" Pichuvy asked him. "Do you remember that the white man killed your father? Do you remember that the white man cut your father up and fed him to the dogs?"

"I don't remember anymore," Roberto said. "He died, and that's it!"

"You want to die here," Pichuvy said. "I'm going back to the forest. Let's go back to the forest. Pio?"

But Pio liked the white men. He came to see Apoena and Chico almost as surrogate parents, ever willing to take care of him, to teach him. The truth was, they were far more affectionate than his own father had ever been. They encouraged him to call them *papai*—"daddy"—and he liked this. On one visit, Chico gave him the first shirt that actually fit his tiny frame. A photo from this time shows him in a crisp, short-sleeve button-up, cream-colored with a red lozenge pattern. Looking curiously at the camera, he appears no older than nine or ten. He is a full head shorter than Roberto Carlos, who wears a new-looking red T-shirt with white and navy stripes, smiling faintly as he ties a toy balloon in Pio's hands.

Chico invited Pio to join him on a plane ride. To load the aircraft as full of provisions as possible, Funai agents removed the seats and sat on sacks of *farinha* or tins of cooking oil, without seatbelts. Pio didn't know the difference. He listened with excitement at the tentative chop, chop, chop of the propeller, which became almost invisible as it reached full speed. The plane accelerated, the passengers jostling as the wheels skated over potholes in the short, packed-dirt runway. At the far end were the carcasses of planes that had attempted to land but failed to stop. Pio saw the ground falling away just in time. They rose fast, and the temperature dropped just as quickly, and every time they plunged into a cloud, he felt like a leaf in the wind. Below was a sight Pio had never seen: the forest canopy that had always been in its rightful place above him, a seemingly endless expanse of green, interrupted only by the squiggle of the Roosevelt, its rocky tumult reduced to a minuscule dappling of white.

Even Westerners familiar with air travel found these bush planes terrifying. One reporter wrote that they "seemed a lot like flying sardine tins." Sometimes a storm would gather out of nowhere, and they were forced to land on highways; sometimes the planes crashed in the forest, and Funai agents perished. The pilots liked to joke: "In-flight service? Rosary, holy water, and the communion wafer." The macabre joke would have been lost on Pio—and anyway, he was too thrilled to care. For the first time, he saw where the forest ended. He saw the vast road that Oita and Roberto had told him about, with its "houses that move," as well as the unthinkably large settlements that sprouted from it: another world. *Oh, my God*, he would recall thinking. *I'm going to get to know all of this stuff.*

CHAPTER 9

A KIDNAPPING

Among the survivors who showed up at Posto Roosevelt was Oita's half-sister Maria. Her travails hadn't ended after the feast. At João Bravo's village, she'd gotten her first period. Tradition mandated that she spend three months in a separate little structure of wood and straw, so cramped that she couldn't stretch out fully. Obliged to spend day and night making necklaces, she couldn't ask for food, no matter how starved she felt, because, her grandfather warned her, someone might poison it. Now and then she might be offered a morsel in exchange for a necklace; she could eat that. Otherwise, even when she smelled monkey being cooked, she had to lower her head and pretend she wasn't hungry. Her only companion was a dog given by her family, who told her it had dropped from a passing plane. Ordinarily, pets were never killed or eaten, but during a feast the dog was taken from her and shot through with arrows. Many years later, even amid everything else that happened to her, this memory was one of her most painful.

And then, seemingly out of nowhere, João Bravo murdered her uncle. Young as she was, Maria had no inkling of the intrigues playing out around her, of João Bravo's paranoid attacks. All she knew was that she had to escape once again. She was wandering in the forest when Oita found her and brought her to Posto Roosevelt. With her long black hair, perfectly parted down the middle to reveal a shy hint of a smile, she made an immediate impression. Her friend Joana would recall, "Everyone wanted Maria, whites and Indians both. We called her Maria *parir*"—the Cinta Larga word for "beautiful." It was a Funai worker who dubbed her Maria Beleza, and when her documents were drawn up, this became her actual legal name. If her official birthday was at all accurate, she would have been fifteen at the time.

By now Maria was already on her second marriage, nothing unusual for a Cinta Larga teenager. Her first husband was an old man from the Stream of the Blackflies, killed in a forgotten feud. Her current husband also lived at Posto Roosevelt, but they had no children.

Unlike Pio and Roberto Carlos, Maria found life at Posto Roosevelt difficult. It didn't help that Chico and Apoena had left the camp in the care of far less enlightened men. In February 1972, three months after Possidônio's killing, Apoena had written a resignation letter in which the tragedy of his dear friend's death seemed to contaminate his hopes for the Suruí and the Cinta Larga: "It will be too difficult for me to watch the extermination of yet another people, and to contemplate the senseless destruction of my dreams, the crazy dreams of my youth, which were never possible....In less than four years their lands have already begun to be devastated, epidemics have already left their mark, and many of them have already fallen on the first kilometers of the long road where they will find misery, hunger, the prostitution of their women, the end of their dreams." Apoena, like his mentor Antônio Cotrim, didn't want to go down in history as the Indians' "pimp," as "a spectator to their plunder, exploitation."

Apoena's letter was leaked to the press (possibly by Apoena himself). It should have been the last straw for the military regime. Funai's own president, a general, once called Apoena an "enfant terrible" with "communist ideas." But Funai needed Apoena, because he was so good at what he did. Building new highways across the Amazon, the government wanted to avoid any more condemnation for failing to protect Indigenous people. Instead, after a brief suspension, Apoena was transferred to another contact effort. The truth was, he was eager to move on. As he wrote in his diary, "Really nothing in this region excites me. I have already traveled all the paths. I am left with no other alternative but to go in search of new missions....I could very well remain absorbed with my books...but an unstoppable desire burns within me for adventures, conquests, victories, or even defeats." As for Chico, his health continued to decline; he died in 1973.

In their place, a Funai agent named Alceu was put in charge. He insisted that all the kids wear clothes and flip-flops, but Maria was never the type to blindly follow an order. In this way she was following an age-old Cinta Larga tradition—never to submit to another man's authority. This tradition didn't really include women, but Maria would always draw inspiration from her grandmother, whom she remembered as a kind of *zapiway*. Maria hated the long flowery dresses that Alceu pushed on her; she accepted only the underwear. "Maria! Clothes!" Alceu would shout. If she dawdled, he beat her with a belt. Still she kicked off her flip-flops. Eventually he tied them to her feet.

Other kids had it even worse. Alceu demanded that everyone start using a pit as a latrine. When he caught one of Maria's friends defecating in the trees, he smeared shit on the kid's face as punishment. Another friend suggested they secretly cut some of Alceu's sugarcane crop. Maria was too scared to go; her friend was caught and took the beating of a lifetime.

Even Alceu was better than Sapecado, the prospector, who returned to take over as head of the post. He became obsessed with Maria, despite her young age. Claiming to have met her before, he showed her a photo of a naked Indian girl and said it was her. She even came to believe it was Sapecado who'd grabbed her hand at the feast, though other Cinta Larga didn't remember seeing him there. Funai, for its part, couldn't approve of any such relationship. Indigenous people were considered wards of the Brazilian state, "legally children," as one newspaper put it. In April 1973, when Sapecado made an official request to marry Maria, Funai responded that the Cinta Larga remained at a "very primitive cultural stage"—and that, anyway, there were already too few women for Cinta Larga men. What remained unsaid was that Funai couldn't afford another scandal of the sort that had sunk the original Indian Protection Service.

Funai ordered Sapecado removed from Posto Roosevelt, but he didn't go easily: when a new agent showed up to replace him, they exchanged gunfire. He continued to roam Cinta Larga country. One newspaper described him as "an illiterate cowboy who knows all the Indian footpaths in Rondônia"; another observer called him a "savage from the city." Even the Cinta Larga saw him this way. "All he carried was shotgun shells," Tataré would recall. "He ate jungle game without salt, just like us." On the Amazon frontier, it was never easy to separate rumor from fact, but one Funai agent discovered that Sapecado was wanted for nine homicides in nearby Presidente Médici.

Plenty of Cinta Larga wanted to escape the brutal conditions at Posto Roosevelt, but in Joana's recollection, when she and Maria left, it was to meet up with Sapecado and another white frontiersman, a third girl's love interest. Joana and Alzira, Oita's sister, both believe that Maria, similarly, *wanted* to be with Sapecado. And indeed, it's possible to imagine the allure, to a young girl who knew nothing of the outside world, of this blustering, cocksure gunslinger. But, of course, she was just that: a girl, barely adolescent. In later years she'd express nothing but revulsion, saying she never wanted anything to do with him at all.

Whatever their reasons, it was a difficult journey for three girls on their own. To avoid being caught, they skirted the usual mule path and walked through the forest, where they noticed jaguar tracks. Unable to hunt or improvise shelter, they had to spend a hungry night in the rain. But Cinta Larga girls could also be brave. People told of a group of women who'd gone to retrieve their husbands' bodies after an Enawenê-Nawê attack, hauling them back home with the head strap they used to carry root vegetables, even as their enemies watched in shock. Then there was Roberto Carlos's sister, widowed by disease only for her new husband to refuse her children; she escaped into the forest and raised them on her own, hunting and growing crops without any man's help. Maria's grandmother, in other words, wasn't the only exception to the rule of feminine passivity. At last the girls reached a road where they found Sapecado. He was on horseback, with mules to carry the girls to a Funai base in Riozinho, which doubled as a free dormitory for Indians passing through.

Roberto Carlos, now a full-time employee of Funai, witnessed their arrival. No one attempted to stop Sapecado from staying, and if there was any commotion that night, Roberto slept through it. In Maria's recollection, she woke in the dark to find Sapecado clamping an ether-soaked rag over her mouth—and the next thing she knew, they were on the road.

*   *   *

For all Maria's willfulness, she had no way to overpower her kidnapper. Sapecado took her first to the dusty boomtown of Vila Rondônia, where Raul the Spaniard lived, a hundred miles northwest on Highway 364. Raul's men often brought Indians by his house, instructing them (not unlike Chico and Apoena) to call Raul "Daddy" and Raul's wife, Maria Graça, "Mommy." Maria Graça, who was in her early twenties then, would remember Beleza as "striking, very pretty, very, very young, very, very shy"—in contrast to "big, ugly" Sapecado.

Whenever Sapecado was away from Vila Rondônia, prospecting in Cinta Larga country, he kept Maria Beleza locked in a house with a chain around her ankle, long enough to reach the bathroom and the kitchen. He got her to wear the dresses that Alceu had failed to. Once he brought back a doll and said they would have a child just like it. Another time he returned with gold, tossing a nugget on the table. Maria had no idea what it was, but he said the shiny metal would provide a future for their children. She was picking up Portuguese but there was much she didn't understand. He didn't call her Maria or even Beleza, much less what her parents had called her, Mabeuíti. He called her *nega*, a Brazilian term for a dark-skinned woman, which she came to think was her name. ("Sapecado" referred to a mixed-race man with fair skin and kinky hair; his real name was either José João Santana Filho or José João Pereira da Conceição.)

From what Maria Graça understood, Beleza had been a "gift" from an Indian chief. This may have been a tall tale told by prospectors, but arrangements like these weren't uncommon. At an attraction post in the eastern part of Cinta Larga country, one Funai agent wrote: "I report a new marriage between the Gavião interpreter and the daughter of one of the chiefs. We gather that their intention is to give women to all of us. We failed to dissuade them of this idea." The idea was to forge alliances with tool-rich outsiders, an old strategy; in the 1600s, the Tupinambá had ceded their daughters to French colonists.

Whatever the truth, most Cinta Larga saw Maria as Sapecado's "wife," no matter that she was his captive. Women kidnapped in battles with enemy groups, like Mankalu's Zoró bride, were also considered legitimate spouses, willing or not. A woman was just about the only possession one could "steal." This was the word used even when a woman ran off of her own accord with a man she hadn't been promised to—rare romances that almost always sparked a violent reaction by her male relatives.

As a rule, a Cinta Larga woman couldn't actively choose her partner, only veto an unacceptable one, asking her father and brothers to take her back. She did, however, enjoy a safety valve. As the anthropologist Carmen Junqueira later observed, "As soon as her husband takes a nap, a woman will allow another man to contribute to the formation of the child in her womb"—as they believed not in a single act of conception, but in a necessary accumulation of semen. These dalliances were usually an open secret. Upon childbirth, the rightful father would make a show of wanting to kill the baby until a relative calmed him down. Still, the theatrics overlaid a quieter everyday violence. In marriage, domestic abuse was common. Outside marriage, while there were plenty of genuine seductions, it was risky to refuse an advance. "In the old days, there was no flirtation," a slightly younger woman, Peneta, would recall. "A man would come and grab her. If she didn't accept it, he'd kill her later with poison."

Maria Beleza lacked any kind of safety valve. Far from her family, she had no recourse to male relatives, no possibility of escape. One year bled into another. Sometime in the mid-1970s, Sapecado took her to live at a ranch downstream from Posto Roosevelt. Paranoid she might sleep with his cook, he forbade her from going into the kitchen. Once, when she thought Sapecado was away, she went to the kitchen for a drink of water. Somehow Sapecado found out. He beat her, chained her up again, said he didn't want to see her face anymore. Even when he allowed her to accompany him outside, the abuse didn't stop. Once he abandoned her in the territory of another, almost certainly hostile Indigenous group. A rubber tapper, thinking she was his daughter, brought her back to him.

Sapecado's ranch was located in an area where the Cinta Larga had yet to be officially "pacified." Winning them over with the usual gifts of metal tools and sugar, he persuaded them to build an airstrip. Sometimes he flew off in a bush plane, and another prospector visited, telling Maria, "You don't deserve this. You're so beautiful, you deserve to be treated like a queen. I'm going to steal you away from him." But he never did.

Maria was washing clothes in a stream when some of the local Cinta Larga came upon her. Amazonians outside the reach of Western society were sometimes thought of as "isolated," but Maria had experienced a much more radical kind of isolation, so intense that she could scarcely speak her own native language anymore. Thinking she was a rubber tapper's wife, her own people nearly killed her.

Finally the day came when Maria went into the kitchen while Sapecado was watching from afar, and he came and struck her so hard, she lost consciousness. When she came to, armed Cinta Larga men had come to her aid, and Sapecado had run off. Bleeding from her nose, ears, and eyes, she thought she might die. She couldn't find her flip-flops, and was unused to walking barefoot, but she managed to follow them into the forest. The whole way to Posto Roosevelt, a few days' walk upriver, she was convinced Sapecado was coming to kill her.

Maria arrived at the Funai camp very skinny. But a nurse told her, "You have a baby inside you."

CHAPTER 10

INTO THE WORLD

Before Apoena moved on from Posto Roosevelt, he'd asked his workers to "prevent the Indians from traveling to Highway 364, to prevent them from contracting diseases and entering into contact with individuals lacking in morals and sensitivity." The Suruí were already visiting the road to try out some of the few Portuguese words they knew: "Give me axe. Give me machete." Some came away with beatings from white settlers, but those who got what they wanted were possibly even less fortunate. One group lived near a settlement known as Espigão d'Oeste, where they became full-time beggars.

When Pio decided to leave, it wasn't because of the conditions at Posto Roosevelt, which he would remember fondly, but because he was curious about the wonders of "the city." An older boy, Barroca, asked him, "Shall we escape?" They sneaked away at night, walking for two days until they reached Espigão. It was barely a town, much less a city, with more tractors than cars on its bumpy dirt roads. Yet the bustle came as a shock to Pio. Realizing that the "house that moves" was a vehicle that carried people, he wondered, *Why are white people always on the move? Why don't they stay home and relax?* He also marveled at Espigão's central square, which inverted the logic of a Cinta

Larga village. Trees were in the middle, houses on the edges—so many houses, with pitched metallic roofs that gleamed in the sun. One had wide-open doors and shelves of packaged sweets. Thinking them free for the taking, he tried to grab some, but the store owner stopped him.

At one point a man approached Pio on the street, such as it was. Everyone called him Tonho Castanha because he traded *castanha*, the nuts known as *maam* to the Cinta Larga. "Are you an Indian?" he asked Pio.

"I am," Pio said.

"Do you want to come live with me?" Tonho asked. "I have a son your size."

Pio, ever trusting of white men, responded simply, "I do."

In Pio's recollection, he went to live in Tonho's own home. Tonho himself died long ago, but his daughter Cleusa would remember it differently: while Pio sometimes visited, he slept at a free "hotel" where workers from nearby ranches could unload their pack mules and string up a hammock. In any case, Tonho took care of Pio, even sending him to the school where Cleusa was a teacher.

It wasn't long before Pio felt the itch to move again. *What am I doing here?* he asked himself. *All day looking at this square [chalkboard], being asked to do things. Writing is hard.* Also, he missed his people. He left for the Funai base in nearby Riozinho, where he reunited with Roberto Carlos.

One of Pio's most profound regrets, later in life, was that he didn't give school more of a chance. The head of the Funai base also sent Pio to classes, this time at a school in Riozinho, and despite his relative lack of education, he received top marks. "I didn't make trouble, so the teacher liked me," he would recall. In the two or three years he spent there, he learned to read ("more or less") and even got along with the white kids. The rest of the time he worked for Funai, weeding the banana grove, planting vegetables, and occasionally accompanying an agent to transport supplies. One of the Funai agents started teaching Pio to drive the base's jeep—and this is what, in Pio's words, "ruined" him.

"If I'd known that I could have achieved more with an education, I might have stayed," Pio would lament. "But I had no father, no mother, nobody to tell me if school was good or bad." The teacher tried to persuade him to stay, saying, "Don't go back to the jungle. Stay here. You're my best student."

Now, though, Pio had a dream. He wanted to earn enough money to buy a car of his own.

PART TWO

THE TIME OF HARDWOOD

1980s

CHAPTER 11

CHIEFS

By the time Pio figured out how much trees were worth to white people, he'd spent a decade trying and failing to save his earnings as a Funai employee. Early on, he couldn't even tell the difference between the various bills—green, red, yellow, each with its own value. To the delight of many a white store owner, he'd hand over a large-denomination note and not wait for change. It didn't help that Brazil was in the midst of a long-running inflation crisis in which the currency, the *cruzeiro*, lost three-quarters of its value in the space of a year, only to be replaced by a new currency, the *cruzado*, which got rid of three zeroes, and then by the *cruzado novo*, which removed another three zeroes—only for the *cruzeiro* to return once again. Every time Pio visited town, prices were wildly changed.

Eventually Pio learned to do the math. Still he failed to hold on to his earnings. In the forest, clothes and boots fell apart fast—and he liked to dress well, favoring polo shirts. He also blew money on cookies, candies, and canned sardines, even though there was honey for free in the forest and plenty of fish in the rivers. He always wanted to try new things. The first time he tasted soda was at a bar in the city of Cacoal. It was a little blue bottle of Guaraná Antarctica, a popular

Brazilian beverage. At first he thought it was awful; the carbonation burned his tongue. But he came to love sugary sodas, all the more so when ice-cold, a pleasure he'd never known in his pre-electrified childhood.

Now in his twenties, Pio no longer marveled at the sight of Espigão d'Oeste, with its wooden shacks and bumpy dirt roads. Settlements had sprouted all along Highway 364, some swollen into sprawling cities like Cacoal, with a population of eighty thousand. Pio also learned about the world from his white coworkers at Funai. They taught him how to play soccer, and he fell in love with the sport. After matches, they would go to a bar to eat and drink beer together. Rondônia was too much of a backwater to have its own premier-league team, so like most people in the Amazon, he came to root for one of the big squads in southeastern Brazil—Flamengo, from Rio de Janeiro—thus stumbling into a kind of national tribe without ethnic boundaries. Suddenly he could connect to white people with whom he shared little else in common.

Though his official role was to cook or perform manual labor, Pio also acted as a go-between, trusted by whites and Indians alike. Partly this was because he was one of the few Cinta Larga who spoke decent Portuguese. He also felt a genuine affinity for men like Apoena Meirelles, who dedicated their lives to the Indigenous cause. It was the start of an enduring confusion in which he felt caught somewhere between the old world of his father and the new world of white society.

In the late 1970s, Pio had worked at the Serra Morena attraction post, in the eastern part of the territory—where many Cinta Larga were still "wild," including the renowned warrior João Bravo. Like the so-called cargo cults of the South Pacific, which attached religious meaning to military airdrops, João had once built an imitation runway to lure planes with Western goods. Still, when he showed up at the attraction post with a large entourage, Pio recalled, "I was afraid that they were going to kill everyone....I explained that Funai was good, that it was there to protect the Indians." Though they would later become rivals, at the time João knew Pio only as the son of his former companion in arms. It helped that Pio never got excited, never raised his voice; he was always calm, and his calmness put others at ease. Soon enough, João, too, would come to live at the attraction post. As Pio put it, "I helped to tame my relatives."

Over the years, Pio spent time at various Funai posts, even helping out with the Suruí, those historic enemies. By the time he was transferred back to Posto Roosevelt, around 1980, the onetime prospectors' camp had grown into a village—Roosevelt Village—with forty Cinta Larga residents, perhaps a tenth of their population at the time. Apoena had taught Pio to see the *chefe de posto* "like a father"; now this position was held by one Benedito Brígido da Silva, who, Pio recalled, "beat people to the point that I once saw someone's head bleed." Yet he also made sure that everyone performed their labors, and the result, in Pio's words, was "plenty." They made their own manioc flour and grew so much rice, beans, and squash that they sent the surplus to the Suruí.

Still, Pio came to feel there was something fundamentally wrong about this arrangement, and he wasn't alone. One day he was at the Funai base in Riozinho with his old friends Pichuvy and Roberto Carlos. Like Pio, Roberto traveled around working for Funai, spoke good Portuguese, and knew how to get along with white men, though he'd never roll over for them. He still had the same long flowing hair of his crooner namesake, but was also developing a belly, thanks to a diet newly rich in white rice, sugar, and processed food. Pichuvy, who stayed closer to Roosevelt Village, remained trimmer. He had a charisma similar to Pio's, but spoke less Portuguese. He still hadn't really warmed to white men, even if he couldn't help yearning for their luxuries. In

Riozinho that day, he and Pio were talking about their burning desire to own a car—and even fly a plane—when Roberto, with his peculiar brand of thoughtfulness, announced, "One day I want to be chief."

Pio himself had always wanted to be like his father, that great *zapiway*, or "owner of the house," from back in the days when a village was basically that: a house. As all three young men knew, though, those days were gone. No one could be said to "own" Roosevelt Village in the Cinta Larga sense of the word, which was less about property than the initiative to build it and care for those who lived there. In addition to some thatched-roof houses where the Cinta Larga slept, there were other buildings where Funai staff lived: who owned those? It was also more of a Western agglomeration, sheltering individuals from various families, lineages, regions, whoever showed up fleeing mass death at home. How to unite all these people without the automatic bond of crisscrossing marriages?

In the old days, if people were unhappy with a *zapiway*'s leadership, they would simply leave, defecting to another village or founding their own. The notion of a despot, foreign or otherwise, had always been unthinkable. Now, while a few individual headmen still held sway in scattered villages, most Cinta Larga had gathered at attraction posts—and for all its beneficence, Funai was unquestionably an alien authority. Pio recognized this. So did Pichuvy. The only question was: who would take charge?

"Roberto, leave the room," Pichuvy said, closing the door behind him. From the other side, Roberto heard Pichuvy say, "Now we're going to see who will be the chief of Roosevelt Village." Then he heard a loud smack as Pichuvy knocked Pio to the ground—an episode that people would laugh about for decades.

The plan wasn't to overthrow Funai, whose help they still welcomed, but for Pichuvy to lead the Cinta Larga at Roosevelt Village while Pio, with his knack for Portuguese, acted as a kind of foreign minister. "Whenever there's a problem," Pio explained to the others, "I'll deal with the white people." It wasn't a form of leadership his father would have recognized, but his father never had to deal with such complex diplomacy, with such a powerful rival. Just about everyone supported the idea.

Pio quickly demonstrated the knack for leadership he'd first revealed as a little boy. Raul the Spaniard was still combing the region for diamonds, and the next time he motored up the Roosevelt, Pio (though it didn't exactly fit with his newly invented role) led a contingent of warriors to "arrest" the legendary prospector, seizing his boat.

In the old days, no one would have thought to take hostages. But Pio saw an opportunity. He agreed to return the boat only after Raul bought a milling machine to process their rice.

*   *   *

It was 1984 when Cinta Larga warriors made an alarming discovery. In the northwestern reaches of their territory, near a river Brazilians called the Fourteenth of April, they came upon an area where all the trees had been knocked down. In their place, a few skinny humpbacked cows grazed on foreign grasses. A little farther along was another area with plots of manioc and corn. Most of these tracts were small, with a single wooden shack that played home to subsistence farmers. Some tracts, though, were incalculably vast, stretching all the way to the horizon, complete with sprawling ranch houses and packed-dirt airstrips, as well as cattle that numbered in the hundreds. This time it seemed the white men had invaded not to collect latex or prospect for diamonds but to establish permanent settlements, to take over Cinta Larga country and make it their own. *If we don't remove them*, Pio thought, *more will come.*

After more than a decade of death, disintegration, and disarray, the Cinta Larga were regaining a sense of themselves as protagonists of their world. In many ways it was a return to a reflexive, age-old pride. It also helped that some new friends questioned the idea that, as Theodore Roosevelt once put it—to the enthusiastic agreement of Cândido Rondon—Indians "must be the wards of the nation." One left-wing Funai agent, an Afro-Brazilian named Hugo Flores, assigned to Roosevelt Village in 1983, was shocked when Pio offered to carry his luggage and called him "Daddy," just like he'd learned with Apoena and Chico. There was a little school at the village, but the teacher spent more time fishing than teaching. Hugo took it upon himself to provide a civic education, and Pio came to understand that whatever aid Funai provided wasn't charity. On the contrary, the government owed them this—and more, as reparations for past injustices. Not long afterward, Pio defiantly told a Funai administrator, "You're here to serve *me*."

The Cinta Larga also gained white allies from outside the government. Some, like Carmen Junqueira, came as anthropologists and ended up as activists. Others, like João Dal Poz, came as volunteer health workers and ended up as anthropologists. In the heyday of the military dictatorship, their advocacy might have gotten them in trouble with the secret police. But after two decades in power, the regime was moribund, thanks in no small part to the ongoing economic crisis. All kinds of social movements were making their voices known, and the cause of Indigenous rights held more sway than ever before.

The most important victories came in the fight for *demarcação*, the official designation of lands for the exclusive use of Indigenous people. In this, too, the Cinta Larga were no longer content to be passive subjects of history. Several young men, including Roberto Carlos and Pio's old friend Tataré, joined official expeditions to define the limits of their territory, flying in bush planes to identify waterways and hacking paths on foot to mark land borders. Despite having lost a few large chunks of land to white settlers in the 1970s, the Cinta Larga ended up with four official *terras indígenas*, which together encompassed 6.7 million acres, an area nearly as large as Belgium. It was one of the largest Indigenous areas in Brazil—or for that matter, in the Western Hemisphere.

These victories were all the more remarkable given the pressure to develop the Amazon frontier. In 1970, Rondônia's official population was around a hundred thousand; a decade later, half a million. Even more settlers came after the BR-364 was finally paved with a half-billion-dollar loan from the World Bank. USAID financed bridges. Each year, new roads branched off from the highway, forming a fishbone pattern, with fresh fields spreading out, in turn, from each road. The point was to make the land "productive," but Amazonian soils proved paradoxically thin, as most nutrients were absorbed before they even reached the ground. Cash crops like coffee didn't thrive here. Instead the Brazilian government endlessly subsidized cattle pasture. In Rondônia alone, settlers had already razed five million acres of rainforest. The smoke that Pio had seen from his village as a boy now amassed each dry season, turning the sky beige for weeks on end. Even miles from any fire, ash would fall like alien snow.

Many newcomers simply ignored the prohibition on entering Indigenous areas. Who was going to stop them? Not the local police, firmly on the side of the settlers. Local government officials were usually settlers themselves. To be fair, some settlers didn't know they were trespassing. Signs were rarely posted. It took just a few years for jungle to reclaim the paths that marked the borders, and you could hardly tell the difference between the forest on one side and the forest on the other. Then there were the *grileiros*, con artists who sold forged land titles—so named because they stored their fake documents with *grilos* (grasshoppers) whose excrement aged them faster. In the region of Espigão d'Oeste, the most successful were four brothers, the Melhoranças, who marketed tracts with a map that falsely labeled Cinta Larga lands as their property. To assuage would-be settlers' fears, the map claimed the group had already been "in peaceful contact with civilized people for more than six years (enjoying work)."

One settler who ended up in Cinta Larga country was a pale-faced man with a jet-black mustache, Eloi Balbinot, who arrived from Brazil's South to join his brothers in search of opportunity. As far as he knew, the land west of the Roosevelt River was public and thus free for the taking, though technically he should have made an application with the agrarian reform agency. He helped to chainsaw a path through the trees, twenty-five miles in a straight line, just wide enough for pack mules. He was one of many who claimed plots on either side by marking the surrounding trunks and putting up signs—until the day Cinta Larga warriors showed up. One who spoke some Portuguese—a "civilized Indian," in Eloi's words—said, "You all can leave. This here belongs to the Indians." Eloi heard about one family who ignored three orders to depart, and paid for it with their lives. Preferring to avoid trouble, he obeyed.

* * *

Even in their newfound leadership roles, Pio and Pichuvy were neither heads of state nor commanders of an army. The Cinta Larga never bowed to any king-like figure; the warriors were nothing like soldiers. Their only allegiance was to their conscience, so all the two young chiefs could do was cajole. Though not afraid of violence, they wanted to avoid it—another way in which Pio diverged from his father, whose very name, Mankalu, came from the group he'd wiped out. Mankalu never lived in a world ruled by governments, a world in which (at least in theory) homicide was taboo, and the state claimed for itself (albeit tenuously) a monopoly on violence. Pio, by contrast, had already spent more than half his life among white people, and as a government employee. He understood the power of the Brazilian state, with its seemingly endless resources. Hoping to keep the government on his side, he tried—as he would always try—to go through official channels, at least at first.

The director of the Aripuanã Indigenous Park, Francisco ("Chicão") Assis da Silva, was all too happy to help, and not too concerned about procedure. With a revolver on his hip and a heavy gold chain around his neck, he was notorious in the region as a swashbuckling Indian agent in the mold of Apoena, his personal friend. "Our greatest pleasure, as *indigenistas* back then, was to remove prospectors, loggers, invaders, any white person who entered Indigenous territory," Chicão would recall. He and his men teamed up with Cinta Larga warriors to remove the settlers without bloodshed, and within a matter of months, the vast majority—thirty-nine families—had abandoned their claims. One settler had already been evicted from another Indigenous area by one of the same Funai agents. "I don't know whether to shoot you," the man lamented, "or to shoot myself in the ear."

Of course, these were just the subsistence farmers. The ranchers proved more obstinate. Roberto Rodrigues dos Santos, a brother-in-law of Espigão's mayor, was allegedly building his own road through Cinta Larga country. He didn't seem to care that this was illegal. Instead he followed the old Amazon frontier law that might makes right—a sentiment that trickled down to the men who managed the estates. When Chicão announced himself at the ranch of a politically connected ex-soldier, Manoel Ferro, the overseer asked, "Chicão who?"

"Chicão from Funai."

"There's no such thing as Funai here," the overseer replied.

Aware that these men had no respect for his employer, Chicão had asked one of his agents to wear dark sunglasses and pretend he was Federal Police. He even fired two warning shots in the air. Still the overseer refused to leave, declaring, "I'd rather die here."

Very well, then: Chicão set fire to the overseer's little wooden house. As flames consumed the thatch, the would-be martyr leaped out of the window "just like one of those *piau* [fish] that jump up waterfalls," in Chicão's words. The siege, though, was just beginning.

To further pressure the ranchers, Pio and a number of other men set up camp on a packed-dirt road that provided access from the west. "If you don't leave," Tataré told another overseer, "we'll eat your cows." Later the overseer's boss sent a messenger with his response: "I'm going to hire fifty gunmen to kill all of you." One night someone fired a few rounds at their camp.

Pio and Pichuvy decided to try a different tack. With a car and a driver provided by Funai, they traveled to Rondônia's capital, Porto Velho, to see Apoena Meirelles, who was now the Funai superintendent in charge of the whole region. As a young man, Apoena had once declared, "I would prefer to die fighting alongside the Cinta Larga, defending their lands, their rights, to seeing them begging on their own lands tomorrow." Unlike Chicão, however, Apoena was mostly past his thrill-seeking days. Age and experience had tempered his romantic self-image. Now he told people, "I never intended, nor could I, to be the 'savior of the Indians.' I don't even know if I can save myself. The Indian problem can't be solved by [individual] men....The Indian problem is structural." In other words, he'd become one of the bureaucrats he used to disdain. Receiving Pio and Pichuvy at his office, he insisted they wait for Funai to petition a judge, for the judge to issue an injunction, for police to evict the ranchers.

The Cinta Larga didn't have a word for "justice," and they couldn't be blamed for failing to understand what it was supposed to mean.

Tying up the eviction order in court, lawyers argued that the ranchers had arrived before the land was declared *terra indígena*, and none had seen an Indian until Funai supposedly "imported" some (even though the Cinta Larga and other Tupi-Mondé groups had been roaming the area for centuries, if not millennia).

By December 1985, Pio and Pichuvy could wait no longer. Following tradition, they gathered sixty men—perhaps one-eighth of the entire Cinta Larga population at the time—for a feast at Roosevelt Village. They painted themselves with jaguar spots, creating a magical association with the forest's apex predator. They danced all night, drank *i* until they vomited, then drank more. Some of their wives cried, fearing they would be killed. Pio himself was married to a Cinta Larga woman with whom he had two small children. But the mission was far too important to abandon. In the morning, the warriors set off with a light insomniac buzz, carrying their traditional six-foot bows and six-foot arrows.

In one important way, the war party wasn't traditional at all: the two young chiefs insisted that no one was to be killed. To that end, their timing was perfect. It was the week before Christmas, and the ranches were largely unoccupied. Those workers who remained were easily run off. An official complaint from the ranchers described it as "guerrilla warfare": "The horde of aboriginal vandals slaughtered dozens of cattle from our herds, in addition to hundreds of pigs; they plundered many of the installations on our lands, cravenly expelling the peaceful farmers with nothing but the clothes on their bodies....Then they installed themselves in our houses, consumed what was inside them, cut down fruit trees from our orchards, stole approximately ten head of horses and mules....[They also] destroyed fences, burned gates and corrals, stole our furniture, domestic utensils, machines and equipment of all kinds...."

With this one blitzkrieg, Pio and Pichuvy had reclaimed a hundred thousand acres of their people's land. In celebration, the raid became a feast. For the next week, the warriors barbecued the ranchers' chickens and pigs, cooking so much meat that you could smell it from miles away. They didn't eat much of the cattle, though. At the time the Cinta Larga thought that the animals smelled of grass, and that beef wasn't suitable for human consumption. Instead they left the dead ones to rot. The live ones were allowed to escape; to this day, feral cows roam the area.

*   *   *

Resentments over this raid would simmer for years. In their complaint to the authorities, the ranchers presented an upside-down view in which Funai and its wards held all the power: "We landholders, victims of this attack, apart from being victims of the Indians, are victims of the indiscriminate pro-Indigenous policy that now reigns not only in our state, but in the entire country....Funai transforms large swaths of land into Indigenous reserves and parks, taking fertile lands, some already occupied and productive, without any kind of rigorous analysis, without respecting the rights of the white people who inhabit these lands...and worst of all is that those who are expelled are called 'invaders.'...We would like to remind you that we landholders, victims of this insidious and craven episode, are the colonizers of the state of Rondônia...encouraged [by the government] to conquer the Amazon and build a new, strong country. We are the anonymous heroes of this, the last human epic of conquest of the last great empty space on planet Earth. And what do we get for our sacrifice of nearly two decades of work and suffering? What will become of us and of the future of our children?"

Some of the ranchers' claims were fantastical, the stuff of conspiracy theory, though they reflected the beliefs of many whites on the

Amazon frontier, then and now: "We cannot believe that this was the exclusive initiative of the Indians. Surely they were instigated, instructed by Funai's radical leaders." The ranchers even claimed that the warriors were armed with "modern weapons....38-caliber repeater rifles, 12-, 16-, and 20-gauge shotguns, in addition to .38 revolvers...all brand new!" Roberto Carlos, for his part, would recall that they carried only bows and arrows. But this was just one item in a paranoid litany: "Where do they get [these weapons]?...Who is really behind this rampant proliferation of Indigenous reserves in Rondônia? Why are they all located in areas rich with minerals[?]...What does the WORLD BANK have to do with the Indigenous reserves in our state?"

Funai agents were used to the dangers of uncontacted Indians; now they also faced hostile settlers. Once, when Chicão went to lunch with Apoena in Espigão, he had to eat with his left hand because his right hand was holding a revolver in a folded-up newspaper. Locals whispered about ambushing them later on some dusty, potholed road. On another occasion a settler told Apoena flat out that he was going to gun down the Indians. The two ended up brawling—"a serious fight," as a reporter described it, "the stuff of rolling around on the ground, [even though] the guy had some thugs with him, a gun and a blade in his pockets."

Pio faced these same threats whenever he went to town, but in his mind, the trouble was worth it. The raid would forever be one of his people's proudest moments, a rare example of victory through unity, courage, and restraint. Their feelings about what came next were far more mixed. Next to one of the roads that wound through the illegal estates, several enormous tree trunks had been laid out, one atop the other, in a kind of pyramid. Each trunk must have weighed multiple tons. Many were wider than a person was tall; all ended in the perfect plane of a chainsaw slice. Down the road was another stack, and another, and another. All told, it was a staggering quantity of hardwood, around eight hundred trunks—all mahogany.

So dense it could hardly be cut with axes of stone or even steel, *nekúvat*, as the Cinta Larga called it, was useless for making bows or longhouse girders. Its wide, gray-barked trunks were simply part of the forest architecture, pillars that seemed to hold up the canopy, rising two hundred feet from the ground. Given their lifespan of three centuries or more, the older ones predated the earliest events in Cinta Larga oral tradition, with the exception of origin myths—as well as Brazil's independence as a nation. Of course, it was precisely its hardness that made mahogany so valuable to Westerners. Resistant to rot and largely devoid of pockets, it was ideal for the slicing of boards to be used in dinner tables, outdoor decking, and boats. In the United States and Europe, its dark brown hue was practically a cliché of aristocratic wealth. It was one of the priciest hardwoods on earth, already harvested to exhaustion across much of the Americas.

Initially, Pio just reported the discovery to Chicão, who planned to seize it all. Logging, after all, was illegal on Indigenous lands. Normally the contraband would be auctioned off, with the proceeds going to Funai. But another Funai agent told Pio that it rightfully belonged to the Cinta Larga—that they had, in essence, won the lottery. Trees, it turned out, weren't just trees. They were also *madeira*, which means "wood" in Portuguese but, when imported to the Tupi-Mondé language, came to refer to its new nature as a commodity.

"That there is worth a lot of money," this agent told Pio. "Don't let it go to waste. Sell that stuff."

CHAPTER 12

POOR PEOPLE

A decade after escaping Sapecado, Maria Beleza, the renowned Cinta Larga beauty, still believed he was "hunting" for her. And with good reason. He continued to roam the region, becoming ever more deranged in his crimes. Always searching for diamonds and gold, he brought in prospectors who dug up the Cinta Larga's manioc and even "stole women," which is to say, committed rape. He himself was believed to have impregnated three women (apart from Maria) who gave birth to half-white babies. Another woman, three months pregnant, had recently turned up dead, her body burned almost beyond recognition; the Cinta Larga were sure Sapecado was to blame.

After Maria had given birth to their child, a daughter, Funai seemed to see the baby as a problem. Any records have been lost, but there's little question that, if the media had found out, it would have been a scandal—and as Roberto Carlos remembered it, "Funai said they weren't going to take care of a white man's child." When the baby was a year old, a pilot landed at Roosevelt Village and said he was there to take mother and daughter for a hospital checkup. "I'm not sick, and neither is my daughter," Maria told him. But he insisted. At the hospital, she and her baby were separated. Roberto and Maria would both come to believe that one of the doctors adopted her. Another version holds that the baby died at the hospital. Whatever the truth, Maria never saw her child again.

In the old days, the Cinta Larga rarely built villages near major waterways, instead preferring areas by little streams, more isolated from would-be attackers. Now, though, they needed a presence on their borders, so Pio called for a new village to be built near the ranchers' estates, and Funai promised to support it with the usual staff (possibly the basis for the ranchers' claim it had "imported" Indians). Among them was an Indigenous man named João, from the Pacaa Nova group—Maria's new husband.

Maria hadn't wanted to marry him. She feared he'd beat her like Sapecado. But there were more Cinta Larga women than men, and Funai, in attempting to Westernize them, wanted to end the old polygamy. In Maria's recollection, it was a Funai agent who arranged the marriage, apparently reasoning that, while João might not belong to the same group, he was at least a fellow Indian. On the Cinta Larga side, the men may have seen the marriage as a way to cement their alliance with Funai, as they'd attempted to do previously. When Maria protested, a male cousin threatened to kill her.

Now Maria was pregnant with her second child. A Funai agent's wife suggested she have an abortion, to give Sapecado one less target for revenge. The authorities were clearly powerless to stop him. At the Funai office in Porto Velho, a poster offered a reward for information on his whereabouts, but Sapecado walked in and demanded it be taken down, threatening to kill the agent in charge unless he abandoned the "defamatory campaign." Despite her very real fear, though, Maria refused. She'd already lost one child, and the pain of that loss would stay with her for the rest of her life.

It was August 1984 when Sapecado showed up at an attraction post downriver from Maria's new village. Such was his sense of entitlement in Cinta Larga country, not only did he declare his intention to spend the night there; he demanded food. The Funai agent on duty ordered him to leave, but Sapecado refused, calling Funai worthless, calling it "shit." Putting a gun on the table, he said, "I'd like to see Funai remove me from here."

Sapecado may have become too sure of himself. The next morning, after he went on his way, a group of young Cinta Larga men—adolescents, really—came to see the Funai agent. One was Maria's brother. As a little boy, he'd vowed to kill Sapecado once he was big enough. Now, following the implacable logic of *wepíka*, he said he planned to "repay" his sister's torture, to "repay" the alleged murders. When the agent radioed headquarters, the reply came from the ever-brash park director, Chicão: "Let them do it." Pio was with him; he translated the message into Tupi-Mondé.

A short distance from the attraction post, the young men caught up with Sapecado. Feigning friendliness, they asked to borrow his machete to skin a freshly killed pig. Even then, he didn't realize how thoroughly the Cinta Larga had turned against him. He handed over his blade and sat down to rest. When he wasn't paying attention, Maria's brother brought the machete down on his head, and the others shot arrows into him—four of them. The Funai agent informed the authorities, but the Cinta Larga refused to let the police remove the body, insisting it be left for vultures to eat. Forever after, Maria's brother would be known as Sapecadinho—Little Sapecado—in homage to his act of vengeance.

* * *

Whenever white people showed up at Maria's village, most of the other women were so shy, they acted as if they didn't even notice, sitting wordlessly in their long flowery dresses as they strung necklaces with beads. Maria, though, wasn't afraid to look the outsiders in the face and speak her mind, no matter that she never went to school. Once, when she signed a document with an inky thumbprint, a Funai agent asked her why she'd never learned to read or write. Barely containing her rage, she sputtered, "What?!" After all, it was Funai that married her off before she even knew that school was an option. Instead she would have to care for the seven children she had with João Pacaa Nova, as well as two she adopted.

Maria's birth rate would have been unfathomable in the old days. Partly this was because, before the introduction of Western medicine, infant mortality was higher. But it was also by design, to avoid having too many little mouths to feed and too few able hands to procure food. As Pio knew from personal experience, it wasn't uncommon for mothers to abandon babies they felt they couldn't care for. If a baby was born disabled, the custom was actually to kill it. Tradition also held that, if a father had sex with his wife—or even another woman—before his child could walk, the baby would fall ill. But as Pichuvy put it, "That [taboo] doesn't exist anymore....Now it's the life of the white man."

In the wake of the mass death brought by imported diseases, child-rearing gained new significance. Family had always been central; now women felt a responsibility to ensure their people's survival in the most literal of ways.

The problem was that, for all the promise of Western medicine, it depended on proper facilities, pharmaceuticals, and trained staff. In the 1980s, every Funai post was supposed to have one doctor, one dentist, and two nurses, but few professionals wanted such poorly paid hardship posts. Those who did faced organizational chaos. Vaccination campaigns were often abruptly cut short when Funai decided it needed their bush plane for some other purpose.

Planes were always in short supply. During one pregnancy, Maria

Beleza came down with hepatitis, and went so long without treatment that her eyes turned yellow. When she finally reached the hospital in Cacoal, her son Jorge was born two months premature. Sometimes help didn't show up at all. When Pio was at the Serra Morena post, his first son got malaria. He'd already watched his father succumb to measles from a Funai post; now he watched his son die because Funai failed to send a plane.

A young woman from Brasília, Maria Inês Saldanha Hargreaves, worked for a nonprofit that was attempting to tackle a Cinta Larga malaria epidemic caused by the influx of settlers. "There was so much malaria that even when someone had no fever, they had inactive malaria," she would recall. "Then when a cold or flu went around, it seemed like it lowered their resistance, and suddenly you had two hundred people with malaria at the same time." Despite her efforts to distribute anti-malarials, many died.

The closest available health care was at the Casa do Índio, or Indian House, which grew from Funai's base in Riozinho, five days' walk from Roosevelt Village (and even farther from others). In a scathing report, the anthropologists Carmen Junqueira and Betty Mindlin described it as "one of the worst examples of unwholesomeness in all aspects of Indian care. It serves not only the sick, but also Indians in transit... [who] take up the lodgings and beds of the sick. In spite of there being twenty officials at the Indian House it could not be dirtier. No one ever sweeps it. The two large unsegregated lodging houses separate not the sick from the sound but the Cinta Larga from the Suruí....There are two toilets—one for the officials and one for the Indians who sometimes number 200 in Riozinho. The jungle path between the houses and the river is putrid and impassable....The water from the well is good quality but no one cleans it; there are old shoes thrown in it. Anyone who arrives healthy at Riozinho runs the risk of leaving ill."

Even the hospital in the city of Cacoal was poorly equipped for complex cases. One day Pio went fishing in the Roosevelt River and the hook got stuck on something. He yanked and yanked until suddenly it came free, flicking straight back into his right eye, which started leaking copiously. This time the plane actually arrived, but by the time Pio was flown to Rondônia's capital, Porto Velho, more than three hundred miles away, the injury was beyond repair. He lost his vision in that eye for good; even with a prosthesis, his eyelid drooped.

With so many health crises, it's little wonder that Maria responded to a novel kind of solace. At the hospital in Cacoal, an Evangelical Christian came to pray at her bedside and invited her to church. The church was little more than a wooden shack, but the experience was powerful. The pastor asked Maria to tell her story of survival, and people stood up and shouted, "It's a miracle!" Maria agreed to be baptized, to have her soul washed clean, "to remove the animal that was eating me from the inside," she would recall. "That's when I became a believer." She was one of the first; the rest would follow.

*   *   *

With the rise of Western medicine came a decline in traditional remedies. After Maria escaped from Sapecado, she'd had to relearn her own native language. One Funai agent said no one should give her salty food, so she could remember the old ways. But her people had their own methods. For a while she was "adopted" by a respected elder who went by the nickname Rondon (because he was rumored to have shot the founder of the Indian Protection Service, Cândido Rondon, with an arrow). Rondon and his wife prepared a medicine from a long leaf that burned Maria's tongue. They put the head of a baby bird in her mouth, too. Others laughed at her discomfort. "But I began to speak," Maria would recall. "Easier words first. Then, all of the sudden, my mind expanded."

The Cinta Larga knew as many medicines as poisons. There were plants that helped the hunter enter the mindset of his prey. There were plants for curing ailments of the heart and the blood and the skin, a plant for cleaning your teeth, another for headache relief. There were plants, too, for shortening menstruation, preventing pregnancy, and boosting fertility. There was even one for curing impotence, which they would come to call "jungle Viagra" and occasionally sell to outsiders.

Part of the reason these remedies fell into disuse was simply that elders were susceptible to disease, and when they died, their knowledge often died with them. Younger Cinta Larga came to see the traditional way of learning, through observation and osmosis, as secondary. Lacking a word for "education," they adopted the Portuguese word *educação* along with a Western sense of its purpose. Even Pio, whose apprenticeship in hunting was so cruelly cut short, wanted his own kids to master the world of letters and numbers, to absorb the secrets of white success. But the education at Funai posts was, like the health care, limited enough to be all but useless, with teachers often barely literate themselves. The other option was to go to "the city," but that required money the Cinta Larga didn't have.

Isolation had once been the foundation of their well-being. Now they were not isolated enough to avoid diseases, but too isolated to receive care. No matter Pio's love for Chico and Apoena, he couldn't help but see the disconnect between their promises and the reality of life under the Brazilian state. Apoena and his father had brought a vision of a life sheltered from day-to-day violence, extended and improved by Western medicine—a life of abundance, even, with access to Western goods: shotguns for hunting, motorboats for fishing trips, individual houses, fridges, TV sets, cars. In Pio's own words, he came to understand "what it is to be comfortable, to have the resources to live well."

The American anthropologist Marshall Sahlins famously called hunter-gatherers the "original affluent society" because, while they rarely produced a surplus, their needs were few and easily met. Funai's strategy was to bring about the opposite situation, giving ever fewer gifts so as to stimulate new wants, new needs—recalling an older effort, in the United States, to push Native Americans to "wear civilized clothes…cultivate the ground, live in houses, ride in Studebaker wagons, send children to school, drink whiskey, [and] own property." And it worked. To achieve what Funai called "economic emancipation," Pio and Pichuvy tried to develop a cash crop, and men took to roaming the forest, filling little buckets with latex, just like the clothes-wearers once did. But they had to walk all the way to the Indian House to sell it, only to receive a pittance in return.

Women still spent their days making traditional necklaces, bracelets, and rings, even while caring for their children. Maria Beleza found joy in this daily artistry, attaching porcupine quills to hardened palm-fruit beads, stringing together sharp little monkey teeth and fearsome jaguar fangs. Sometimes they came up with new designs, such as a duster made from a monkey's tail. Sometimes they imported foreign ones, such as the dream catchers that white hippies sold on Highway 364 (which originally came from the Ojibwe of North America). In memos, Funai officials spoke of creating a shop for these handicrafts, to "incentivize" the women to participate in Western society in the most Western way possible. Never mind that Maria still saw money as mere "pieces of paper," lacking meaning or value. How could she sell her wares without a road, without some means of transport?

Back when men used to hunt with bow and arrow, this had limited how much they could kill. Now Funai was teaching them to use shotguns—such a novelty in this part of the Amazon that tapirs, for instance, didn't always run from the sound, instead coming *toward* it to investigate. Meanwhile, the old attraction posts became permanent, breaking the tradition of moving whenever game grew scarce. With each passing season, people had to travel ever farther to find meat, and it became ever easier to stay home and eat rice and beans—crops that, unlike the traditional tubers, required constant tending. This, too, was by design, because hunting didn't fit with the Western logic of investment and reward. Hunting never felt like work to the Cinta Larga; it was closer to a form of play. Funai wanted the Indians to work.

It was shocking how fast certain Westernisms took hold. At Roosevelt Village, the Cinta Larga didn't build traditional longhouses but imitations of the wooden shelters erected by Funai agents. Lacking sawn boards, they made the walls out of mud; lacking roof tiles, they used palm bark. The original they were copying may have been even worse. Unlike the thatched dome that kept a longhouse cool and dark, the standard fiber-cement roofs absorbed the sun's heat and radiated it back inside. A longhouse also allowed smoke from little fires to escape, and smoke kept away insects, while ash sterilized the packed-dirt floor. It was spacious, cathedral-like, compared to the white people's cramped little shacks. Still, these new dwellings allowed individual families to sleep separately, just like white people did. And this may have been the most important point of all. At the Serra Morena post, the Cinta Larga actually burned down their traditional longhouse, because no one wanted to live in the past.

The Cinta Larga weren't alone in their predicament. Across the country, newly contacted Indigenous groups had fallen for Funai's bait-and-switch. They watched their former "affluence" slip away, to be replaced with a life of lack. As the anthropologist Eduardo Viveiros de Castro put it, "The Brazilian state turned Indians into poor people."

CHAPTER 13

ENCOUNTERS WITH THE BUREAUCRACY

B y the time they found the mahogany by the Fourteenth of April River, Pio and Pichuvy were tired of begging Funai for a road. They'd even attempted to build their own. With machetes, axes, and the odd chainsaw, they'd rallied the residents of Roosevelt Village to cut a six-mile path to the edge of the Indigenous area. Without a means to level the earth, though, it was hardly suitable for automobiles.

Pio and Pichuvy had always agreed that it was too risky to allow white men (beyond Funai agents) inside Cinta Larga country, because they might never leave. But the mahogany was already cut down, ready to be hauled out—and that Funai agent had said it was worth a lot of money, maybe enough to build a road. After consulting with the rest of the village, they decided to sell it.

Unsure how to arrange the transaction, they went once again to consult with Apoena. Apoena was all too aware of Funai's shortcomings. He spoke with regret about the misplaced optimism of contact, "the historic responsibility we still owe the Indians." Whatever the idealism of his youth, however, he'd fully adopted his father's pragmatism.

Now he believed the way to avoid ending up like the Xavante—contacted by his father only to become wage laborers on nearby ranches—was through economic development. This onetime romantic criticized the "romantic *indigenismo*" of colleagues who saw the Indians as "bearers of an eccentric, disappearing culture." As he put it, "If we can help the Indian to survive, his culture will never die, and anthropology books will be enriched by facts told by living men, and not just by researchers of corpses." Apoena even detected a whiff of racism in the idea that Indians shouldn't be allowed to choose their own path, if that path clashed with a certain idea about how they should live.

In Apoena's mind, the solution wasn't to ban the hardwood trade but to regulate it so that any transition would be gradual. Otherwise the forest might be devastated, sold "for the price of a banana," with only an elite few (whites and Indians alike) benefiting. Of course, no such legal framework existed yet. And so he said, "You can't. It's not allowed. Let it rot."

Apoena may have hoped to slow the young chiefs down, but they started receiving visits from loggers offering to pay what Funai would not. To prevent this from happening, Funai rushed ahead with an auction, allowing Pio and Pichuvy to dream about how they would spend the proceeds:

1. Purchase of a boat, six meters long, with a fifteen-horsepower outboard motor, [$2,500].
2. Purchase of two horses or mules for transport, [$1,000].
3. Immediate purchase of food, clothing, footwear and other necessities, [$4,000].
4. Purchase of barbed wire for fencing, [$200].
5. Investment in a savings account for the Cinta Larga Indigenous Group, [$12,000].
6. Purchase of fuel, [$400].

Disappointingly, the plan didn't include a road. The expected revenues were laughable, a tiny fraction of the true value of the hardwood. But it hardly mattered, because the auction results had to be thrown out after Funai's own president was accused of colluding with the winning firm, Comexmad. One Funai agent who refused to go along with the scheme was transferred to another state; that was the usual fate of idealists in government.

Pio and Pichuvy didn't see why any of this should affect them. "Don't give us the runaround," they said, when Funai agents explained that they didn't have the money. Apoena relayed one conversation in a telegram: "The Indians demand payment in cash for the 800 trunks of hardwood felled on their lands, [and they do not care] who is responsible for it, which [in their view] is Funai's problem." Setting aside his personal feelings for Apoena, Pio joined Pichuvy in making a threat: if Funai didn't keep its word—and fast—they'd burn down every single official building on their lands, along with all the vehicles. It was perhaps the first example of what would become a vital quality in Cinta Larga leaders: the willingness to *brigar com autoridade*, as they phrased it in Portuguese— "to fight with the authorities," showing they weren't cowed.

Hoping to avoid chaos, Funai rushed through another auction. Surreally, though, Comexmad again won the bidding. Amid the confusion, a new Funai president said he wouldn't allow the mahogany to be sold at all. For the Cinta Larga, it was an important lesson: the Brazilian state was not to be trusted.

*   *   *

No buildings were burned down. Instead, Pio and Pichuvy decided to go over Apoena's head and lobby Funai's new president to let them sell the wood themselves. On the newly paved Highway 364, it took just a couple of days to travel the twelve hundred miles to Brasília. But what they saw was another world. By now they were used to the noise and bustle of Porto Velho; with a population of 1.2 million, the nation's capital was an order of magnitude larger.

Built from scratch in Brazil's high plains in the 1950s, the city grew from the utopian visions of modernist architects. At one end of the so-called Monumental Axis, past a vast square of manicured lawns and manmade lakes, two towers of dark glass and white cement rose more than three hundred feet in the sky, flanked by two enormous white cement bowls, one face down, the other face up, where the two houses of Congress met. The Presidential Palace and the Supreme Court looked humble only by comparison, with white cement pillars that curved almost like the roots of an Amazonian tree toward their base. The overwhelming feeling was one of space, expansiveness, inaccessible power. On a subsequent visit, one Cinta Larga would be heard saying, "So this is where the guys who steal live."

The Cinta Larga lacked the money to pay for a hotel, but managed to find lodging at a convent thanks to the one person they knew in Brasília, Inês Hargreaves, the onetime health worker. In her description, they treated the visit like an anthropological survey: "They'd grab a taxi, drive around the whole city, and visit government buildings, monuments, even whorehouses," before returning to the strict regime of the nuns to get some sleep.

They arrived at a time of rare ideological upheaval. After two decades in power, the military dictatorship was ending. A new constitution was to be drafted, and thanks to a backlash against the right-wing generals, unionists, landless peasants, and advocates for Indigenous rights exerted more influence than ever before. Perhaps most surprising of all, given their usual role as passive subjects of politics, Indigenous people themselves had a say. Brazil had even elected its first Indigenous member of Congress, Mário Juruna, a Xavante.

For the first time in Brazil's five hundred years of colonization, a truly national pan-Indigenous movement was taking root. What they wanted was nothing less than the full citizenship long denied them as legal "wards" of the state. They wanted to overthrow the policy born back when Cândido Rondon created the Indian Protection Service: that Indigenous people must be assimilated into national society, made into workers, made into white people—a policy that classed them as primitives from an archaic phase of human development, rather than as adults capable of choosing their destiny.

It was a testament to the scale of the upheaval that, despite the enduring power of Brazil's landowners, the movement achieved much of what it asked for. At least on paper, the new constitution would enshrine their right to maintain their own cultures and, even more important, to occupy their lands—a victory vital to the Cinta Larga's own future.

But Pio and Pichuvy had more immediate concerns: invasions, health crises, material deprivation, and what they saw as a solution, the mahogany. Alas, Funai's new president wouldn't budge. Over the next year, the agency would go through three other leaders, and the two young chiefs would make this same journey over and over again, always betting on an opening, always coming away empty-handed. They may have gotten their hopes up when Apoena was named Funai's president toward the end of 1985. But in the absence of regulation, he refused to allow the hardwood to be sold.

* * *

Finally, after two years of this, Pio was fed up. "I decided to sell without permission," he would recall. "The wood was already chopped down!" To avoid problems with the Federal Police, he cut a local Funai agent in on the scheme. Then he went to a sawmill in the town of Pimenta Bueno, owned by a bald man who clearly saw Pio as an easy mark. As payment, the man handed over a huge burlap sack bulging with cash. "I already knew a little about sums of money, how much a thousand was, how much two thousand was," Pio would recall. But it took him a while to realize that the volume of bills didn't necessarily match up with their value, especially in times of hyperinflation.

Still, Pio would maintain, "It was very good for us." He and Pichuvy followed the original plan for the auction, buying clothes and a truckload of rice, beans, oil, sardines, sugar, and even salt—once inedible, now indispensable—for Roosevelt Village. They also bought medicines for the clinic, chickens and pigs to keep in corrals, a generator and the diesel to fuel it. Best of all, part of the mahogany's price was to be paid in kind. For the logger, it was no great ask to build a road, as he would need one suitable for a semi truck to haul his product to the BR-364. Driving a tractor, he widened the crude path from Roosevelt Village to the edge of the Indigenous area, leveling it into a packed-dirt "highway" that finally provided access to the hospitals, pharmacies, and shops in nearby towns. The logger also agreed to build a dozen Western-style houses at Roosevelt Village. Though the floors remained naked earth, they boasted walls of wood from the surrounding forest, painted a bright cyan, and roofs of the Eternit brand of asbestos tiles favored on the Amazon frontier.

For Pio, the sale fulfilled two ambitions. Not only was he living up to the model of the *zapiway* he knew from his father. At long last, he also got his car, a Chevrolet sedan. Admittedly, it wasn't much use in the rainy season, when the new "highway" became a quagmire. But it was a luxury few of his people would ever enjoy, and it allowed Pio to carry out his evolving duties as chief, visiting white associates in town.

The windfall might have been a one-off if not for a change at the top of Funai in Brasília. Apoena lacked the tact to stay in the capital for long. A few months into his presidency, he plainly told a reporter, "Funai in Brasília has turned into a central station for lobbies"— companies hoping to extract resources from Indigenous lands. In one phrase, he made the central government look bad, well-connected businessmen worse. He was out in May 1986, replaced by an exemplar of the exact problem he'd denounced, a mustachioed operator named Romero Jucá, who had no actual experience with Indigenous people.

Whereas Apoena saw economic development as a way for Indigenous people to protect their lands and even thrive, Jucá saw it as a moneymaking opportunity. He latched on to an idea then becoming popular: that their lands were a kind of financial asset owned by the government. It was an evolution of the policy of "economic emancipation," which, in the era of Ronald Reagan and Margaret Thatcher, was rebranded *rentabilização do patrimônio indígena*—basically, "making Indigenous patrimony profitable." The idea wasn't without its true believers, even among Funai officials. But it also provided a screen for more cynical machinations.

Though Jucá wore wire-rimmed glasses and a suit and tie, he was basically a modern version of an old Amazon figure, the *bandeirante*, who opened up the frontier by pillaging it. In the lands east of the Roosevelt River, he sold off 40,000 cubic meters of mahogany without even bothering to tell the Cinta Larga who lived there. Inês Hargreaves, who'd since become a kind of independent *indigenista*, dug up the contracts—and the reaction, in her words, was "outrage." With sawmills offering $50 per cubic meter, the contract was worth $2 million even before the wood was sliced into boards and shipped abroad. All the loggers had to give the Cinta Larga was a school, a clinic building, a few wooden houses, and roads they needed anyway. The deal was even worse—far worse—than Pio's with the bald man. Pio and Pichuvy gathered everyone at Roosevelt Village to discuss what to do, and a common refrain was "Funai is stealing from us!"

Pichuvy still didn't want loggers on their lands. As ever, he feared they would never leave. Pio, though, saw that his own resistance had been pointless: "Why should Funai get to sell our hardwood?"

CHAPTER 14

UNITY AND BETRAYAL

In the early 1980s, Oita was working at Funai's Serra Morena post, in the eastern part of Cinta Larga country. By now he understood what Maloqueiro—Rapscallion—meant, and vowed to kill anyone who insisted on calling him that, almost as if the old name taboo persisted. People still said it behind his back. They even whispered that he "stole" women, having affairs with other men's wives, the ultimate Cinta Larga motive for homicide.

People would give various explanations for why Oita had left the Roosevelt post, all pointing to his tendency to live up to his nickname. According to Roberto Carlos, Oita had threatened to kill him over an imagined affair with Oita's then-wife. Oita himself would later admit that he was *muito encrenqueiro*, that he liked to court trouble, pick fights. But in his own telling, Apoena sent him away because he was such a trusted interpreter, and was needed among the Gavião people, who spoke a similar language.

If Funai had hoped to keep him out of trouble, it didn't work. An American linguist, Denny Moore, went to live at the Gavião post in 1975, and in his recollection, Oita was constantly threatening people: "One time he wanted to kill *me* because I didn't bring baby shoes for his daughter." In time, though, Oita warmed to him, much like he had to the idealistic Possidônio, forging a friendship he would treasure for the rest of his life. "I told him he had to stop talking about killing people," Denny would recall. "He got quite annoyed. I said, 'I'm just your friend, trying to help you.' No one wanted to go out hunting with him alone."

Denny wasn't afraid to go into the forest with Oita, who taught him how to hunt monkey. There is a photo of the two, each brandishing a shotgun; Oita holds a dead monkey up by the neck, while Denny holds another by the tail. Oita, probably in his early twenties, looks younger than his age. He wears a baseball cap and a green-and-white-striped T-shirt, and a faint smile curls one end of his mouth.

Denny found productive outlets for Oita's propensity for conflict. In one instance, he would recall, "We did a survey of a road and took Oita with us in case we had problems." When they encountered livestock corrals inside the Indigenous area, Oita helped smash them to pieces. On another occasion, a rubber tycoon known as Tarzan had invaded the lands of the Arara, and Oita helped seize Tarzan's stock of latex, rolling the heavy white balls all the way back to the Funai base.

Denny departed a few years later, leaving Oita, once again, without a counterpoint to the outlaw style of Sapecado, his onetime "teacher." In Funai records, his name was often associated with trouble: "We report [that] Indian Oita Matina Cinta Larga, employee-interpreter based at [Posto] Serra Morena, formed a group [of other Cinta Larga] and, taking control of two canoes donated by prospectors and a shotgun belonging to...Funai, escaped early this morning destination unknown." (The adventure culminated in the death of a Cinta Larga woman who caught the flu.)

Much like he'd wandered from village to village as a young "castoff," Oita now roamed across Rondônia and neighboring Mato Grosso, sometimes working for Funai, sometimes freelancing. He had no qualms about using a little deceit to get by. "I came up with anything to make money," he would recall. "I decided to paint houses, and I charged some guy [$200] even though I didn't know how to paint. But the guy liked it." He also worked for Brazil's geological survey on expeditions to map mineral deposits. ("From my time there, I know where there's gold, diamonds, from one end of this territory to the other," he would brag.) Unlike the majority of Cinta Larga, for whom clothing was functional at best, Oita acquired a taste for dressing well. In a photo from 1981, he wears a white collared shirt, buttoned low, and Ray-Ban-style aviator sunglasses.

Oita was always searching, even if he couldn't necessarily say what for. In town one day, a pastor called out to him: "Hey, Indian. Come to church today." Inside, the church was packed. Amid the impassioned preaching, Oita would remember thinking, *My God, what is this?* At one point, though, the pastor called out to him again, in front of everyone: "Your time has come! God chose you among your people. Many times, He spared you from death." That gave Oita pause. He thought about how he'd survived the white man's disease at the fateful feast, about the gunmen who'd killed his father, and wondered, *How does he know?* Still, when he left, he said to himself, *Ah, it's all lies!* He went to a bar and got drunk on *cachaça*. Someone punched him in the face. *If God had known about this*, Oita thought, *He could have prevented it!*

Oita already knew what other people thought of him. Pio would recall an episode in which Pichuvy's radio disappeared, and Oita blamed another Indigenous group for the theft, though in reality *he* had taken it. When they discovered Oita's duplicity, men from the other group gave him a beating. At the Serra Morena post, meanwhile, the ill will was even stronger. At one point a cousin told him, "People are waiting for the moment to kill you. Get out of here!"

"One day I passed by and saw Maloqueiro at peace," the anthropologist Carmen Junqueira would recall. "People were playing flutes, lying in hammocks. Then, all of the sudden, everyone started running." Half a dozen Cinta Larga men came after Oita with machetes and axes. He bolted into the trees but they caught up with him. He put up his hands to defend himself, so they slashed at his arms. They sliced open his face and head. When he turned onto his stomach, they hacked at his back. Then they left him for dead.

Oita's clothes were saturated with blood, but he was still breathing. With no doctor at the post, the Funai agent on duty tried to fix him up himself. He spent five hours stitching up Oita's face, until the sutures ran out; then he used fishing line. He radioed for an airlift, but none was forthcoming, so he put Oita in a hammock and gave him intravenous saline solution, hoping for the best. Junqueira stayed with him to ensure no one came back to finish the job. Eventually, miraculously, he recovered.

The Cinta Larga figured there was no way a normal human could have survived such an attack. Oita, then, must be a *wãwã*, a shaman, like his father. Oita himself cultivated this impression, saying that his father had taught him the way. But he wasn't the type who cures disease by blowing smoke in your ear. "When a shaman wants to kill someone," Oita would say, "he doesn't do it as a person. He turns into a snake and bites them. Or he turns into a jaguar." His scars would remain visible into old age.

*   *   *

After an attempt on his life, another Cinta Larga might have sought refuge among his family, his lineage, if only to gather a posse for revenge. In the old days, it was simply unthinkable to turn your back on your people as a whole. Oita, though, felt like more of a loner than ever. As much as he resented white men for the deaths inflicted on his family, he increasingly sought their approval, hoping to find the recognition he never received back home.

As always, Oita kept on wandering, searching for something. Having been so close to death, he came to see that pastor's words in a different light. He started attending services at the Assemblies of God, a popular Pentecostal denomination, and while he never learned to read himself, he asked people to read the Bible aloud to him, and lapped up the stories. His independent streak actually fit very well with Evangelical Christianity, with its emphasis on personal experiences of God. He decided to be baptized, born again. He even began to give his own sermons, relating his stories of survival and weaving in the voice of the Lord. In his telling, as he lay dying from his wounds at Serra Morena, he'd ascended to Heaven and met God and Jesus. God pulled out a big book and said, "Your name is here. You are my chosen one. Your people like you."

Oita objected: "My people killed me!"

"I allowed it to happen," God said. And then He sent Oita back to bring His word to the Cinta Larga.

Despite his reputation inside Cinta Larga country, Oita felt he couldn't ignore God's message. He wasn't the first to attempt it. In the 1970s, an Englishman named Clive Sandberg went to the Roosevelt post as part of the Summer Institute of Linguistics, a California-based Evangelical organization that translated the Bible into Indigenous languages. In Pichuvy's description, he "showed up to mess with the Indians' heads. He built a church and everything....He said we can't drink [*i*], we can't dance....And we believed him, you know?" Sandberg didn't last long, though. Paranoid about foreign influence, the government expelled the SIL in 1977. As Pichuvy put it just a few years later, "Now we forgot what that American [*sic*] said." One newly formed

Cinta Larga myth even held that, long ago, they'd killed the Bible's Adam, "father of the civilized ones."

Little wonder that, when Oita took his sermons to Roosevelt Village, no one understood what he was talking about, at least back then.

* * *

Oita was on assignment for Funai in northwestern Rondônia, far from Cinta Larga country, when the hardwood trade started to spread back home. Other headmen had heard about the new roads, wooden houses, and truckloads of food at Roosevelt Village. Lacking experience with white people, they were only too grateful when Pio or Roberto Carlos arranged the deals, earning a kind of commission for their efforts. Apart from the car he kept for himself, Pio was known for redistributing whatever came in (or at least most of it). "If there was no nurse," one Funai agent would recall, "he'd pay for a nurse." Pio was also learning to invest, a habit he noticed in white men. He bought dairy cows and hired a farmer to teach how to milk them. "Pio was always thinking of his people," the agent said. "He wasn't, like, 'This is mine.' Instead it was: 'This is ours.'"

Roberto, meanwhile, earned a new nickname in those years: Robertinho Rico—Rich Little Roberto. He bought his own modest wooden house in Riozinho and decked it out with consumer goods, like a color TV, that were luxurious even for white Brazilians at the time. Forgetting his disdain for Pio's dream of acquiring a car, he came to own a Toyota pickup truck emblazoned with the phrase "Many thought it was impossible, but I managed it." He even hired a white driver to ferry him around.

Pichuvy, as chief of Roosevelt Village, also received a Toyota, as did the headmen of other, smaller villages. Automobiles soon became so vital to Cinta Larga life that, according to the anthropologist João

Dal Poz, a new figure emerged, akin to the traditional *zapiway* ("owner of the house"): the *carro-iway* ("owner of the car"). Whenever the *carro-iway* made a trip to town, people would pile into the bed of his truck to visit the shops or see a doctor or just get to know the white man's world. Some tried to drive themselves, but never learned how to shift out of first gear, and destroyed their transmissions. Nor did they learn to top up the motor oil or engine coolant. Like the axes and machetes that were their first Western goods, cars were seen less as an asset or an investment—concepts from capitalism—than as a resource you used up, like those from the forest that naturally replenished over time. Often, when a car stopped working, it was simply abandoned. Dal Poz also observed how, unlike the English expression "to make money," in which your earnings were implicitly the result of *work*, the Cinta Larga spoke of "getting money," which recalled the old relationship between hunter and prey.

In some ways, logging fit surprisingly well into the world the Cinta Larga already knew. Unlike ranchers, loggers didn't raze the forest to the ground, instead seeking to remove only the most valuable specimens. Others were inevitably knocked down when a large tree keeled over, but the surrounding flora would soon surge into any gaps. The disturbances could almost seem natural, as the sunlight drew pale yellow butterflies to alight on bulldozers parked in clearings.

In other ways, the Cinta Larga's conception of their environment was profoundly altered. Though not as valuable as mahogany, the tree known to Westerners as Brazil nut was sought after by loggers, with sawmills in Rondônia paying as much as $24 per cubic meter. Its wood was exceptionally dense, and the largest specimens were more than a hundred and fifty feet tall, with trunks exceeding fifteen feet in diameter. To the Cinta Larga, of course, this was the *maam* tree from which Pio's lineage was said to have emerged, prized for the heavy pods it dropped near the start of the rainy season, with those large, delicious nuts inside. The nuts were also food for the rodents known as agoutis, which liked to bury them for later. Some forgotten nuts would sprout into new trees that could live five hundred years, providing sustenance to generation after generation of people and forest fauna—including orchid bees, the only insects capable of pollinating them, which is why these trees could reproduce only in their native habitat, never on a plantation. Logging cut that cycle short for an immediate payday.

Loggers were quick to realize that one of the surest ways to win over a headman wasn't with material luxuries but with access to *brancas*—white women. Often this took the form of trips to brothels, though genuine romances also sprouted, as well as relationships that blurred the line between the two. Sometimes loggers offered up their own daughters as "wives," forming alliances that were already familiar to the Cinta Larga, and effective, though the marriages usually didn't last long.

Women had always been a source of status for Cinta Larga men, even as they lacked status of their own. In a world without money, a man with multiple wives enjoyed a kind of wealth, and a *zapiway*'s influence grew from the number of children and grandchildren he had. Now white women became a "prestige item," as one pair of anthropologists phrased it. Though already married to a woman at Roosevelt Village, Pio wasn't immune to the temptations. He and Chicão, the freewheeling Funai agent, used to drink together at bars and nightclubs—and as Chicão later put it, referring to himself in the third person, "Pio and Chicão were trouble." Pio became involved with a *branca* known in whispers behind her back as Tamalíap, the Cinta Larga word for a species of long-necked bird with tall, spindly legs. She gave birth to a son, whom Pio helped to raise. (Later in life, when asked how many children he had, he would say "seven or eight" because he wasn't sure about one that came later.) Roberto Carlos also had a son with a white woman, paying child support for seven years, until a Funai lawyer got him off the hook. (He stayed on good terms with the kid, jokingly calling him his "imported son," as if he were a luxury car.)

Gradually Cinta Larga life fell into a new cycle. People even began to think about time differently, gauging it by the stages of the logging season rather than by the fruits that ripened at different parts of the year. As the rains petered out in May, loggers would come bearing gifts, promising to build new roads and houses. Once they'd delivered their haul of mahogany to sawmills, they would hand a small percentage of the cash to village headmen. Then, as the rains resumed in November and December, and roads became too muddy to navigate, their largesse waned.

Loggers complained that the Cinta Larga didn't follow the Western logic of contracts, agreeing to terms in advance and sticking to them. What the Cinta Larga did understand was the concept of leverage. Unlike ranchers, who could defend their claims with armed gunmen, loggers ran small crews deep in the forest, where they were easily ambushed. Sometimes a headman promised access to an area that another headman claimed as his own, and the logger would have to pay both or risk having his equipment seized. Other times a headman would approach a logger when he was at his most vulnerable, stopping a truck loaded with hardwood on the eve of the rains to wring some extra diesel for the village generator.

Loggers knew their access depended on the chiefs' goodwill. Even in the rainy season, they tried to keep the Cinta Larga happy with little handouts, a bit of food or cash for an emergency medical visit. Departing from the unabashed prejudice of most settlers, they were performative in their friendliness, gushing with flattery, especially for Pio, given his leadership role. At a birthday party for one of Pio's daughters, Inês Hargreaves watched in horror as a parade of loggers showed up, clapped him on the back, and said: "Hey, chief, do you need anything?

Hey, chief, are you making enough money? Next year we're going to make even more..."

The Cinta Larga had never been the type to make threats, but they hardly needed to. Everyone knew about loggers who'd refused their demands. Some were tied up and held hostage until they relented. Those who went so far as to cut without permission might pay with their lives. In the eastern part of Cinta Larga country—where the Massacre of the Eleventh Parallel took place—the first peaceful contacts had come later, and people still hewed more to traditional norms than to Brazilian laws and taboos. One sawmill owner spoke of the need to respect "the law of the Indian," given that, in those days, no prosecutor would bring a case against a recently contacted Indigenous person. Brazil's justice system still considered them "relatively incompetent," like children or the mentally disabled—even for a charge of homicide.

*   *   *

Oita would later deny he ever dealt in hardwood. But NGOs, sawmill owners, and family members all cited him as a major player. It seems he quit Funai and moved to Riozinho just to get in on the game. Unlike other Cinta Larga, he didn't need Pio or Roberto Carlos to arrange his deals, because he spoke fluent (if ungrammatical) Portuguese. Also, he had no village to maintain. He did ultimately have five children with his then wife, a woman from another Indigenous group, but in her recollection, "He didn't spend his money on us, just on booze and women"—even while working as a traveling preacher.

Loggers saw Oita as "dangerous," a *matador*—a killer—even though he'd spent more than enough time in town to know the law of the white man. "I used to be bad," he would say in later years. According to rumor, he'd gotten his name by murdering a white man named Ita, rather than from Raul the Spaniard's prospectors. Like with his reputation as a shaman, though, he cultivated the image. He liked to show off his gun collection, and continued to be liberal with death threats. Unlike younger Cinta Larga, he still knew how to follow an enemy's scent. One day, patrolling a fresh road in the forest, he detected the stale sweat of a white man. A shotgun slung over his shoulder, he sat down and waited—and the logger, when he finally rounded the bend, jumped with fright. Without even moving, Oita muttered, "If I wanted to kill you, you'd already be dead."

In Oita's mind, none of this contradicted his newfound faith. In a certain light, his approach to the hardwood trade, like any other business, actually fit just fine with Protestant notions of individual effort and reward. According to one estimate, the total value of the hardwood extracted from Cinta Larga country, each year, was $45 million. Little wonder that loggers hardly seemed like outlaws. They even became landowners, filling vast estates with cattle. Oita wanted what they had—to be respected, admired, at last.

* * *

One day in the dry season of 1988, two buses arrived at a federal checkpoint meant to stop settlers from entering the lands of the Zoró, just northwest of Cinta Larga country. A man from the Apurinã people worked there, and in his recollection, Oita hopped down with a bow and arrow, announcing with authority, "These buses are going through and nobody is going to check them." When the Apurinã refused to bend, Oita pointed an arrow at him and drew his bowstring taut. But the Apurinã was close enough to grab it with his hand, saying, "You're going to have to respect the rules." Oita, clearly humiliated, had little choice but to stand down. The settlers carried all their belongings, including farm tools. When the Federal Police interrogated them, they said Oita had told them it wasn't Indigenous land at all.

The Zoró had been contacted far more recently, in 1977. With a population of just a hundred and fifty, they'd been unable to prevent an illegal settlement, Paraíso da Serra ("Paradise on the Hill"), from taking root inside their borders. It had already swollen to a quarter-million acres; the Zoró were vastly outnumbered. Funai had petitioned to have the invaders removed, but the case was mired in the usual bureaucracy.

In the old days, the Cinta Larga might not have cared what happened to their neighbors, hated enemies. But Indigenous people across Brazil were realizing that, whatever their historic divisions, they were all "Indians," with radically different interests from those of the "white man." Inspired by their connections in Brasília, they were forming associations to engage with the government, nonprofits, and even private businesses as formal collectives. In Rondônia, the Suruí did this under the guidance of an Indigenous intellectual named Ailton Krenak—and the Cinta Larga noticed. The two groups were already used to encountering one another at the Indian House in Riozinho. Now, when the Cinta Larga wanted to set up their own association, the Suruí helped. (Roberto simply copied their charter, replacing "Suruí" with "Cinta Larga" when necessary.)

It was a moment not only of intertribal solidarity but of unprecedented unity among the Cinta Larga themselves. Their association would be called Pamaré—literally "that which is ours"—and at the meeting to create it, many spoke of putting aside the old internal divisions between Maam, Kaban, and Kakin. "Our war now is with the white people," one participant said. "Let's come together to confront the white people's stealing."

When it came to selecting Pamaré's first leader, the choice was obvious. Pio was already admired for his diplomacy, even beyond Roosevelt Village. In the eastern part of Cinta Larga country, he'd helped to negotiate indemnity payments for a newly built hydroelectric dam.

He even risked his life to mediate disputes. When one headman was clashing with a rancher, Pio had gone to negotiate. The rancher's men detained him; one put a .38 rifle to his head. But Pio talked his way out of it, and managed to arrange a truce. Now he was made president by popular vote—a Western import that felt well suited to their new circumstances. Some called him *cacique geral,* or "general chief," almost certainly the first time the Cinta Larga had recognized such a figure, though Pio himself never felt comfortable with the title.

Oita never joined Pamaré, because in his words, "Dealing with people only brings headaches!" He didn't mind partnering with white men, though. Paraíso's founder, a logger named Américo Minotti Filho, had enlisted him to consolidate his claim in Zoró country; as payment, he would receive not only cash but a ranch of his own there. His main job was to win over the Zoró, who spoke a similar language—and on a visit to one of their villages, he riled them up, saying, "Funai won't remove the settlers. Funai no longer cares about the Indians!" Instead, he argued, the Zoró should accept a deal. If they allowed Paraíso to continue, Américo was prepared to build a road linking their main village to the nearest town. In return for access to hardwood, he would also give them a bus for transportation, and "keep the Indians constantly supplied with provisions and all manner of clothing." Once a year, he would even send thirty men with chainsaws to clear fields for crops, sparing the Zoró their most arduous task.

Oita's speech struck a chord with the aging Zoró chief Paiô, who'd already spent years begging Funai to remove the settlers. There was just one other condition: the Zoró would have to kick out all the Funai agents from their territory. Promised his own jeep as an additional enticement, Paiô agreed. A few days later, he led a group of Zoró warriors to burn the checkpoint to the ground, forcing the feds to retreat.

Not all Zoró were on board with the deal. A dissident group sought the help of the Cinta Larga, who already feared how the invasion might grow. This time Roberto Carlos led the war party, gathering three hundred Cinta Larga, Suruí, Gavião, and Arara—an alliance without any known precedent in their long history as neighbors. White workers were already building the promised road; the warriors tied them up and drove them to the edge of the Indigenous area with orders not to return. When the war party encountered Paiô, Roberto briefly had *him* tied up, too. Pichuvy, whose own mother was Zoró, declared his intention to kill Oita, finishing the job begun at the Serra Morena post.

One settler would describe Roberto's campaign as a "revolution." As usual, the warriors slaughtered animals and burned down houses so that settlers would have nothing to come back to—and within a few weeks, two hundred families had fled. In response, some of América's men formed a posse, piling into two trucks to hunt for Indians. At one point they came across an unsuspecting Suruí named Yaminer, who hailed them for a ride; they shot him to death, carried his body into the jungle, and set it on fire to destroy the evidence. Finally they found Roberto Carlos and several of his warriors at a nearby ranch, and a battle ensued. Armed with a shotgun, Roberto managed to take down one of the white *pistoleiros* before fleeing into the forest. His friends and family thought he was dead until, four days later, he made it back to Roosevelt Village on foot.

In later years, Oita would deny he was involved in América's scheme. Yes, he received a ranch, but it wasn't even on Zoró land, he insisted. In his version, the other Cinta Larga were simply too ignorant to understand the white man's dealings. Still, he acknowledged that his own people had wanted him dead. Asked why, he would reply with a single word: "Envy."

"Three hundred fifty Indians against one," he would say with evident pride. "When I heard they wanted to kill me, I went to Bolivia and bought an AR-15 assault rifle. Little Roberto was their leader.... When I saw him in front, I took aim, but a voice said to me, 'Don't do that,' and lifted the rifle barrel. I shot into the air, *ba-ba-ba-ba-ba*." It was, in Oita's description, an intervention from God. "To this day people are afraid of me," he would add. "They failed to kill me because God didn't allow it. That's the real story."

Hearing this version told back to him, Roberto himself would scoff: "If he'd been shooting into the air, it would have shredded the leaves" in the trees overhead. "The bullets hit the ground"—where Roberto was taking cover. Still, given the chaos, he remained unsure as to whether Oita had been there at all.

Roberto's war party was unable to remove all the settlers from Paraíso on its own. But the campaign made headlines. Forced to intervene, the government finally transferred those who remained off Zoró lands.

Oita, despite his later bravado, made himself scarce. He and his wife spent a few months hiding out at a ranch near Cacoal, as guests of its white owner. Only after passions had cooled did they move back to Riozinho. Oita's old friend Tataré was living there, working for Funai; he was first to welcome Oita back into the fold. He didn't believe Oita had fired his gun that day, reasoning that, if he had, this student of Sapecado wouldn't have missed. And indeed, Oita's version may just be self-aggrandizement.

Whatever the truth, Tataré could never forget how, when he was wandering with Pio after the measles outbreak, Oita had provided fresh meat to fill their empty bellies. In his words, "Oita saved us." And so he gave his friend fresh clothes and some cash to get back on his feet.

There were few others in the world who'd been through what they had. Oita, even with all his faults, made Tataré feel less alone.

CHAPTER 15

"WHO WANTS TO BE CIVILIZED?"

For a while it seemed like Pio had gotten what he wanted. Within a couple of years, roads crisscrossed Cinta Larga country, and his people hadn't lost any of their land to invaders. They were finally tasting some of the Western things they'd yearned for, not least Pio with his Chevrolet. Pichuvy, though, was having a harder time with it. He'd always been more ambivalent about the white men's world. Now he sometimes drank to the point of becoming aggressive; once he even pointed a shotgun at Pio, his dear old friend.

The Cinta Larga were far from the only Indigenous people to sell the riches of the forest. In part this was because they acted like ambassadors for the trade, even teaching their onetime enemies the Nambikwara how it worked. Other groups, though, were far more divided on the issue. Among the Suruí, some made deals with loggers, but a young man named Almir would become internationally renowned for his environmental activism. It wasn't that the Cinta Larga had no interest in such things. Pio loved the forest, his home. But whereas Almir had Ailton Krenak, the Indigenous intellectual, as a mentor, Pio's guidance came mostly from white men willing to break the law to make money. Even Apoena lacked a better idea for how the Cinta Larga could support themselves.

The bonanza brought its own problems. In September 1987, two government officials visited a logger and a sawmill owner who worked with Pio. Identifying themselves as advisers to Romero Jucá, Funai's mustachioed president, they threatened to confiscate the businessmen's equipment unless each handed over $30,000. Jucá was signing away hardwood from Indigenous areas across the region, and it appeared he wanted a piece of the Cinta Larga's business, too. One of his advisers had previously met with Roberto and some other headmen to buy them off, but Roberto not only turned them down; he held the adviser and two Funai agents hostage, painted their bodies red, and took their official vehicles. Justifying this later to a reporter, Roberto said the men had been using the vehicles to tour brothels instead of doing their job: to help the Indians.

Allegations about Jucá's dealings were published in a magazine piece titled "Índio dá dinheiro"—roughly, "Indians Are Profitable." It was a national scandal, and likely hastened the end of Jucá's tenure at Funai. Before stepping down, though, he had Roberto Carlos, still a Funai employee, fired along with two other agents who'd denounced the scheme. Jucá himself called the allegations "frivolous" and was never charged with a crime. Nor did his career suffer. The following year he was named governor of the newly created Amazonian state of Roraima. For the Cinta Larga, it was another kind of informal civics lesson: despite its high-minded rhetoric, the Brazilian state was basically cynical.

Gradually it dawned on Pio that their white associates were taking advantage of them. Eloi Balbinot was one of the settlers who'd lost their farms in the Fourteenth of April area, but in just a few years he'd become a successful logger, living in a house of Brazil nut wood on a new property just outside Cinta Larga country. With the profits from just eight mahogany trunks, he'd bought a brand-new car—and in an average season, he cut down hundreds. If the Cinta Larga made as much as he did, Pio realized, they'd all have cars! Visiting Espigão d'Oeste, he could see that a whole economy was sprouting—shops, restaurants, mechanics—thanks to their resources. Eloi's brothers were loggers, too, and just as successful. The central square was named for their father, Nilo Paulo Balbinot.

Pio wondered what would happen to Espigão if he cut off access. But he needed the loggers, too. Instead he sent Cinta Larga men to accompany them and learn their ways. The first step was "research," tromping through the rainforest to find the most valuable specimens—not just mahogany but *cerejeira* and *louro freijó*, known abroad as Brazilian oak and Brazilian walnut. Marking the trunks with a few whacks from a machete, the men would then open a trail connecting them all. The next step was to create a "patio," using chainsaws to clear an area large enough to store a hundred trunks. Meanwhile, another team would build a road wide enough to accommodate a flatbed Mercedes-Benz semi, which could carry half a dozen logs at a time. Eloi did this job with a Komatsu crawler, a bulldozer with tracked wheels like a tank, allowing him to advance a half-mile through the forest in a single day; when he hit a stream, he and his men would construct a bridge out of freshly cut sections of tree.

The work was both hard and dangerous. A shift typically lasted twenty-five days, with nights spent in hammocks right there in the forest. On one occasion Eloi watched as a falling tree hit a branch, catapulting it into a worker's head and killing him instantly. On another, after they'd knocked down an enormous specimen, a man sat down to rest in the earthy scar, and the uprooted trunk fell back into place, crushing him to death. At least for Eloi, though, it was worth it. The business was highly profitable. He and his brothers also owned a sawmill, where the wood could be sliced into boards for the export market, for even wider margins.

In the timber industry, the standard unit is the cubic meter of usable wood. To keep his associates honest, Pio hired other loggers to train his people in making these measurements; then he posted Cinta Larga "inspectors" to track what was hauled out. Under his leadership, the Pamaré Association would even acquire a sawmill of its own, thus vertically integrating (in the jargon of the business world) the Cinta Larga hardwood trade. "Now everything is going to work out," Pio told a friend. "We won't depend on the loggers anymore. We're going to make the loggers go broke!"

*　*　*

Around that time, elders started telling a myth that hinted at a deep ambivalence about Western goods. Recorded by the anthropologist João Dal Poz, it sought to explain why the white man possessed such advanced technologies: Ngurá—the Creator—"created the axe, created the machete, created everything." And then He said, "Who wants to be civilized? Who wants to be knowledgeable? Whoever wants to be civilized, come to me." Ngurá pulled out his penis. The white man agreed to suck it, but the Cinta Larga refused. And so the Cinta Larga were left to make their own arrows, baskets, hammocks, necklaces.

Even Pio had misgivings. As much as he might indulge in the temptations of white society, as much as he might make white friends, he never felt truly comfortable in their world. He saw other headmen forgetting who they were, where they came from, and he didn't want that for himself—or for any Cinta Larga. At Roosevelt Village, people no longer made the flutes known as *orê orê áp*, whose melodies worked as a kind of Morse code, recalling known lyrics. Noticing this, Pio cut one from hard green bamboo and started playing: *"Father, Daddy, where did you go?"* So many others followed his lead, the trilling of nostalgic songs seemed to erupt from every corner.

Even as the entire village population moved into Western-style homes, Pio and Pichuvy decided to build one traditional longhouse, transporting the thatch in a truck gifted by loggers, on roads built by loggers. The purpose was to hold a Feast of the Pig like in the old days, and in 1987, two hundred people would attend, many coming from far-flung villages. Pio's father-in-law, the respected elder known as Rondon, made sure the feast followed the traditional format with improvised songs, gifts of beautiful arrows, and the killing of a pig. Yet Rondon couldn't ignore how much his people had changed in the short time since contact, with so many wearing flip-flops and T-shirts along with headdresses of black curassow and brown tinamou feathers. Some went naked except for the traditional belt of bark, but most at least wore Western underwear. While they remained muscular, incipient paunches could be seen, thanks to their changing habits. Pio, who now spent much of his time in town, was getting particularly round.

Around this time, an architect named Leda Leonel Lima came to study Cinta Larga longhouses. She ended up recording hours of conversations with Pichuvy, which later became a book. Pichuvy spent most of the time recounting myths and stories of contact, drawing on the memories of elders who didn't speak much Portuguese. But he also told of more recent encounters with white men, without letting on that he and Pio had forged alliances with them. "Loggers are removing hardwood, but they are wrong," he declared. "It ruins everything.... When you cut down a tree, the trunk won't grow anymore....Now all the game is disappearing." He even speculated that deforestation would cause the Amazon's rivers to dry up—years before climatologists, using advanced computer models, would arrive at a similar conclusion.

"The white man wants land to make money," Pichuvy went on. "The Indian doesn't need money....The Indian needs to hunt...needs to fish...gather honey....That's all the Indian needs. But there's no need to cut down trees. If I were a white man, I wouldn't cut down trees.... It's no good for the Indian."

Pichuvy shared Pio's concern that his people were losing their identity. "The Indian got used to wearing clothes because white people wear clothes," he lamented. "That's why the Indian is no longer interested in Indian life....The Indian wants to be just like the white man."

And yet, when Pichuvy wasn't at Roosevelt Village, he partook in the exact behavior he denounced, drinking and cavorting with *brancas*. Late one night in June 1988, he was driving the Toyota he'd received from a logger. With him were two white women—one his girlfriend, who lived in a house he paid for in town—and a Cinta Larga named Renato. That night he was drunk, too drunk. Driving on Highway 364, he crashed straight into a Mercedes-Benz truck loaded with Cinta Larga mahogany. Pichuvy and the two white women were killed instantly; Renato was taken to a hospital but couldn't be saved.

Among the Cinta Larga, Pichuvy would always be considered a great leader and fearless warrior, central to their campaigns to kick out invaders. Pio, like everyone else, mourned his friend's death. But his love affair with money was just beginning.

PART THREE

THE TIME OF DIAMONDS

2000s

CHAPTER 16

OLD LUCA

On the morning of April 10, 2004, the day before Easter, a taxi packed with Cinta Larga was spotted in Espigão d'Oeste. The driver was about to fill up with gas for the drive to Riozinho when a hundred white people surrounded the car. Among them were several women, wives and girlfriends of prospectors who'd recently gone missing inside Cinta Larga country. Three bodies had already been found in an area known as the Gully of Tranquility, but the word around town was that the dead numbered far more, maybe twenty, maybe as many as sixty.

A rock broke through the taxi's back windshield. One of the Cinta Larga, Donivaldo, would later tell the police he knew nothing about what had happened at the gully, but his face was known to prospectors because he sometimes joined Funai agents on patrol. Now he opened the door and tried to escape, but someone smashed a brick into his face. Before he knew it, he was being dragged down the street. At Espigão's central square, he was tied to a tree. A crowd formed, and he heard shouts of "Kill the Indian!" and "Show him his place!" The mob tore at his clothes, pummeling him with rocks and pieces of wood. Blood started streaming from his forehead. Half a dozen cops showed up, but whether out of complicity or fear, they didn't intervene.

The Federal Police were alerted but claimed to be short of agents. Funai lacked the manpower to do anything but warn other Cinta Larga to stay away. In the meantime, a TV crew showed up. The head of the local prospectors union said there was no way the missing men could be lost in the forest or hiding from the police: "These are family men. They were seen tied up and never made it back to town." A woman named Sandra, the wife of a prospector known as Baiano Doido, took the lead in negotiations with the authorities. Baiano himself had been breaking the law, digging for diamonds on Indigenous lands. But now he was missing, and Sandra demanded an official search in return for releasing Donivaldo. She also wanted three prospectors to come along so that Funai couldn't "eliminate the evidence."

Another rumor took hold: a hundred Cinta Larga warriors were on their way to free Donivaldo by force. Local police set up checkpoints to head them off. It was dusk when the mob relented, allowing Donivaldo to be cut free and escorted to an empty gym to await rescue. To secure his release, the authorities had agreed to some of the mob's demands. But passions hadn't cooled. People kept grabbing at Donivaldo even as the cops attempted to form a wall around him, and a rock hit an officer, who had to get ten stitches in his scalp. A Federal Police detachment finally arrived around midnight to transfer Donivaldo to another city.

Pio's friend Barroca heard about the incident from a Funai agent. An old warrior, he said he wasn't afraid. But the agent told him, "Go back to Roosevelt Village. You'll be safe there. That's your place."

* * *

When Pio thought back to that time, when it seemed like the whole world was against them—not just prospectors and their allies in Rondônia but politicians in Brasília and media across the country, prosecutors and Federal Police—he could hardly believe it had started with the arrival of an almost comical figure at the office he now kept in Riozinho. It was the start of the rainy season of 1999. The man was in his eighties, his leathery skin mottled albino-white from vitiligo, and he dressed all in black, including his hat. Speaking Portuguese with an unplaceable accent, he introduced himself as José Lucas de Bonfim, though like most prospectors, he was better known by his nickname, Luca Pintado (Spotted Luca). He wanted to look for diamonds in Cinta Larga country.

By now, Pio had heard too many pitches like this one. To locate the legendary Mines of Urucumacuã in the early 1990s, he'd partnered with a white man who claimed to be a geologist. They'd traveled all over Cinta Larga country and into Nambikwara lands, tracing the footsteps of successful prospectors past—Raul the Spaniard, Sapecado—but found nothing. Pio belatedly realized that his partner was little more than an adventurer, if not an outright grifter. After that, Pio financed two dredges, rafts from which divers combed the Roosevelt like the original prospectors in the 1960s. Again, nothing.

Pio was ready to brush Luca off, but the old man reminded him they'd actually met before. The first time was probably in 1981. Pio was alone in the forest near Roosevelt Village, looking for honey, when a few bedraggled white men emerged from the trees, Luca among them. They claimed to be lost, so Pio escorted them to the edge of the Indigenous area. A couple of years later, Pio was fishing on the Roosevelt when Luca and his crew appeared once again. Just like before, Luca claimed to be lost, so Pio ferried them across and pointed them to town. But Luca was nothing if not persistent. Pio was hunting for armadillos just a few days after *that* when he heard a bush plane buzzing low. Pio knew the Funai plane that brought supplies to Roosevelt Village, and this wasn't it. He followed the sound and saw the plane dropping packages somewhere near the Stream of the Blackflies. Approaching quietly, he spied

Luca and his companions in a fresh clearing. There was a woman who seemed to be a cook; four men were building a crude dam out of rocks and straw to divert the water, the better to dig into the stream bed. The packages were full of provisions, mostly sweets, to fuel their labor.

Pio came back with Chicão, the swashbuckling director of the Aripuanã Indigenous Park, and two other agents. With his usual brashness, Chicão told the prospectors, "You have two weeks to get out of here. We'll be back in two weeks, and if you're still here, you're all going to jail."

Luca tried to negotiate. "*Senhor*," he said, "you could be a rich man. Richer than the owner of a bank. So rich, so rich, that the banks won't even be able to hold all your money. If you give me thirty days, I'll write you a check that not just any bank can cash."

Chicão laughed, and Pio, uncomprehending, asked what the prospector was saying. Luca ignored Pio and repeated his offer to Chicão. One of the other agents said, "This man is shameless, isn't he?"

"If I come back and you're still here..." Chicão began, before switching gears: "I won't even need to come back here, because these Indians will kill you all. And then they'll eat you." (The threat worked.)

If Luca looked bedraggled then, he hardly inspired confidence now, with his thick glasses and wiry, aging frame. Little wonder he'd gained a new nickname: Old Luca. He'd driven down from Porto Velho with a young man named Mococa, whom he called his son though they looked nothing alike. They had all their belongings in the back of an old Fiat pickup, but none of it was special equipment, just shovels, pickaxes, and sieves. Luca couldn't even offer money up front. Yet he declared with utter certainty, "I'm going to make you rich."

Pio remained skeptical: "How many people have searched around here and found nothing?"

Luca didn't pretend to be a geologist. He had no formal schooling at all. Born in the Dutch colony of Suriname, just north of Brazil, he'd moved with his mother to Macapá, a Brazilian city near the mouth of the Amazon River, when he was around seven. He never met his father. (A joke he liked to tell was: "Do you know who your father is? No, you don't. You can only know for sure who your mother is.") Even as a child he bounced around in search of work, once walking all the way from Cuiabá to Porto Velho, a journey of nine hundred miles. He claimed to have worked under Cândido Rondon himself, resettling tribes for the Indian Protection Service in the 1930s—even though the great explorer wasn't actually in Rondônia at the time.

Luca's name was absent from histories of prospecting in Rondônia. But he also claimed to have been a kind of forefather to pioneers like Raul Moreda. "This Raul the Spaniard stuff is a bunch of monkey crap," he said, "because I'm the one who brought them here." Luca said he'd discovered some of the richest prospects not only in Rondônia but across the Amazon region. He said he owned maps where Rondon had indicated all the most promising mineral deposits, including the Mines of Urucumacuá. If that wasn't enough, he boasted of a sixth sense that allowed him to "see" precious metals and stones beneath the ground: "The power of the mind is a power that passes through everything. If you have this power, you pray, you blow on the world, and you can do whatever you want....It's a God-given gift, you see?"

If Pio swallowed half of what Luca said, he was far from alone. Belief in magic, spirits, and the occult have always thrived in Brazil, and not just among poorly educated country folk. Luca later became friends with a high-ranking official at the National Department of Mineral Production who testified under oath that he possessed "supernatural powers" for locating diamonds.

"You'll see," Luca said to Pio now. "You're going to be the richest Indian in the world."

Pio might have wondered why, with all that Luca had going for him, he was so broke. Describing past successes, Luca boasted of hauls of gold weighing five, thirteen, sixty kilograms—and at the prevailing market price, a single kilo would be worth around $10,000. "Pocket change like that—three hundred thousand, four hundred thousand— never lasted long," he explained. "I could spend fifty thousand, a hundred thousand in a day."

On what?

"Whores. I'd become the 'owner' of the brothel. I'd say, 'This is mine, drink up.' The men would drink until everything was gone, and then I'd pay the bill. Crazy life, but that's the way it is."

*   *   *

Luca's luck was that Pio was desperate for a new source of income. Bowing to pressure from environmentalists, the government had banned all trade in Brazil nut wood in 1994, and was about to do the same for mahogany. At least in Cinta Larga country, though, it was already too late for this. After years of frenzied logging, just about all of the mahogany within easy reach of a highway was already gone. What remained was so deep in the forest that the cost of hauling it out would exceed any revenue. Loggers started going after the less valuable species they used to disdain, such as *ipê*, whose bright yellow and pink flowers punctuated the canopy. But even this tree became scarce. Scrambling for the same dwindling resources, Cinta Larga headmen butted heads over turf.

Pio's plan to "make the loggers go broke" hadn't turned out well, either. Under his leadership, the Pamaré Association had acquired a sawmill from a logger named Luiz Turatti. But the Cinta Larga still lacked tractors or trucks. Forced to rent them from Turatti himself, they became Turatti's debtors, and sold the sawmill at a loss.

Despite these setbacks, the association ended up with the equivalent of $50,000 in the bank. Then, in 1990, the government announced a half-baked plan to attack hyperinflation by freezing savings accounts. By the time the freeze was lifted, inflation had so weakened the currency that people's savings were practically worthless. It was a national trauma for a whole generation of Brazilians, and showed the Cinta Larga, once again, that the government couldn't be trusted.

The Cinta Larga had also tried to accumulate another form of capital, popular on the Amazon frontier: cattle. In the early 1990s they had a few hundred head grazing on pastureland cleared by the invaders in the Fourteenth of April area. Like money in a savings account (except more reliable), it was capital that reproduced itself, literally, with freshly born calves. Apart from some ears of corn kept in a little village storehouse, the Cinta Larga never used to maintain any kind of surplus. The Western concept of investment was still mostly foreign, and this attempt to learn it likewise met with failure. A Funai agent told them their cattle were infected with brucellosis, a bacterial disease that can be passed to humans. But he was in cahoots with a rancher who offered to take the cattle off their hands for a measly Volkswagen Fusca (the Brazilian equivalent of the Bug). In town, the police found that the registration had been falsified, and seized it. The Cinta Larga couldn't even turn to Apoena, as their old ally had long since moved on.

Fifteen years in, Pio's people had little to show for all their logging. Their population was edging past twelve hundred, possibly exceeding its level before contact, but this brought problems, too. In the aging wooden homes at Roosevelt Village, once-vibrant paint jobs were sun-faded and peeling, and whole families would sleep in a single room, on grubby mattresses laid out on packed-dirt floors. The population was also largely children, which meant more helpless mouths to feed than ever before in their history.

Pio already regretted quitting school as a boy. But he wanted to send the next generation to college so they could become doctors, lawyers, teachers, agronomists, and maybe even politicians, to find new ways for their nation to sustain itself, to protect their lands with the white man's tools. To that end, he'd picked two promising youths, Panderê and Rondonzinho (Little Rondon, a son of the respected elder), to send to school in town. "It wasn't easy to sit there with a bunch of non-Indigenous kids," Rondonzinho would recall. "Whenever I spoke, they'd make fun of me. They said I should go back to the village because Indians belong in the jungle." What really derailed his education, though, was discovering *brancas*. Cinta Larga children had always been taught to be self-reliant, allowed to roam free—but they were also allowed to make their own mistakes, even if it meant cutting themselves on a sharp blade. Now Rondonzinho and Panderê both shacked up with white women, abandoning their studies to try and make money, like Pio had done. Pio was profoundly disappointed.

In some ways the Cinta Larga were actually worse off than before the hardwood trade. Game was already scarce near villages, with their newly permanent populations. As loggers crisscrossed the territory, building roads wherever they went, their chainsaws scared off tapirs, deer, curassows, and countless other animals, forcing hunters to travel even farther to find game. This was one reason Pio had hopes for prospecting. *If we find diamonds*, he thought, *we'll work only in one spot.* The rest of the forest would remain undisturbed, thus preserving, maybe even restoring, their longtime hunting grounds.

There was another reason Pio would admit to only later. "I'm the guy who did everything first," he would say. "I was first to get a car and learn to drive. I was first to fly on a plane." Yet there were things he still wanted to experience: to travel to big coastal cities like Rio de Janeiro, to stay in five-star hotels and eat in fancy restaurants, no matter how weird the food. In short, he wanted to be rich. And so he decided to see what Old Luca could do. *As long as we can control it*, Pio said to himself, *it will be good.*

CHAPTER 17

THE STREAM OF THE BLACKFLIES

When Oita heard about Pio's deal with Luca, he decided to visit the old man's camp on the Stream of the Blackflies. He actually had prospectors of his own searching for diamonds nearby. As usual, he was going it alone, without any other Cinta Larga in on the deal. As usual, he was looking for recognition, respect—and in the new world of Brazilian society, this meant making money. At the time he was married to a white woman named Alba Gomes, who would recall a succession of schemes: "For a while it was hardwood, for a while it was heart of palm." None worked out.

Loggers had long feared Oita's violent reputation, but he also became known for deceptions. One settler had sold Oita a car; Oita said he could collect the payment from a lawyer, but the so-called lawyer disappeared—just one of many such stories. Still money ran short. Alba sometimes had to take their children to her parents' for dinner because there was no food at home. Other times Oita's old friend Tataré helped out, buying groceries with his Funai salary.

Alba had moved to Riozinho as a kid in 1986. Her father was an underemployed construction worker, and when Alba turned fifteen, she helped out by taking a job in Oita's home, cooking, cleaning, and caring for his children. It should have been obvious that Oita had an eye for young girls. He'd married his Indigenous wife when she was fourteen and he was in his early thirties. Now he started complaining to Alba about her, claiming they'd separated, though they still lived together.

Oita seemed to have a plan. He offered her father a job tending his fields in Cinta Larga country, and the whole family relocated to a wooden shack near Roosevelt Village. Alba quit school. Even as she washed clothes in a stream, she couldn't help but notice when Oita was watching her. His wife mostly stayed in Riozinho, taking care of the kids, but one day when Oita was away, she showed up and demanded to know where he was sleeping. To Alba, a devout Christian, the implication was obvious: she was being accused of adultery. Later in life, she would realize just how hotheaded and naive she was then. She flew into a rage and said, "You think I'm sleeping with him? Fine. Starting today, if he wants me to be his wife, that's what I'll be."

Other Cinta Larga men, of course, had multiple wives. But when Oita proposed this to his own wife—a devout Christian herself—she refused, and retreated to Riozinho. Observing all this, Alba's father became nervous. He saw an opportunity to escape a few days later, when the family was at Roosevelt Village and a truck stopped on its way to town. He hadn't even collected his wages, but he asked for a lift so his family could go home. That's when Oita showed up, gun in hand. He sat on a log some distance away, silent but menacing. Tataré, the village chief at the time, went to speak to him. In later years Tataré would wonder why his old friend never changed, never stopped threatening people. At the time, though, he just wanted to prevent anything bad from happening. He returned with Oita's message: Alba's family could go, but she had to stay.

Alba tried to explain that she'd spoken out of pique and wanted to go home. But Tataré said that if she tried to leave, Oita had promised to kill her whole family—"and he'll do it." It was then that Alba realized, with a sinking feeling, just what she'd gotten herself into. She told her parents to go. Some would later whisper that Alba's father had "sold" her to Oita, but Alba knew better. Once back in town, he went to the police, but the officers said they had no power to enter Indigenous territory, which was under federal jurisdiction.

That same afternoon, Oita took Alba back to the shack by his fields. For a whole month he didn't leave, paranoid that someone would steal her from him. He said she must never joke around with another Cinta Larga man, mustn't even make conversation, because it would be seen as an invitation to sleep with her. Jealousy had always been a blot on Cinta Larga life, but Oita took it to another level. Even in the old days, women had never been so thoroughly reined in. Like when Maria Beleza was kidnapped by Sapecado, there wasn't a single person Alba could turn to. Ten months later, she gave birth to a son, whom they gave the Biblical name Ezequiel—the first of five (in addition to the five he had with his Indigenous wife, and four others along the way).

There is a photo of Alba holding Ezequiel as she lies in a hammock. She looks even younger than her seventeen years, like a kid taking care of a baby sibling. When they moved back to Riozinho, people would ask if she was Oita's daughter.

For all his suffering in the time when he lacked any power, Oita didn't hesitate to make others suffer when they were under his control. According to Alba, he beat her during an argument just two weeks after the birth of their second child, a daughter. She tried to leave him, taking their two babies to her parents' house, but her father naively invited Oita over to make peace. Friendly at first, Oita put Ezequiel on his lap. Then he picked the baby up and left, effectively holding their one-year-old son hostage. Alba tried to enlist the police, again to no avail. Ultimately she saw no choice but to go back to him. Hoping to protect her parents, she decided to leave them out of her troubles. (In later years, at least two other partners would say he beat them, too, but Oita would refuse to speak about any of it, even to give his own, self-flattering version.)

Alba found solace at church, submerging herself in prayer. Because of her faith, she felt a duty to be not only a good mother but a good wife, even ironing Oita's shirts. (As always, he liked to look polished.) Yet she felt false when she watched his sermons, and he acted like their life together was wonderful. She was never sure whether he knew this was a lie. "In his head it's like everything was normal," she would recall. But then she would correct herself: "He knew what was right and what was wrong. And the Bible says that if you know the difference between right and wrong, you're responsible for what you do...whether you're an Indian or not."

* * *

At the Stream of the Blackflies, Oita couldn't help remembering the day he'd brought the prospector known as Pamapat—Great Death—to that long-ago feast. Most Cinta Larga were stoic when they told the story, but Oita would break into sobs; after all, it was he who'd brought the white men's disease into their home. It helped that there were no longer any traces of the life that once flourished there. All the old longhouses had long since fallen apart, becoming forest once again. Now it was only loggers who haunted the area, searching for the last few trees of value.

The area wasn't unknown to geologists. Since developing South Africa's Big Hole, De Beers had become a global monopoly. Kimberlites, those columns of cooled magma, weren't actually so rare once you knew where to look: in the oldest geologic provinces, known as cratons. All told, more than six thousand kimberlites would be identified around the world. But only one in seven contained diamonds—and of those, only a fraction were economically viable. In the 1970s, before mining companies were banned from Brazil's Indigenous lands, De Beers had located five in the southern Amazon, but chose not to explore them, whether because the stones were too small and impure or simply not plentiful enough to justify a mine. Typically measuring less than a mile in diameter, kimberlites were easy to miss. The company failed to notice the one Brazil's geological survey later dubbed Cinta Larga-1, which lay isolated from the rest, in a so-called intrusive suite of coarse-grained igneous rock, below a little tributary labeled Igarapé Lajes on maps.

In a typical twist of Brazilian Portuguese, the word *igarapé* is one of many borrowed from the Tupian languages once spoken by Indigenous groups on the coast (who themselves shared an ancestor with the Cinta Larga). Literally "canoe path," it has come to refer to any small Amazonian waterway. A *laje*, meanwhile, is a smooth, flat stone. The stream probably got its name because, at its mouth in the Roosevelt, it flowed over a wide bed of water-smoothed granite, so shallow that the water turned translucent before a moment of white-tipped turbulence where the river swallowed it up. How many prospectors had motored by without realizing this was the source of all the Roosevelt's diamonds? Despite its name, the *igarapé* could hardly be navigated by canoe, much less by a hulking dredge. It was narrow enough that a pilot flying overhead would see little more than the odd flash of reflected sunlight peeking through the canopy.

Waterways were everywhere in this forest, born as springs in tree-covered hills and collecting in countless little valleys. What made this one different was that it passed over Cinta Larga-1, which, by an obscure accident of geology, had brought up diamonds pure enough to be world-class gems. Two hundred million years of weather had since acted upon it. Every time an Amazonian deluge burst through the canopy, water seeped through the tangle of vines and spongelike mosses and down to the shallow roots, saturating the soil and soaking up a few grains of the kimberlite's uppermost layers. Every once in a while, a diamond was dislodged, and the diamond had no choice but to follow the path of least resistance, Igarapé Lajes—the Stream of the Blackflies—for twenty meandering miles, all the way to the Roosevelt.

Luca would never reveal what intuition led him there, time and again. Perhaps it was blind luck. Until Oita showed up, the old man's plan was just to start at the stream's mouth and work his way up, stopping now and then to dig a hole. He and Mococa used the same tools of prospectors in preindustrial times. With a shovel and a pickaxe, they broke up the earth, dropped it into a sieve, and rinsed it in the stream. Whatever remained, they sorted through with fingers. Finding nothing, they moved on to dig another hole. And another. And again nothing. And again. But in Pio's words, "Prospectors are stubborn creatures." For weeks they kept at it, sleeping in hammocks slung between trees with nothing but a plastic tarp to shield against the elements. There was no relief from blood-hungry *Simuliidae* flies, whose larva attached themselves to rocks in the stream bed (hence the waterway's Cinta Larga name).

Lacking the funds for a pilot to airdrop supplies, Luca relied on the Cinta Larga to bring the occasional package of rice, beans, and oil. If they wanted to eat meat, they had to hunt it themselves. "Oh, what suffering," Mococa would recall. "My God, nothing but problems." His brother had come along, too. For days on end, they failed to catch even a monkey. One morning they heard the call of a curassow, and the two young men went looking for it, only to come upon two black jaguars. Luckily, judging from their distended bellies, the jaguars had just eaten. Mococa could have shot them but didn't have the heart. For the next couple of nights, they heard the jaguars purring, stalking them. Luca finally decided to go after them with a shotgun. Mococa didn't want the old man leaving camp in the dark, but Luca managed to shoot and kill one—meat, at last.

When Oita showed up at their camp, he said he'd had a dream. Recounting it in later years, his voice would go soft, quiet, striking a balance between whimsy and profundity—his pastor voice, perfect for entrancing his audience. In the dream, God spoke to Oita: "My son, come walk with me. Do you remember where you used to walk when you were a little boy?" Oita said yes, so God took him there, to the Stream of the Blackflies. And then He said, "I left all the riches here for you. You are a blessed man upon this earth....I'm going to show you that it is your God who is speaking to you."

Oita drew a diagram in the dirt, indicating the place where, according to his dream, Luca and his men would find what they were looking for. Luca suspected that Oita planned to rob them when they went to sleep. Oita, for his part, may have hoped to misdirect the old man. After all, he had his own prospectors working nearby. Other Cinta Larga had seen the dredge while fishing on the Roosevelt. They called Oita crazy, saying he'd be better off hunting to put some food on the table. He'd teamed up with a "geologist" who never finished college, and ultimately turned up but one *chibiu*, a diamond weighing less than a carat. As Luca would soon discover, though, Oita had somehow marked the exact location of the motherlode.

* * *

As a child, Tataré had always listened to his elders' stories, saving them for future generations. Now, as an adult, he ended up writing new chapters of his own. It was early in the dry season of 2000 when

Pio sent him to check up on Luca and his men. They'd already scoured some ten miles of the Stream of the Blackflies with nothing to show for it. Tataré got straight to the point: "*Senhor* Luca, here's the deal. You haven't found anything, so we're going to remove you."

Luca told Tataré to open his hand. Tataré noticed that the old man's skin was stippled with swollen reddish sores—even the corners of his mouth. In the middle of each sore was the off-white nub of a bot-fly larva. Tataré got the impression Luca didn't bathe, despite having the stream right there. Still, he opened his hand, and Luca placed four tiny crystals in it. They were mere *chibius* like the one Oita had found. But Luca said, "This is just the beginning."

A week later, Tataré returned to meet the prospectors at a new camp upstream, arriving just as Luca was plopping muddy gravel into a sieve. Luca dipped the sieve into the water and shook it with a practiced, rhythmic whirl, repeating the movements until all the dirt washed away. Amid the little rocks that remained, there sparkled several *biris*, diamonds weighing one, two, three carats. Luca repeated the process until Tataré noticed a clearish stone the size of a girl's fingertip. Luca began to tremble with excitement. Eyeballing, he guessed it weighed ten carats.

How could they know these crystals were truly diamonds? Some prospectors would put a stone in their mouth to test it. If they took it out and it stayed all steamed up, it was probably not a diamond, because diamonds repel moisture. If it stayed warm, it was probably not a diamond, because diamonds dump heat five times faster than copper. If that test failed to convince you, you could pick it up with tweezers, hold a lighter under it, and drop it into your hand; then if it didn't burn you, it was almost certainly the real thing. If it did burn you, well, everyone knew that the prospector's life was mostly suffering.

The only confirmation that mattered, of course, was a buyer making a purchase. But Luca wanted to avoid that as long as possible. He knew the frenzy that would ensue once the usual gossip circulated. For all his bluster, he truly had sparked at least one rush before. Funai blamed him for a social and environmental disaster in northwestern Rondônia in the early 1990s: "Senhor José Luca[s] do Bonfim...has been, for the past two years, prospecting for gold in the region....His prospecting has led to 'gossip' and in the last thirty days six hundred men with more than twelve pairs of machines have invaded twenty kilometers deep into the Uru-eu Indigenous Area. Blinded by gold fever, they are savagely destroying forests, rivers, and lives....The situation at the mine is grave....Mercury is being used indiscriminately."

Luca agreed to show the find to Pio, at least. Back at the Pamaré office, he spilled some stones on a table. The association's white administrator, Claudiney Souza, had never seen diamonds before; to him, they looked like flecks of broken glass. According to Luca, the whole lot was worth around $70,000—and that wasn't even all of it, as he'd secreted some away.

Pio didn't want to spread the word either. As ever, he worried about invaders—not to mention that mining, like logging, was illegal on Indigenous lands. He did need proof that Luca was for real, though. Cacoal wasn't a hub for precious stones, but Luca had stayed at a hotel whose owner, Josias Ascaciba da Silva, happened to dabble in prospecting. Offered a single stone, he bought it for $7,000. Pio was impressed: this rock, so small you could hide it in your shoe, was worth more than a whole truckload of hardwood!

The Cinta Larga cut was just 10 percent at that point. If they wanted more, they'd need proper equipment, regardless of any worries about gossip. Conveniently, Josias himself was eager to invest. He already had a dredge on the Machado River. He'd just have to bring in his business partner. And one other prospector. No one else.

171

CHAPTER 18

A SMALL OPERATION

When Olide Marafon started his farm, on a hilly plot by the Roosevelt River, the Cinta Larga used to show up on boats and declare simply, "I want a pig." They might hand him some money, but they seemed not to understand the numbers, sometimes offering half the pig's market price. Other times they had no money at all. But Marafon thought, *Well, they need it more than I do.* And he liked to be a good neighbor. He just asked which one they wanted, and even killed it for them, so they could take the meat back to their families. Gradually a friendship bloomed. One day they invited him to the village to play soccer. He played with them for years, until he got too old to keep up and started refereeing instead. After one tournament, they gave him a medal for best ref.

In the 1990s, Pio asked Marafon's permission to build a dirt road through his land, linking Roosevelt Village to the tiny outpost of Vila Bradesco, farther south. Marafon gladly assented; roads were always welcome. He soon became accustomed to the sight of Mercedes-Benz trucks hauling lumber in the dry season. He didn't mind; he himself had once owned a sawmill. But then came the night in 2000 when a truck came not to remove something from the forest but to drop

172

something off. Any vehicle passing through Marafon's land had to stop at a wooden gate that kept his cattle from escaping. He heard the diesel engine's breathy idle, then the gate swinging open. But the truck didn't continue on its way. Instead, right there on the roadside where Marafon's cattle grazed, workers unloaded an array of generators and pumps and stacks of plastic tubing, a few barrels that sloshed with fuel, and a boxy, heavy-looking contraption he'd later learn was a jig, for sorting diamonds.

The workers didn't ask Marafon's permission or even greet him. They simply threw a tarp over the machines and left, returning the way they'd come. Then, around dawn, a tractor rumbled down from Roosevelt Village and carried it all away. It wasn't long before another shipment arrived, and then another, until Marafon lost count. Sometimes there were three or four in a single night. He didn't like to complain about other people's business, but as the dry season gave way to the rains, the endless parade of trucks turned the road into a swamp.

Other strangers, carrying little more than a backpack, occasionally showed up at Marafon's ranch and paid him to drive the rest of the way to the village. Among them was a fifty-something Belgian who didn't speak Portuguese, instead communicating through an interpreter. Another Belgian spoke some Portuguese, but for some reason he went by the nickname "American." There was also a young, quiet, skinny "oriental" Marafon guessed to be Korean. Sometimes he watched as they handed over a few neat piles of cash and received a rattling section of bamboo with the ends taped shut.

Marafon wasn't the type to ask questions, but it was impossible not to realize that something big was happening in the Indigenous area. He continued to receive visits from the Cinta Larga, but now they had wads of cash to offer for his pigs, and even bought whole cows. He'd take no more than what was fair. Sometimes they offered him precious stones as payment, but Marafon, not having any clue how much they were worth, said he preferred hard currency. That was no problem. "Indians have money now," they said. "Indians have a mine."

*　*　*

Pio had tried to keep it small. As usual, he'd held a meeting at Roosevelt Village, and in the words of a Funai agent who participated, "Pio wanted something that would be exclusively theirs, because he worried about losing control." All the other Cinta Larga agreed: the Pamaré Association would act as sole intermediary, selecting who would be allowed in and collecting a flat fee, or "toll," along with a percentage of sales.

At first the only prospectors authorized were Old Luca, Josias, and Josias's partner on the dredge, Mauro Pereira dos Santos (better known as Lobão, the Big Wolf), as well as a car salesman named Ubiratan Hass de Paula (who was also suspected of moonlighting as a drug dealer). The three newcomers fit a profile common among investors in Amazonian mines: local businessmen with no real knowledge of geology, no special acumen for prospecting, and not the faintest inkling of Indigenous culture—just some capital, an appetite for risk, and a casual disdain for the law. They set to re-creating the system that reigned in informal mining prospects across Brazil. They didn't necessarily do the work themselves. Josias apparently never visited the mine at all, and while Lobão and Ubiratan were broadly considered *garimpeiros* ("prospectors"), they weren't manual laborers but rather *donos de máquina* ("owners of machines") who oversaw operations.

Their first step was to set up camp. Shelter was just some sturdy branches lashed together and covered with a blue tarpaulin that gave the inside a moody, azure tint. Everyone strung up hammocks to sleep in. Cooks tended to enormous aluminum pots full of rice, beans, and meat when it was available, on fires fueled by heavy canisters of lique-fied gas. Ubiratan tossed a few tubes of lipstick into the stream out of an obscure superstition that this would bring good luck, and thus their first area came to be known as Grota do Batom, Lipstick Gully.

The next step was to clear an area with chainsaws, knocking down the trees to expose the ochre soil. Each team set up what was known in Brazilian prospecting lingo as a "pair of machines," which used water to separate minerals from worthless sediment. The method traces back to Ancient Rome, when engineers used aqueducts to fill reservoirs, opening floodgates to wash away the earth and reveal the ore. In the nineteenth century, during the California Gold Rush, prospectors constructed so-called holding ponds, channeling water into hoses to achieve the same effect. Now, at the Stream of the Blackflies, diesel engines were hooked up to pumps that sent water through a tube to a high-pressure nozzle—the first machine in the "pair." The jet was so powerful, the worker known as the *jateiro* leaned forward at a seemingly impossible angle. His job was to spray away the "overburden," the layers of mud and clay atop the "pay gravel," where diamonds could be found. Gradually a "sink" of reddish-brown water formed—the pit where a team would do its work. Machines were fixed to rafts of wood and empty fuel barrels.

In Pio's recollection, Lobão initially brought in four pairs of machines. Josias and Ubiratan brought in several more. As each team created its own pit, the noise drowned out every other sound, making normal conversation difficult. It was a chorus of roaring engines shuddering with combusting diesel, drive belts spinning the gears of hydraulic pumps, plus the higher-pitched note of the jets. Day by day the pits widened until they reached perhaps a hundred feet in diameter, deepening until, around fifty feet down, they could go no deeper. Wet and unstable, the Amazonian earth would collapse if you went too deep, so prospectors had no hope of reaching the underlying kimberlite, like in South Africa's Big Hole. Still they pushed the limits as far as they could, and sometimes farther, clambering up and down ramps that gave way beneath their feet.

Given that each pit required four workers (almost always men) and a cook (almost always a woman), the number of white people quickly multiplied. In addition to the *jateiro*, there was a *maraqueiro*, who operated a device that aspirated the muddy gravel—the second machine in the "pair." To avoid clogging, he modulated the suction with a foot pedal, while a third worker tossed large rocks from the pit with a pitchfork. The fourth and final worker stayed above to tend a sluice box that caught the suctioned slurry. Resembling a carpeted water slide, a sluice box featured a series of obstructions known as riffles, meant to catch heavier minerals like diamonds and gold while lighter rocks and dirt washed over it. The apparatus was imprecise, often ejecting precious stones along with worthless tailings. In those days, though, it hardly mattered, because those were the smaller stones.

Pio often visited the operation. Looking down into a pit, he could hardly tell one person from another. Mud-men waded in muddy water high enough that there was little use in wearing boots, the clear spray of the water jets turning muddy brown as it raked the pit walls, then the rebound spray like a horizontal mud shower. At the end of the day the men might dunk in the stream, but their clothes inevitably took on the mud's rusty hue. To avoid losing shoes and flip-flops to the mud vacuum underfoot, most went without, so it was easy to cut yourself on the refuse that accumulated: broken bottles, snapped drive belts, damaged sections of tubing. At one point Pio stepped wrong and injured his leg, leaving him with a permanent limp.

Even then Pio could see it was only a matter of time before the secret got out. A single generator could burn through more than twenty gallons of diesel a day—and with so many generators running, they would soon be forced to raise cash.

*   *   *

From the hardwood trade, Pio had learned to monitor his white business partners. For those Cinta Larga who still had limited experience of the outside world, he explained the task didactically. Once or twice a day, the prospectors would empty the contents of the sluice box to count their haul. "You're going to stay in their tent and keep an eye on them," he told his old friend Barroca. "When they're rinsing the gravel in a sieve, you have to stay on top of them. Prospectors are very clever. That's when they'll try to grab some diamonds for themselves and hide them." He even gave Barroca the official title "inspector." Barroca watched as prospectors plucked out little crystals. The larger ones were weighed individually, the smaller ones as a group. Each lot was sealed into a *picuá*—any kind of tube, whether a section of hose or bamboo or even a large animal bone, with a makeshift plug, perhaps a piece of wood, secured with tape.

Barroca wasn't the only one enlisted. Roberto Carlos was living in the city of Juína, near the eastern edge of their territory, when Pio called and asked him to bring his truck, saying, "Let's make some money." Like Oita, Roberto already knew the area intimately, having grown up on the Stream of the Blackflies. Also like Oita, he'd acquired a taste for the finer things in Western life. But when he arrived at the mine, he couldn't help remembering those terrible days in the late 1960s. Hearing the mechanical racket, he imagined what the place would look like if his village—and so many others—hadn't been wiped out. He pictured the many Cinta Larga who would be going about their lives, tending their crops, bathing in the stream, or just hanging out trading stories of great hunts and battles.

Other traces of their history emerged in more tangible form.

Sometimes the prospectors stumbled upon fragments of the clay pots women once used for cooking, or dulled stone axe heads, the wooden handles having long since decomposed. At night in a prospector's tent, lying in a white man's hammock beneath the blue plastic roof, Roberto tried to sleep but felt his throat close up. He knew that white people talked about things that happened long ago as "sacred." To him this place was just that. At the very least it could be fenced off, he thought, out of respect for the dead. Whatever his profligacy during the logging boom, he'd always been a sensitive soul. He agreed to help Pio, but tried to spend as little time as possible at the mine itself.

Some Cinta Larga inspectors brought their whole families with them. Tataré's son Diogo, who was attending school in Cacoal, visited on school vacations; other kids skipped out on classes altogether. Unoccupied pits doubled as makeshift swimming pools. Diogo and his friends would happily kick off their flip-flops and dive in, climbing out to play in the mud piles. Sometimes they sprayed each other with the high-pressure hoses, soaking their clothes. Once Diogo found a diamond in the mud; another time he spied a cook bathing and surreptitiously watched her.

Hoping to keep the mine as orderly as possible, Pio banned prostitution, firearms, drugs, and hard liquor, and three dozen warriors policed the mine. "Warrior," of course, had never been a discrete profession; traditionally it was the obligation of any able-bodied man. As in the old days, though, they painted their bodies with jaguar spots—and prospectors were terrified of them. Many barely spoke Portuguese. They tended to hail from the east, where contact had come later, and the "white man's law" remained a distant concept. Despite Pio's status as "general chief," he still lacked any power to tell them what to do. They saw the world more like Pio's father had—as a world in which there were few friends beyond their borders, and only a man's conscience could determine what was right. Some carried pistols or hunting shotguns. Others had spent their whole lives wielding a bow, still made their own arrows, and shot with startling accuracy. Their ranks also included teenagers, who made up for their inexperience with a gameness for action and were, for this reason, just as terrifying.

*   *   *

There are different versions of how the gossip may have spread. Local Funai agents were among the first outsiders to learn of the prospect on the Stream of the Blackflies. One heard Ubiratan, the car salesman, saying, "Let's spread the word! That way it'll blow up and no one will ever be able to shut it down." The agent tried to dissuade him: "What you should do is keep very quiet with the Indians there, and once you're rich and the Indians have also done well, you get out. And you don't even say you were there." Ubiratan apparently didn't heed this advice, instead trumpeting the find to anyone who'd listen.

Washington Cordeiro, a mining technician who knew Luca, would tell a different story. In nearby Juína, a business called the Bolsa de Diamantes, or Diamond Exchange, had been founded in the 1980s. The region sat atop a cluster of kimberlites, most yielding the dark little stones known as bort, which are useful in drill bits and circuit board heat sinks but not as gems. Diamonds aren't like gold, which is infinitely fungible, a chemical element that can be melted down and cast into any number of shapes, the value deriving entirely from its purity and weight. Even when carbon atoms are arranged in the "diamond cubic" lattice, the structure repeats in seemingly random ways, creating a variety of shapes, so that no two diamonds are exactly alike.

Instead a diamond's price is determined by the four C's: carats, clarity, color, and cut. The first is a straightforward measure of weight, with a carat equal to two hundred milligrams. But because larger stones are exponentially rarer, a ten-carat stone is typically worth far more than ten times as much as a one-carat stone. "Clarity" is perhaps the most important factor, and the most subjective, rising in inverse proportion to the number of so-called flaws, such as "feather inclusions" (small internal cracks) or "pinpoint inclusions" (tiny spots caused by the presence of smaller crystals within the stone). A very dense profusion of flaws, however, can actually increase a diamond's value by effectively turning it black.

More commonly, a diamond's color derives from the presence of other elements within the crystal. Blue diamonds, for example, are tinted by traces of boron, a rarity that makes them even more coveted. Yellow diamonds, stained by nitrogen, are physically the hardest, making them ideal for industrial purposes, but they are also the most common, making them the least valuable as gems. In Brazil, they are sometimes known as *diamante xixi*, or "piss diamonds," though sharper marketing minds also came up with the terms "champagne diamonds," or for stones with a browner hue, "cognac diamonds."

"Cut" refers to the precision and artistry with which a rough stone has been chiseled and polished into a gem (nowadays, mostly in dank warehouses in Surat, India, though this work was historically done by Jewish families in Antwerp, Amsterdam, and London). First a cutter will draw up a kind of blueprint dividing the original amorphous shape into a round brilliant, a radiant, a pear. The next step is "bruting," cleaving the stone in separate pieces, typically with the aid of another diamond. Then each piece is sliced into angular facets—in the case of the round brilliant, thirty-three on the crown, twenty-five in the underlying "pavilion." Half a stone's weight might be sacrificed for the sake of reflective brightness, "fire" (the scattering of light into the colors of the rainbow), and "scintillation" (sparkle). While this C isn't exactly applicable to raw product, a stone's original shape will heavily influence its final size. If the rough stone is a so-called flat triangle, it will yield a gem that is only a small fraction of the starting weight.

Most of a diamond's price, then, is entirely subjective—the quintessence of modern capitalism, in which monetary value is divorced from effort or actual usefulness. De Beers, the international diamond cartel, has always been as much a marketing operation as a mining company. Starting in the 1930s, it hired New York admen to promote the idea that, as the slogan went, "A Diamond Is Forever," and a diamond engagement ring is the truest expression of love. Such was the campaign's success, the idea came to seem ancient, traditional, in consumers' minds.

Storytelling is essential to the creation of a diamond's value; the $350 million Hope Diamond, for instance, comes with a rich history dating back to seventeenth-century India. This became even clearer with the advent of synthetic diamonds, formed through industrial processes that mimic what happens down in the earth's mantle. Lacking even trace amounts of foreign elements such as nitrogen, they are actually purer than any natural diamond; otherwise they are indistinguishable. Yet they command a lower price, because they also lack the mystique of a crystal forged by God's own hand over billions of years.

Diamonds have always been thought of as scarce, but even this is something of a fiction. When new mines emerged in Siberia in the 1950s, De Beers invited the Soviets to join its cartel so as not to flood the market—and whenever supply exceeded demand, De Beers itself often purchased the excess. Meanwhile, to keep secondhand diamonds from weighing on prices, jewelers buy them back from consumers at a steep markdown, discouraging resales.

Black-market stones, such as those from Cinta Larga country, sell at a discount to make up for the costs of dodging the authorities. Smugglers capture much of the value by spiriting the product abroad; a sixty-five-year-old Israeli-Belgian was caught trying to leave Brazil with condoms full of cotton-wrapped diamonds inside her vagina and rectum. Then there are the middlemen who transform the contraband into a legal commodity. One method is to use an officially licensed mine to produce fraudulent documentation for an ill-gotten stone. In Brazil in the 2000s, this was so easy to do that so-called blood diamonds, produced in African conflict zones, were actually smuggled *in* before being smuggled out again, to reappear in a European jewelry store with papers declaring them conflict-free.

The Cinta Larga could be forgiven for failing to grasp, at least at first, how diamonds were priced. In time, though, many chiefs would learn to value them by eye—and Pio would be left to wonder how their lives might be different, given the chance to apply their wit to more constructive ends.

At the Stream of the Blackflies, even lifelong prospectors had trouble valuing their product, and would greedily seize upon bluish-violet stones that turned out to be amethyst. In the Juína region, the diamonds were of such low quality that they typically sold in bulk, say $40 for a lot of a hundred carats—compared to perhaps $10,000 for a single, high-quality, one-carat gem. Still, some buyers at the Bolsa de Diamantes knew how to recognize a jewel. According to Washington Cordeiro, when Luca and Lobão decided to raise cash, it was to these buyers that they turned. While most of their stones were small and yellowish—piss diamonds—more than a few were large and clear. The Juína men could see they were among the best that could be found in Brazil, on a par with the best in the world.

Some of these men ran operations of their own, complete with jigs, which were pricier than sluice boxes but far more precise in sorting diamonds. Luca and Lobão tried to keep their source secret, but in Cordeiro's version, one of the buyers took them for a night on the town, got them drunk, got them laid. Before they knew it, they'd agreed to take a scout from Juína to the Stream of the Blackflies so he could report back.

The scout was stunned by what he saw. He called his boss and said, "Stop everything you have running out there. Bring everything over here."

CHAPTER 19

THE RUSH

Maria Beleza, the renowned beauty, wanted nothing to do with the mine. She was living in Riozinho, where her children attended school, and she'd found a joy in motherhood that almost made up for her regret that she never got an education herself. One of her sons had applied to be a police officer; she had high hopes for him. "Anyone who has a child," she would explain, "has a dream."

Maria also lamented that she never found the true love said to exist in white society (at least in telenovelas), though she mostly tolerated her husband, João Pacaa Nova. Still employed by Funai, he felt it was too risky to get involved in the mine himself—but thought it was an error for the family to stay out entirely. Money was tight. Sometimes they didn't have enough to buy groceries; their children's clothes were ragged. Also, one of their sons was deaf and needed special care. Maria and her husband argued bitterly over it, until one day Oita showed up with some food and a gift of $50 to soften them up. Her sons were on school vacation, and Oita, as their uncle, wanted to hire them as inspectors at the Stream of the Blackflies. He already had two of his own sons working for him there.

True to form, Oita was one of the first to go around the Pamaré

Association with his own, independent deal at the mine. This time, though, he wasn't alone. Once the gossip was out, prospectors flocked to Josias's hotel by the Cacoal bus station, the Jardim das Oliveiras (Olive Tree Garden), and accosted any Indian they could find. Seeing an opportunity to make some money, many Cinta Larga, in turn, came looking for prospectors. One fortune-seeker, known as Bola (Ball) because of his roly-poly build, was working as a mechanic in Juína when he heard about the mine from prospectors buying diesel generators. Turning up at the hotel, he met a Cinta Larga who asked for just $1,000 up front—an unbelievably good deal, given the quality of the diamonds.

"Pio didn't authorize any of it," Claudiney Souza, Pamaré's white administrator, would recall. "But there was nothing he could do to stop them. It was almost a coup d'état." Not that Pio was ever a head of state to begin with, as he still lacked any means (beyond the force of his own charisma) to enforce the rules. The warriors, for their part, tended to feel that any Cinta Larga man should enjoy an equal right to bring in outsiders.

Some Cinta Larga actually performed manual labor themselves down in the pit. Tataré's son Diogo was only thirteen when one of his brothers asked him to take over the *maraca* while he went to take a shit; he handled the job well, so he was allowed to continue, and he used his earnings to buy a personal computer. Tataré didn't want his teenage daughter, Bete, staying the night there, but she visited just the same. So many diamonds were turning up that her uncle gave her and her friends a cup full of stones he deemed too small to bother selling. Buyers now visited the mine directly; the girls received around $1,000 each from the sale.

Never mind that everyone else was doing it—Maria wasn't won over by Oita's offerings. She'd never been the type to blindly accept a man's will. "I don't want my children handling heavy machines," she insisted. "They're studying." Her children, though, felt old enough to make their own decisions. Four of her sons decided to try their luck at the mine. "I don't even like men, but God gave me all these male children," Maria would complain—except that one of her daughters also went to work as a cook.

Pio did what he could to maintain a semblance of control. If he couldn't stop people from freelancing, he would at least demand a concession: 5 percent of any sale must go to the Pamaré Association for wider distribution. Prospectors continued to approach Pio at his office in Riozinho, but since it was too late to keep things small, he didn't turn them away. Instead he partnered them up with Cinta Larga of his choosing, who would keep another 15 percent for themselves while Pamaré received the "toll." (Thirty percent of the revenues typically went to the five-person team at each pit, while the remaining 50 percent went to the owner of the machines, who paid for fuel, food, and repairs.)

Pio was quick to grasp the concept of supply and demand. Initially he set the toll at a mere $750 per pair of machines. In October 2000, he doubled it; then in December, he doubled it again. Interest didn't flag in the slightest. Pio was amazed to see how fast the gossip traveled, even in those days before most Brazilians had internet access. On one level, it was exciting: a glimmer of future wealth. On another, of course, it was terrifying—that seemingly bottomless hunger. In any case, Pio saw little option but to manage the chaos, directing as much of the money as possible to his own people.

It was thanks to Pio that Maria finally got a prospector, too. Her children, after all, were already working there. Once Pio arranged the partnership, though, she had to fend for herself—and as Maria would acknowledge, "I had no notion of money back then." Her associates took advantage of this. Police later seized the records of a diamond buyer who listed Maria Beleza among his sellers. According to one entry, she sold him 136 carats for a mere $750, even though, according to the next entry, someone else sold him a similar quantity for $15,000. Without knowing the quality of the stones, it's hard to say if she got ripped off. In other cases, there was little question. At the mine once, she showed Pio two tubes full of diamonds and asked him to help her buy a car. "Sure," he said. "When you're in town, find me and we'll buy it together." But the prospectors diverted her, to stiff her without interference. More than once, when prospectors found a good stone, they simply disappeared.

Once word got out that the Indians were flush, it was open season for white opportunists. One Cinta Larga reportedly traded ninety diamonds for a Toyota Hilux even though they were worth enough to buy ten. Despite his reputation as a killer of white men, João Bravo became a favorite target. Once, he was said to have handed over $120,000 for a plot of land worth $30,000. On another occasion, a buyer offered him $400,000 for a lot of diamonds but João, thinking he was playing hardball but not so good with large numbers, insisted on a price that was half that amount. As in Pio's early hardwood deals, white middlemen quickly figured out that the physical volume of cash often made more of an impression than its numerical value, and would hand over fat stacks of low-denomination bills.

There was more cash going around than any Cinta Larga had ever seen or even thought possible. At one point Maria's son Haroldo received an astonishing $200,000 from the sale of a single large stone. He gave her $50,000, and she bought her own modest house in Riozinho. For all the money she lost to deception, people would remember Maria as a rich woman at the time. She took to wearing a large, heavy watch of the sort that was fashionable in the early 2000s. A driver for the Indigenous health service once asked her for the time. She looked at her watch for a while, trying to decipher the meaning in the position of the hands, before finally telling him, "Buy your own watch!"

*   *   *

Other women got in on the action, too, with mixed results. Often they had husbands from other Indigenous groups, who lacked the same automatic access to the mine. Oita's sister Alzira was married to a Suruí; she teamed up with a prospector named Camargo. One day Camargo found a large green diamond; Alzira's cut of the sale was $15,000, and she gave $1,000 to each of her sons for helping out. Because she didn't have her own bank account, she asked her husband to deposit the rest. She'd hoped to buy a refrigerator, but in her words, he "devoured it all." Then he left her. "Prospecting is no good," she concluded.

Tataré's wife, Peneta, initially went to work as a cook at her nephew's pit. In the two months she was there, her nephew made more than $35,000 but paid her only $300. Much like Maria, she admitted to having "no understanding of percentages"—until her marriage fell apart, and she met a white prospector named Celino, who set her up with her own pair of machines. Some whispered that Celino was only with Peneta to gain access to the mine, but they would remain together for sixteen years.

For a young woman like Bete, Peneta's daughter, who grew up watching Brazilian TV—which was never wildly progressive but did show women becoming ever more independent, whether in telenovelas or on the news—this chain of events may not have seemed so remarkable. For her mother, born into a world where women were treated like possessions, it was a revolution.

Maria Beleza eventually left her husband, too—and for the first time in her life, she tasted a kind of freedom. She even gained some of the authority she'd always associated with her grandmother, whom she remembered as a female *zapiway*. Others might say this figure never existed, but in the new world, it was possible. At meetings with government officials, Maria was asked to speak for Cinta Larga women—no small thing in a society where women had always kept quiet in village discussions. Though she was given the bureaucratic title "women's representative," she came to think of herself as a kind of "chief," too.

To be sure, the vast majority of Cinta Larga women stayed with their spouses. But they became increasingly discontented, complaining that they were being "traded" for white women. Visits to prostitutes were nothing new, but now the debauchery reached a grandiose scale. João Bravo's sons set the tone. One of them, Marcelinho, used to take his prospectors to a brothel where they'd boast about money and mining and women over blaring country music, wrists heavy with thick gold bracelets, necks laden with thick gold crosses on thick gold chains, eyes glassy from a combination of whiskey, Red Bull, and cocaine. In a country where the monthly minimum wage was $75, Marcelinho could spend $2,500 in a single night. He wanted to be, as he later put it, *o patrão*—"the boss." He wore a T-shirt that read 100% PARTY PEOPLE; on the front was a cartoon of a generic Indian wielding a bow and arrow. His benders would go for two or three days straight, until he had a heart attack and swore off partying forever.

Far exceeding the time of hardwood, these men bought four-wheel-drive Toyota Land Cruisers and Hiluxes and Ford F-150s. People heard Panderê say his dream was to own a different vehicle for each day of the week; he fulfilled it. Panderê, of course, was one of the young men whom Pio had sent to school, so this was a second disappointment. Pio also saw the other young man, Rondonzinho, learning what he called "the white man's guile." Pio's own sons would eventually start prospecting, dashing his hopes they'd get the education he never had.

Pio didn't object to the luxuries per se. After all, he still wanted many of the same things. Albeit more quietly, he, too, bought cars and properties, one in Riozinho and another in a well-to-do neighborhood in Cacoal. His lament was that these men thought only of themselves. They came to be known as *caciques*, the Portuguese word for "chiefs," but they never followed the old way of the *zapiway*, caring for their people in general. Instead they hired bodyguards (some of whom were off-duty cops) and asked them to pick up prostitutes.

"Lots of whores got rich from that mine," one observer would recall. Another of João Bravo's sons, Raimundinho, would admit he used to "close down the brothel." Like Old Luca in his heyday, he'd arrive with his entourage and hand over a large sum—perhaps $25,000—and all the other men would have to leave so that his crew could have the brothel to themselves. The amounts were all the more shocking given how decrepit these places looked. One favorite, Noturnos—literally Nocturnals, though it was open all day—was a one-story wooden building with peeling white paint a few blocks from Highway 364. The men would park their car in a dirt lot and enter a dim, low-ceilinged bar with a slot machine and a pool table. Young women waited in short shorts and tube tops, ready to usher them into one of the private rooms accessible from a long porch, like at an American motel. Sometimes the chiefs tried to outdo one another; Raimundinho would remember a night when Oita and Panderê insisted, "This one's on us." It was a strange evolution of the old Cinta Larga feasts, now reserved for a select few—more like the displays of Rio de Janeiro drug lords or Wall Street traders. "A money fever," Pio called it.

Sometimes the revelry came back to the village, and people heard pounding techno music issuing from Panderê's house. Worse was when the men brought sexually transmitted diseases, or came home drunk and beat their wives. João Bravo apparently indulged in white women, too, despite having six Cinta Larga wives. One was Maria Beleza's daughter Neide, who said she felt "abandoned" and "thrown away." Another woman, Lúcia, was married to the chief of Roosevelt Village. He tried to bring a white woman into their house, and as Lúcia succinctly put it, "She was a prostitute. I grabbed her and gave her a beating. He got upset and left me."

Fed up, women from Roosevelt Village staged an act of resistance. For two days they blocked the road to the mine, seizing their husbands' vehicles—another unthinkable event. Not that it brought the change they hoped for. Bola, the mechanic turned prospector, once accompanied his Cinta Larga business partner to a brothel. When the Cinta Larga's usual woman approached, he told her he couldn't be with her anymore, out of respect for his wife. She beseeched him to change his mind before finally saying, "I'm in love with you. If you want me to fall out of love, you'll have to pay me." She set a price of $2,500, and he met it. But it was only a matter of time before he went back. Some men, faced with complaints from their wives, simply bought them off, handing them $10,000 in cash and saying, "Be quiet." As Pio put it, "People thought the money would never end."

This time around, Pio didn't engage in the same displays (at least not on that scale). He'd long been separated from the white woman known as Tamalíap and also his Cinta Larga wife. At the Funai base in Riozinho back in the 1980s, he'd noticed a girl named Rute, whose mother was from the Apuriná people. Her stepfather worked for Funai, and while she was only fourteen at the time, and very skinny, she helped out cleaning. Pio admired her work ethic. He started wooing her in the traditional way, bringing her parents little gifts and giving them money to spend at the market. Soon he was using his hardwood earnings to support much of their extended family. Rute had no interest in Pio at first, but when she was around eighteen, she agreed to a date. Six months later they got married at the local notary. Pio, wearing a suit and tie, held a reception in town. In his words, he was the first Cinta Larga ever to be married "on paper, just like a white person."

* * *

As a white woman herself, Oita's wife, Alba, couldn't expect much solidarity. Like other wives, though, she joined her husband at the mine to help out as a cook even while watching after their kids. In her recollection, even though they had five pairs of machines running, Oita's prospectors failed to produce any diamonds in those early weeks. Eventually they ran out of diesel, so Oita went to town to scare up some more. While he was away, an experienced prospector from a nearby pit offered to lend Alba a hand. Later in life, she would conclude that he was the only person who ever helped her out of pure generosity of spirit, without an ulterior motive. Rather than leave the five pairs of machines sitting idle, he suggested she negotiate supplies from other teams on credit, and even offered to oversee the machines at night. When at last they began to turn up diamonds, he also taught her how to select the best ones, what qualities to look for, what price to ask.

When Oita returned a few weeks later, he was surprised to see the machines running. But he could hardly argue with the results: four hundred carats and counting. With the help of Alba's new friend, they contacted a buyer in Cacoal who paid $500,000 for the lot. And as Alba would remember it, "Oita went crazy"—making the other chiefs look almost frugal. Whenever he got bored with one car, he'd buy another, continuously adding to his fleet. He made sure the windows were tinted, and wore dark sunglasses to match. He also took to wearing a gold chain around his neck, tight enough that he could undo the top button of his shirt to display it. Unlike Pio and Roberto Carlos, he remained trim, cutting an elegant figure.

When it came to Oita's extramarital activities, Alba looked the other way. But her prospector friend warned her not to let all that money go to waste. It's hard to say why Oita let her invest—whether because the suggestion came from the kind of clever white outlaw he'd always idolized, or because there was so much money coming in that he simply didn't care. In any case, with her friend's guidance, Alba spent $175,000 for a three-hundred-acre ranch and put 224 head of cattle on it. She also purchased a sprawling home in the center of Cacoal for $125,000. Though the price was modest by US standards, it was a veritable mansion, with six bedrooms, three living rooms, three *quartos de empregada* ("maid's rooms"), a pool, a hot tub, a sauna, and a barbecue area, all surrounded by the sort of high wall that was standard for affluent Brazilians. It was by far the most luxurious piece of real estate purchased by a Cinta Larga in those years. Maria Beleza's house was a glorified shack with unfinished cement floors, and neither of Pio's was especially lavish; apart from its high walls, his Cacoal home could have been a lower-middle-class dwelling in any small US town, except its yard was dirt rather than grass.

The other difference was that, while other chiefs hired some staff, Oita and Alba amassed an army of maids, chauffeurs, and private security. Even white people started calling Oita by the honorific *doutor*, which literally refers to a doctor but is also a term of respect for judges, lawyers, rich people. At long last, he achieved the recognition he was searching for, having never received it from his own people. And it went to his head. Tataré complained that—despite all they'd been through together in the contact era, despite having been the first to welcome Oita after his betrayals in Zoró country, despite having helped him through his tough times in the 1990s—when he asked to borrow a piddling $1,000, Oita gave him the runaround. Tataré had to make an appointment just to speak with him. One day Tataré's son and son-in-law dropped by Oita's house in Cacoal. They were met by two guards, who said only one could enter. On another occasion, Tataré's then-wife, Peneta—who'd helped take care of Oita's son Ezequiel when he was a baby—visited with a friend. They were made to wait for Oita in the kitchen. An hour later, he still hadn't shown up, so they gave up and left.

Oita's status extended to his children. Since the school at Roosevelt Village was so inadequate, he and Alba enrolled their kids at a private school in Cacoal, run by the Assemblies of God. Ezequiel was driven to school by a white chauffeur in what seemed to be a different car every day. At one point, according to one of his friends, Ezequiel stumbled upon a bag full of cash in a closet, and started pilfering fifty-*real* notes (worth roughly $25) to buy snacks for all the white kids.

Oita and Alba also agreed to set aside the 10 percent tithe that was the obligation of any Evangelical. Their business might be illegal according to the laws of man, but it allowed them to build a church at Roosevelt Village. This time Oita made the impression he'd hoped for when he tried to convert his people in the 1980s. Built with poured concrete and painted a pleasant cream color, the building was among the largest in the village, and the only one with glass windows. For its inauguration, Oita and Alba invited the mostly white congregation of their Assemblies of God church in town, and a band played trumpets, saxophones, and rock-and-roll drums. Oita took to preaching there along with visiting white pastors, while Alba led Bible classes for kids. Despite Oita's poor standing among his own people, gradually the pews filled with Cinta Larga captivated by the inflamed Pentecostal style. More than a few felt the Holy Spirit enter them, and spoke in tongues that were neither Portuguese nor Tupi-Mondé.

Outsiders would sometimes wonder why the Cinta Larga were so quick to accept the white man's religion—a question rarely asked of the rest of the world's two billion Christians. In some ways, it wasn't much of a leap. The Cinta Larga already believed in a single Creator, Ngurá; now they called him Deus. They used to say they'd killed the Bible's Adam, but that was different from believing he hadn't existed. Many converts never actually abandoned their former world of myth; they just made room for new myths. Absent the longhouse where everyone used to live together, sleeping in crisscrossing hammocks, the church became the space for collective experiences, for the energy of the old feasts. They'd always sung songs; now, while they could never quite master the melodies, they translated Evangelical songs into Tupi-Mondé.

Some whites credited the church for finishing the job that Funai had started, "taming" the Cinta Larga. This time around, when pastors said they couldn't dance, couldn't drink *i*—that these were sins— many listened.

At least in those days, though, there were plenty who remained, as the Cinta Larga themselves put it, "wild."

CHAPTER 20

LOSING CONTROL

In November 2000, a bush plane carrying Funai and Federal Police personnel took off to investigate the gossip. Compared to gold mining, in which mercury is used to separate the metal from the surrounding ore, diamond prospecting is relatively clean, requiring only water. Still, the agents could see that the mouth of the Stream of the Blackflies, once clear, had turned brown. For five miles of the stream's meandering course, a half-mile margin of trees had been cut down, and the water had been diverted into a honeycomb of muddy, stagnant pits. There were at least 180 machines in operation, with nearly five hundred prospectors working them, their blue tarpaulin shelters half-hidden in the surrounding trees. The ridges between pits doubled as makeshift roads where motorcycles wove between diesel-powered pumps and hulking jigs, under and around the thousands of feet of plastic tubing that crisscrossed it all. On the edges, fresh pits were being excavated, new machines being hauled in.

For the authorities, the situation at the mine itself was only part of the problem. Exceeding even the early days of Highway 364, prospectors arrived in Cacoal and Espigão almost daily, some traveling for days on long-distance buses or in the flatbed of trucks, dreaming of striking it rich—or at least putting some food on the table. For every adventurer like Old Luca, there was also a prospector like Antonio Marcos de Almeida, who came because he was unemployed, with a pregnant wife and a two-year-old daughter. One successful prospector was said to have fixed diamonds to his front teeth; plenty of other prospectors had no front teeth. Many were functionally illiterate, some to the point that they misspelled their own names, or signed documents with a thumbprint, like Maria Beleza. These people couldn't afford their own machines, much less pay the hefty toll for entry into the Stream of the Blackflies. Some were lucky enough to find work on a team authorized by the Pamaré Association. The rest had little choice but to wait, filling the region's hotels until whatever meager savings they had ran dry. Then they camped out wherever they could. By the end of the year, five hundred people were sleeping next to the main road into Cinta Larga country. Another thousand, possibly more, were staying in the fields near the Vila Bradesco outpost, just south of Marafon's ranch.

Even Pio could see that most prospectors were desperate folk who came to the mine "out of necessity." He needed to think of his own people first, though. At Roosevelt Village, a few warriors guarded the bridge that led over the river, wearing blue T-shirts that read PAMARÉ ASSOCIATION INSPECTOR. They tried to make sure no one entered without a Cinta Larga overseer or written authorization on Pamaré letterhead. They also carried a Globalstar satellite phone to confer with Pio. But he wasn't always available, and it was hard to check every prospector's claims. One brandished a grocery receipt showing a Pamaré Association purchase of a kilo of sausage—code, supposedly, for authorization to enter the mine, though that may have been a ruse.

The Brazilian expression *pau rodado* refers to a stick carried along by a river current, always moving, going with the flow. At the Stream of the Blackflies, *rodados* were those who sneaked in without permission—wildcats. Marafon saw them arriving on foot to his fields, which came right to the western bank of the Roosevelt. He would watch as they stripped off their clothes, stuffed their belongings into plastic bags, and swam across. From there it was a whole day's walk through the forest to reach the Stream of the Blackflies, a path that became known as the *varação*, or "back door." Despite his friendship with the Cinta Larga, Marafon couldn't resist helping these sorry strivers. He ferried them across in a raft, and they became his friends, too. They called him Velho Canoeiro, the Old Canoe-man.

At the mine, Maria Beleza's tent sat next to Oita's sister Alzira's. They were hanging out chatting as usual when one of the chiefs asked for help clearing out *rodados* before the warriors, those unpredictable men from the east, got to them. Already becoming a kind of chief herself, Maria now became a kind of warrior, too, though her goal was to *prevent* violence. She led a whole group of women, along with a couple of men, in sweeping the forest—no easy task. On their first expedition, they embarked shortly after daybreak with only a thermos of sugary coffee to fuel them. The forest was vast, and Maria had lost the habit of traipsing around barefoot. Her flip-flops got stuck in the mud. All the women wore the usual flowery dresses, which caught on branches and spines. Night was falling by the time they encountered a camp where twenty wildcats were resting, having finished work for the day. Lacking machines, the men used nothing but shovels and pickaxes. At first they fled into the trees, leaving their tools on the ground. They returned once they realized the group was mostly women.

"Do you have children?" Maria asked. "I can see the hole you've dug here, but you don't need to return the diamonds. Just leave."

"For the love of God," Alzira chimed in. "If you want to live, leave this place. The warriors have no respect for life."

In later years, Maria would speak with pride of her days as peacemaker. This role had little precedent in Cinta Larga history, much less for a woman, though Maria would always take inspiration from her grandmother—the one who, with her ability to hunt and fish and fire an arrow, "was like a man," in Maria's words. Even after the massacre that left her grandmother dead, Maria had little appetite for revenge. She would actually come to resent the warriors who were so quick to spill blood, to leave other children orphaned like she'd been—like they'd all been.

The warriors, though, couldn't escape the logic of *wepíka*. Whether or not the prospectors knew it, they fit into an accounting of deaths that went back to the darkest days of contact—and by sneaking in, they were effectively invading, threatening the integrity of the Cinta Larga's ancestral lands. A prospector named Giudo would later describe going in through the "back door," leaving as soon as he realized he could be killed for this. Rumors began to circulate about prospectors stumbling upon human bones and hair in the forest. There were even stories about warriors tearing men's stomachs open to see if they'd swallowed diamonds. As always in the prospecting world, it was hard to separate rumor from fact. No doubt prospectors went missing, but this was all too common in their line of work. Today there's a Facebook group called O Garimpeiro sem Limites de Fronteiras (Prospectors Without Borders), where people post endless photos of fathers, brothers, and sons last seen at some Amazonian dig before disappearing.

Some felt the risk was worth it—if they found a big stone, they could keep all the money for themselves rather than receive the usual 6 percent share for a pit worker. Most, however, were like Giudo. When Maria led her group back the following day, all the wildcats were gone.

* * *

To Pio, it seemed as though he'd barely gotten started, was barely tasting prosperity, when the thing he'd always feared most—invasion—threatened to derail his plans. Every time he visited the mine, it looked more like a boomtown inside Cinta Larga country. Improvised as they were, some shacks became downright homey, with diesel generators powering fridges and satellite TVs. There was even a little wooden church for born-again workers. At night Pio looked out and saw a dark landscape dotted by hundreds of lights; now and then shots rang out. Though white men weren't allowed guns, the Cinta Larga were, and as one prospector remembered it, they "spent a lot of bullets." Partying, some would fire into the air just for fun. Even other Cinta Larga didn't feel safe there. "At the mine," one would recall, "you had to be *velhaco*"—wily. There was a Bolivian named Sidnei, known as "the fake Indian," who joined the warriors on patrol and was said to relish violence. Pio's brother-in-law Paulo once saw him viciously beating someone, and told him to stop. "I better not find you alone here," Sidnei responded.

Prospectors brought guns in, too, despite the prohibition. It was easy enough to hide a .38 revolver among their equipment, and many preferred the risk of being caught *with* one to being caught without. The only exception to the no-liquor rule was special occasions like Christmas and New Year's Eve; the rest of the year, a little bar was allowed to function as long as it sold nothing stronger than beer. But the bar offered *cachaça* when the warriors weren't around. It wasn't only white men who broke the rules; one young Cinta Larga purchased a case of *cachaça* for $5 a bottle, selling at $25 until the warriors made him stop. Drugs were even easier to smuggle in, and Bolivia, a major coca producer, was a day's drive away. Tataré's son Diogo saw prospectors teaching Cinta Larga to smoke crack, which, he would recall, "stank like burnt gasoline." As for Pio's ban on prostitution, sex workers came disguised as cooks; their clientele included whites and Cinta Larga alike.

For a while the chaos seemed worth it. As he had with his hardwood earnings, Pio sent truckloads of rice, beans, pasta, coffee, and sugar, as well as large quantities of soda and packaged sweets, to Roosevelt Village. Another chief even started a canteen to provide free breakfast, lunch, and dinner. They also rebuilt their cattle herd, hiring white workers to plant fresh grass for grazing; each week a cow was butchered for the meat, but the herd continued to grow. To make up for the Roosevelt's depleted fish stocks, Pio had a fish pond put in, too.

Whenever Pio came to the village, he asked what people wanted. Television? Satellite dishes were installed, TV sets distributed, diesel purchased for generators. A soccer field? Workers leveled the earth and erected goalposts. The women wanted a vehicle to travel to the fields where they harvested manioc, and to Espigão for shopping trips, so Pio bought them a flatbed Toyota Land Cruiser and hired a driver. On visits to Riozinho, anyone was welcome to stay at Pamaré's headquarters, and the association would cover the cost of their meals. Sometimes people simply asked for cash; Pio's old friend Barroca would remember receiving $750, just like that. Barroca also wanted his daughters to attend school in town, so Pio had a prospector buy a two-bedroom house for them, and soon young Iara and Patrícia were speaking fluent Portuguese like their father never could.

Of course, people couldn't help but notice that Pio bought things for himself, too. His two new houses in town, though modest by American standards, were palatial compared to the wooden shacks at Roosevelt Village. "The chiefs said not to worry, they would take care of us," one resident muttered. "But I can't even afford to put in a floor." Another complained, "Pio, Panderê, Oita…They're all buying cars and we're still on foot!" Little wonder that you often saw four people packed onto a single motorcycle, a baby in its father's lap peering curiously over the handlebars. It was inequality unlike any they'd known before, as a traditional *zapiway* might have multiple wives but never possessed material wealth of his own. Meanwhile, as people took to watching the nightly news on TV, they picked up on Western notions of democracy, as well as the concept of corruption, that perennial Brazilian problem. They even adopted the Portuguese word *comunidade*—community—to describe the idea of a public to whom their leaders should be accountable.

Elders, too, were upset about the changes. One respected former *zapiway* complained about the trucks rolling through at all hours, interrupting his sleep. Old women complained about the dust that was kicked up, dirtying clothes hung to dry. They also feared new outbreaks of disease, as malaria, once all but defeated in Cinta Larga country, started to return to the Stream of the Blackflies. Worst of all, their own village, that refuge from the dangers of the outside world, now felt unsafe. Sometimes prospectors would stay the night, drink with Cinta Larga men, and leer at young girls. There were whispers about rapes, though victims were too ashamed to report them to the police.

In December, Pio decided to shut the mine down. His plan was to empty it out and raise the toll high enough that only the biggest players could go back in. Thus revenues would remain high, but with far fewer white men to make trouble. At first it seemed to work. Just before Christmas, the warriors swept through pit by pit. No one dared defy their order to depart, though many left their equipment behind, believing they could come back for it later. Bola, the rotund prospector from Juína, always got along with the warriors—"except when they came to remove people. Then there was no such thing as friendship!"

* * *

The problem, now, wasn't the prospectors themselves. As always, Pio could lead only by consensus, holding long village meetings at which everyone could say their piece. But João Bravo—who'd once battled white men alongside Pio's father, and whom Pio had helped to "tame"—considered himself separate from Roosevelt Village. He'd built a new village just east of the river, and considered a large expanse of the surrounding territory to be his domain. At first he'd actually forbidden Old Luca from searching for diamonds at the Stream of the Blackflies, telling Pio, "You can authorize whatever you want, but if he comes over to my side, I'm going to tie him up."

João's claim to leadership was far more traditional than Pio's, which was based on majority vote. Whereas Roosevelt Village was formed by refugees from across their territory, João's was almost entirely related to him by blood or marriage. With his six wives, forty-nine children, and countless grandchildren, not only did he enjoy the loyalty of many sons and grandsons; he also had many male in-laws in his debt for "giving" them his daughters and granddaughters. He was a true *zapiway*, that old "owner of the house." Other men admitted they envied him, wishing that they, too, could have so many wives.

Even outsiders came away impressed. Though João was relatively short, like most Cinta Larga, he appeared much larger, with an impressive belly he almost never covered with a shirt. ("I don't like wearing clothes," he explained.) Famed as a killer of white men, he also had an irrepressible sense of humor. His face could go from deadly serious to hysterical with laughter in an instant. ("Why didn't you bring me any money?" he demanded of a visiting journalist, before letting on that it was a joke.) It was hard not to laugh along with him, whether or not you understood what he was saying. Even younger Cinta Larga could fail to grasp his meaning. João never fully learned Portuguese, instead speaking his own improvised hodgepodge with an outmoded strain of Tupi-Mondé.

João scoffed at the new generation of chiefs, who never learned to dodge arrows, never trained their stamina by treading whitewater for an entire day, and never took these skills to battle. As João later explained it to the anthropologist Nadja Marin, "I didn't become chief by selling things....There are chiefs but they are worth nothing." There's a Brazilian expression, *muito cacique para pouco índio*—"too many chiefs for too few Indians" (akin to the English one about too many cooks in the kitchen). The way João saw Roosevelt Village, this was literally true. In his own village, he bragged, "I am the only one who is chief."

In his conversation with Marin, João didn't mention Pio by name, but criticized anyone who would claim to lead their nation as a whole: "Another man says, 'I am the general chief' just because he lives among white people. He could just say he's a representative of the community....He says he's a general chief but he doesn't take care of his community."

None of this was to say that João abstained from selling natural resources himself. During the hardwood boom, he'd started his own association to oversee the trade in his area—and after he saw what Old Luca's diamonds were worth, he struck his own deals with prospectors. Far from going against his old-school bona fides, he seemed to feel this was his duty as *zapiway*, just as it had been to acquire metal tools in the time of contact, or to gather the best straw for a longhouse roof in the old days. He was proud of how he provided for his village. Not only did he buy the usual food and cattle; he arranged to build a miniature hydroelectric dam so as not to depend on diesel generators. Sadly, the dam proved to be a boondoggle, the contractor just another grifter. In reality, his village wasn't so different from Roosevelt Village, except that only his bloodline could prosper. Pio, for his part, didn't see why he couldn't take the best of both worlds, white *and* Indian. If the result was more democratic, so what if he was breaking with tradition?

Back in the days of contact, João had built an imitation airstrip to lure planes with Western goods. Now he was building a real airstrip so that diamond buyers could fly straight to his village. He didn't want the flow of money to stop. To get around Pio's shutdown, he built a second road to the Stream of the Blackflies that passed through *his* area, and started collecting the toll that previously accrued to the Pamaré Association. In the space of a single week in January, a hundred prospectors entered the mine this way. Given an average of five workers in a team and a fee of $3,000, this meant João had likely received around $60,000 even before his cut of the sales.

Pio remained reluctant to reopen the original road. But with João's access unimpeded, Roosevelt Village had little incentive to keep its own side closed. Even those without prospectors of their own seemed to think it was better to receive an unequal share than nothing at all. In the words of one Funai agent, "Pio was overruled." Not even a month after the shutdown, another Funai agent sent a message from Roosevelt Village: "Cinta Larga leaders have once again put prospectors to work, receiving a sum of money in advance. Seventy-five pairs of machines were installed, plus a total of around five hundred prospectors." Just a week later, no fewer than fifteen hundred fortune-seekers had reportedly entered. Pio increased the toll to $5,000 per pair of machines, and then $6,500. Still more outsiders came. Gas stations in Cacoal and Espigão started running out of diesel for all the machines.

By early February, two thousand prospectors—more than the entire Cinta Larga population at the time—had flooded into the mine. Pio had never imagined that so many people could fit in one place. Watching them swarm in the mud, he was reminded of an Amazonian anthill. When space ran short in the forest, they pitched tents amid the machines. Each day they knocked down more trees and opened new pits, practically obliterating the Stream of the Blackflies for five, six, seven miles. Some machine owners brought in bulldozers with hydraulic backhoes, the better to move huge quantities of earth. With hundreds of diesel generators powering hundreds of pumps and water jets and jigs, the noise drowned out every other sound. Another two thousand prospectors were camped along Highway 364, waiting for their chance to enter—with or without permission.

Realizing there was no hope of hiding all this from the government, Pio, ever the diplomat, tried to keep a channel open for dialogue. An official at Funai's base in Cacoal wrote, "[Pio and Roberto Carlos] came to this office in order to inform us that, because of pressure from the other members of the [Roosevelt Village] community and other villages…they had no option but to authorize the entry of prospectors into the area." The government, they explained, had never provided an economic alternative—and in the meantime, this was their "big chance to earn some pocket money."

Pio and his old friend also emphasized their willingness to *brigar com autoridade*—to fight with the authorities. As the Funai official relayed their message: "Many [Cinta Larga] have made it clear they will not allow any police forces to enter."

CHAPTER 21

NEGOTIATIONS

Even as a crackdown seemed imminent, Pio was trying to make what was illegal, legal—to somehow finagle permission to sell diamonds from Cinta Larga country. "That's what I always wanted," he would say. "Always, always." He didn't like being considered an outlaw for seeking the "economic emancipation" Funai itself promoted. The land, after all, was rightfully theirs—and a mine would be perfectly legal just beyond their borders. Nor did he like giving credence to the racist cliché that, as a member of Congress phrased it, "Indians today are synonymous with obesity, with sloth, with idleness."

Going back to the 1980s, Pio had searched for a way for his people to make a living, to avoid the fate of all those groups that ended up as "slaves to white people," in Apoena's words. They had tried rubber tapping, but it was impossible to compete with a globalized market. They were happy to grow crops but needed tractors, pesticides, and proper transport links to make a profit—things Funai had long promised but never delivered. Self-reliance had always been a Cinta Larga virtue, but they lacked title to their land, and so couldn't use it as collateral for bank loans like white farmers did. "How can the people who live around here say we do nothing, that Indians are lazy?" Pio once complained to a visiting official. "If the government *allowed* us to work, and brought technicians in to teach us, we would be able to survive without depending on…Funai."

Pio had already tried to gain official approval to sell hardwood. Even in the Amazon, some logging was legal, licensed with strict environmental guidelines. Why, Pio wondered, couldn't the Cinta Larga do this, too? It was already happening anyway, outside the law.

The problem, from the perspective of many activists and government officials, was that one exception could lead to another, and deforestation would spiral out of control. Other Indigenous groups, like the Kayapó and the Munduruku, had issues of their own with gold mines; the Paresi had partnered with white farmers to grow soybeans. Where would this end? When Pio was born, Rondônia was a Wyoming-size stretch of near-perfect canopy cover. Now it was one of the Amazon's most heavily deforested areas, with more than a quarter of its trees gone. Settlers were required by law to preserve half their property in its original state, but even when they did, the forest was whittled down to disconnected fragments. The human population had soared past a million; the bovine population was even larger. All along Highway 364, pasture extended to the horizon, flat except for the odd Brazil nut tree, now protected by Brazilian law, though it would be unable to reproduce or even generate nuts in that environment.

Scientists had actually begun to fear that, if enough of the Amazon was cut down—possibly as little as one-fifth of the original area—it could reach a tipping point and start dying on its own. Every time a tree turned sunlight into energy, it released vapor that became fresh rain clouds, and precipitation was recycled so many times that "flying rivers" formed. Less tree cover, then, meant less rainfall, less vapor to cool the air, and less of a canopy to shield against the tropical sun, conditions more suited to savanna—the predicted end state—than rainforest. Not only would this devastate the habitat for 10 percent of the world's known species; it would also fuel global warming, because giant trees suck up far more carbon than wispy grasses.

In Rondônia, people could already tell the climate was changing. Settlers who arrived in the 1960s remembered the penetrating chill of mist and drizzle, weather that was almost unheard-of now. There had always been a dry season, but it was growing drier than ever, and longer, and hotter. The yearly burns to clear fields sparked more and more wildfires—previously feeble, quickly extinguished by the forest's residual dampness, now likelier than ever to spread, putting all that carbon back into the atmosphere.

Though they didn't clear-cut like ranchers, loggers left subtler ravages. In the clearings where they stored felled trunks, the forest did eventually grow back, but not in the same way, with fast-growing vines, bamboo, and hollow, soft-wooded *embaúba* trees dominating, leaving little space for the old giants, mahogany and Brazil nut, to return.

And yet, Indigenous areas remained the best-preserved parts of the Amazon. Seen from above, the difference was improbably stark. On reconnaissance flights, federal agents took off amid neat rows of crops and imported grasses, but soon crossed a border where the shaggy forest began—8.6 million acres of it, if you counted the lands of the Cinta Larga, the Suruí, the Zoró, the Gavião, and the Arara. Even the mine at the Stream of the Blackflies was an almost imperceptible blemish in this ocean of green. "If it weren't for us," Pio said, "the forest would be gone already." Why couldn't they develop a tiny corner of it?

*　*　*

Amid the stream of white men coming to Pio's office, a Lebanese-Brazilian named Khaled Jezzini stood out. Described by one observer as "not doing well financially" and by another as a *pobre coitado* (poor bastard), he was nonetheless very different from other fortune-seekers. For one thing, whereas most prospectors relied on little more than intuition and magical thinking, Khaled had partnered with an experienced geologist named Max Salustiano, who'd previously worked for the government of Mato Grosso and the international mining giant Anglo American, across the Amazon region and in South Africa. Even more important, Khaled also had a plan to overcome the legal obstacles.

The 1988 constitution was vague on Indigenous people's land rights. While they were granted "exclusive usufruct of the riches of the soil," only Congress could authorize "exploration and excavation of the mineral riches." But it turned out that Romero Jucá—the former Funai president who'd been embroiled in the Cinta Larga hardwood scandal, and was now a senator—had already proposed a bill to do just that. It had lain dormant for five years, but Khaled believed the Stream of the Blackflies could serve as a "pilot." Max would draw up the Environmental Impact Study, a first step toward a license. If everything went according to plan, the prospectors would be banned from the mine, and a more orderly operation would be installed. Operating within the law, industrial equipment could be imported to drill into the underlying kimberlite, with its untold wealth of diamonds. Pio also liked the idea that the Cinta Larga wouldn't just sit back and receive royalties but would be trained to work at the mine—a marketable profession.

With Max as technical adviser, Pio filed twenty requests to extract diamonds from areas along the Stream of the Blackflies. Meanwhile, alongside Khaled, he and the other chiefs met with lawmakers, ministers, the head of the National Department for Mineral Production, and the presidents of Funai and Ibama, the environmental protection agency. At times it was obvious that Pio was receiving outside assistance. In a letter to Funai's president, he cited a newspaper editorial that argued, "In Brazil, the supposed inviolability of Indigenous rights prevents [mining] from happening legally; thus, it ends up happening illegally. The only possible course of action, given this reality, is the economic integration of the Brazilian Indian. Their lands should continue to be theirs, but not unconditionally; they should be developed, cultivated, irrigated, fertilized, mined by companies controlled by the Indians." The basic sentiment, however, was unquestionably Pio's: "We don't want to give [this mine] to the white man. We want to set up our own Indian mining company so that we Indians can explore the mine."

Pio's lobbying scrambled the usual political narratives. Among left-leaning journalists and activists, Indigenous people were often described as "forest guardians," living in harmony with nature. Plenty of Indigenous people—such as Almir Suruí, the environmentalist—embraced this identity themselves. But Roberto Carlos, for one, was bothered by the implication that it was the only authentic way to be an Indian. Speaking of one activist in particular, he said, "She wants us to be naked, without cars. She thinks human beings don't grow. You want me to live in the jungle like an animal? I've already done that." Though well-meaning, it was a view that reduced complex individuals to symbols—something like Rousseau's "noble savage," consigned to a timeless past. It was almost the flip side of the old evolutionist view of human society, inherited from the social Darwinists, that inspired Cândido Rondon's quest to assimilate Brazil's "primitives."

Pio, for his part, had long felt caught in some impossible place between the old world of his father and the new world of white society. Speaking to outsiders, he sometimes referred to his fellow Cinta Larga as "the Indians," as if he were separate from them. And in a sense he was: living in town, driving a car, married to a woman from a group that had already adopted many Brazilian norms. At the same time, he also felt deeply Cinta Larga. Though he was fluent in Portuguese, his grammar was erratic, and he still preferred to speak Tupi-Mondé. He was born in the forest, grew up in the forest, and never quite felt at ease in the land of asphalt roads. His confusion was only heightened by the fact that so many other people had their own ideas about what he should be. On the other end of the political spectrum, whites saw Indians as impediments to economic progress. The prime example was Jair Bolsonaro, the congressman who would be elected president in 2018, who vowed to block the demarcation of any new Indigenous areas and even to cancel some that already existed, because they "suffocate agribusiness." He also said, "Indians don't speak our language, don't have money, don't have culture. How can they control 13 percent of the national territory?"

Pio was all too aware of the anti-Indigenous bias in Brasília. But he was pragmatic about it, seeking common ground where he could, emphasizing their common mission to develop the Amazon region. When it came to legalizing the mine, Pio would recall, "The government received us well. They said they would look into it, study it."

Khaled's other asset was his connections to foreign buyers. As part of his deal with Pio, he was, according to a former mining official, first in line to acquire any blue diamonds that turned up. These rarities were exponentially more valuable: one from the Stream of the Blackflies was said to have fetched $1.85 million. Other outstanding stones came out of there, too, such as a clear, one-hundred-carat behemoth that reportedly sold for $6 million. Local middlemen lacked the knowledge, experience, and capital to pay the right price for these diamonds, and big-deal buyers from Antwerp and Tel Aviv never came straight to the mine. They hardly showed their faces in Brazil, much less Rondônia, though they followed the market through intermediaries. In the city of Juína, where Old Luca and Lobão had sold their first haul, an Israeli even set up a makeshift office in his hotel, placing a sign that read IMG COMÉRCIO DE DIAMANTES on the door of his room. (Probably too indiscreet, he was later arrested trying to smuggle out his purchases.)

Khaled almost never revealed who was on the other end of his transactions. But on one of his and Pio's visits to Brasília, he arranged a meeting with investors from abroad—"Belgians, all of them big and tall," Pio's brother-in-law Paulo would recall. Paulo brought a three-carat stone as a sample, hidden in a slit in his shoe. Buyers at the Stream of the Blackflies had valued it at just $11,000, but the Belgians bought it for $23,000. They spoke about investing $2.5 million in total. This, Pio thought, was the way forward.

* * *

While Pio was making headway in Brasília, other parts of the government were panicking. In Brazil, the so-called Public Ministry plays a dual role. On the one hand, it's home to prosecutors who bring criminal cases; on the other, it acts as a kind of government ombudsman, concerned more broadly with social order. Its officials had already appealed to the general in charge of the regional Army brigade and the head of the Federal Police in Porto Velho, asking them to intervene at the Stream of the Blackflies. They wanted to prevent another Serra Pelada—a gold find that brought a hundred thousand fortune-seekers to the northeastern Amazon in the 1980s, forcing the military to take over. The general, though, said he couldn't act without an order from the president. The Federal Police superintendent offered a half-dozen agents—a laughably small contingent, given the scale of the mine.

But then the press got wind of the story. On January 16, 2001, Rondônia's *Diário da Amazônia* printed a dramatic headline on its front page: DIAMOND MINE REVIVES PROSPECTING FEVER. Just below, in bold italics, it read: "*The deposit is one of the largest ever found and the diamonds are considered the best quality in the world.*" National papers followed, each outdoing the other's sensationalism. *O Estado de S. Paulo* referred to Pio's house at Roosevelt Village as a "two-story chalet," as if it were a Swiss mountain retreat and not a wooden shack by an Amazonian river. Rio de Janeiro's *O Globo* claimed that his Cacoal home was located in "one of the priciest neighborhoods," as if it were on Manhattan's Upper East Side rather than a warren of unpaved roads near Highway 364. Banal comforts were framed as lavish excesses, like the trucks said to possess "double cabins [i.e., with both front and back seats], souped up and equipped with air-conditioning units." One journalist marveled that Oita possessed not only a TV but a VCR, a DVD player, *and* a microwave oven.

The *Globo* article was probably the most exaggerated of all. Headlined THE DIAMOND CHIEFS, it said the mine had "transformed eleven of the most influential chiefs of the tribe into diamond barons, with vast powers over a legion of more than three thousand prospectors, and a fortune in stones that, according to expert calculations, may be greater than $2 billion." Never mind that no actual experts had come up with this figure, as even Brazil's geological survey was barred from taking measurements. The vast majority of those stones were lodged deep down in the kimberlite, inaccessible. Other articles cited Federal Police estimates that $20 million worth left the mine each month, but even this was highly speculative, given that all the sales took place on the black market.

Pio himself, though he watched the news on TV, could barely read a newspaper. Needless to say, he lacked even the faintest media training. Speaking to one reporter, he openly admitted to having received $150,000 from prospectors, though he claimed to have spent it all on village improvements. João Bravo was similarly tactless. In that *Globo* article, he was pictured shirtless by one of his six pickup trucks, saying, "I don't have as much money as people say. If I did, I would have bought an airplane." Worst of all, the coverage attracted even more fortune-seekers. In Pio's words, "We let Globo [TV] in and they showed images that told the whole country there were diamonds here."

Perhaps the biggest disconnect came in the coverage of the "drama" of desperate prospectors, charitably described by the *Diário da Amazônia* as "family men…with no money in their pocket." This wasn't necessarily inaccurate, but the media seemed to be waking up to the existence of inequality in their deeply unequal country. *O Globo*, for one, had always espoused a thoroughly capitalist worldview. Even in the opinion section, the paper would never betray astonishment that, say, a CEO earned thousands of times what his workers did. Now, in what was supposed to be a news story, it editorialized that "the chiefs are reveling in a life of luxury and privileges far exceeding the standards of other Indians and most Brazilians." All of which raised the question of what the real scandal was.

The resentment was even more blatant among settlers. Those like Marafon, who saw the Cinta Larga as people like any other, were few and far between. Go to any frontier bar, and you would hear phrases like "The Indians got used to the easy life thanks to their hardwood and diamonds." The settlers, brave pioneers who'd worked hard for their homesteads, didn't hide their envy at the Cinta Larga's Belgium-size reserve. *É muita terra para pouco índio*, they'd say—"It's a lot of land for a few Indians"—and clearly they felt it was unearned. Revealingly, though, they didn't apply the same logic to the white landowners who inherited vast, unproductive tracts across Brazil.

As usual in the Amazon region, fact mingled with fantasy. One conspiracy theory held that Indigenous people received a government "pension" just for being Indigenous (almost as if Funai was actually living up to its promises). Even more fanciful rumors circulated about Pio. He found them deeply upsetting, not only because they were false, but because of what they implied about his proper place in society. "People say I have bank accounts in places I've never heard of, outside the country, that I own buildings, that I own a private plane, a jet," he said, smiling with a look of bitter irony. "I think to myself, man, I really would like to have all that! Is it forbidden for an Indian to have these things?"

*   *   *

The Federal Police moved slowly at first. A few agents visited Josias's hotel, where newly arrived fortune-seekers hoped to find Cinta Larga partners. Echoing the sympathetic media coverage, their stated goal was to carry out "a preventive effort with the objective of raising prospector awareness...[as] prospectors are people without the education necessary to know they are committing irregularities." An attempt to make contact with the Cinta Larga, meanwhile, met with what the agents vaguely termed "hostility." A later video showed what this might mean: heavily armed Federal Police in bulletproof vests descending on the mine in a helicopter, only to be repelled by shirtless warriors with bows drawn. "Next time you're in the city, I'll arrest you!" one of the agents shouted. There in the forest, though, he was outmatched.

The feds caught a lucky break at the end of January, when Old Luca's partner Lobão showed up at a police station in Cacoal to report an accident. One of his workers had attached his hammock to a jig, and according to the police report, the "steel box...ended up falling on top of the victim, who died instantly." Investigators already knew that Lobão was involved in the mine; Luca himself had informed them. Removed from the mine in December, he'd been unable to return, and had grown embittered. In later years he would claim that Pio and Tataré had promised him a gully all to himself, but obscure rivals offered $1 million to have him removed. Others would say, more credibly, that he simply couldn't afford the toll to go back in. In any case, he told the police that Lobão and Josias now ran eighteen pairs of machines at the mine, producing fifty carats a day. He also confirmed that Pio, Oita, and João Bravo were involved.

The Federal Police, responsible for law enforcement in Indigenous areas, was basically a Brazilian version of the United States FBI. Its agents were typically more educated than local police, though this was no guarantee of enlightened attitudes. Sometimes their elite status simply made them over-confident, and they acted like they'd watched one too many Hollywood movies about trigger-happy super-cops. A couple of years earlier, they'd carried out a spectacular raid inside Cinta Larga country, looking for what they thought were coca plants—the raw ingredient in cocaine—but were actually herbs used in traditional hunting preparations.

To be fair, some Federal Police agents truly believed in their work: protecting the Amazon and its original inhabitants. At first they targeted the white suspects, arresting Lobão, Josias, a diamond buyer named Ancelmo Peron, and Claudiney, the Pamaré Association's white adminis-trator. (The latter three would spend years fighting the charges, but Lobão turned police informant—an arrangement that lasted until two prospec-tors threatened to kill him, and he shot them to death on a Cacoal street.)

Of course, the arrests didn't do much to address the larger prob-lem. Across the government, people started warning of "armed conflict." "Countless machines are coming from Juína, Porto Velho, and cities in Minas Gerais state, to search for diamonds in this new El Dorado," one official wrote, adding that "1,200 prospectors may attempt an invasion." In another memo, two Federal Police agents even raised the specter of a certain age-old fixation: "The Cinta Larga people are feared by all as the most aggressive and warlike of all the Indigenous groups in the region, and records show that they practiced cannibalism until a few years ago." (In reality, the last known case took place in 1970, but the broader point stood.)

By February, the Federal Police, the Brazilian armed forces, Funai, and Ibama had started discussing a large-scale intervention. Pio and the other chiefs, all too aware they were losing control, agreed to negotiate. Meeting at the state police barracks in Espigão, they spoke with what one Funai agent described as "the sincerity that is peculiar to them." They wanted new houses, not of wood but of cement, for their grow-ing populations. They wanted hookups to the electric grid to replace diesel generators. Pio was especially emphatic about upgrading their schools so that kids could get an education without moving to town, with all its bad influences. He also wanted the government to deliver on its promises to support commercial farming with roads, equipment, technical assistance, and financing.

The words at this particular meeting have been lost, but many others were recorded, and the basic script never varied. Pio, wearing a spotted jaguar-skin headdress, would remind the government of its own role in getting them hooked on Western goods: "It was the white man who brought these habits to us. Now there's no way to live without this stuff." Not only that, he said, "It was Funai that taught us hardwood could be sold." Despite his differences with Pio, João Bravo would chime in: "Why didn't you leave me naked in the forest? I didn't used to know what money was. I even ripped it up because I didn't understand its importance. Today we need money to buy houses, we need doctors, we need to pay for hospital care, notebooks, private schools. Nowadays there's salt, sugar, coffee—all of this is the government's fault."

After Oita's betrayals in Zoró country, Pio had vowed he would never be chief. Yet no one interrupted the monologues in which he presented himself as a "leader of my people." For all his faults, he was a survivor of contact, and this had to be respected. Also, he was undeniably good at speeches, never reluctant to speak the blunt truth to white men in ties. Sometimes it sounded like he was giving one of his sermons: "Indians aren't animals. They're humans just like white people, they're children of God just like white people." The Cinta Larga weren't *bandidos*, he said: they wanted to live in peace and pay taxes like any other citizen.

Funai's president said he was willing to discuss "sustainable development projects," but only after security forces were allowed inside Cinta Larga country, and the illegal mine was shut down. Though they should have known better by now, Pio and the other chiefs agreed.

CHAPTER 22

BODIES

Prospectors were called to a rally in Espigão's central square—the same place where, in April 2004, Donivaldo Cinta Larga would be tied to a tree and beaten. For such a tiny town, the *praça* was oddly extravagant, with green lawns and cobbled walkways extending out like spokes on a wheel—all of it built, of course, with money made from Indigenous lands. What with the searing Amazonian sun, people rarely hung out there, unless it was in the shade of the motorcycle taxi stand. On this day, though, a squat man in a red polo shirt, Ernandes Amorim, was holding forth. "Indian lands are there to be invaded!" he bellowed, receiving cheers in response.

This crowd hardly cared that Amorim was, according to one newspaper, the "record-holder for crimes in the state"—a man who'd been investigated for cocaine trafficking even as a senator in Brasília, and was ultimately stripped of his seat for campaigning with siphoned-off public funds. They didn't even care that he'd been labeled "an enslaver of minors at a cassiterite mine." There was, after all, no question whose side he was on. Now Amorim was running for governor, but he, too, had once been a prospector. He knew how they suffered, tarred as outlaws even as they tried to make an honest living, contributing to the economic development of the Amazon.

The government takeover had proved surprisingly anticlimactic. Federal agents were brought in from across the country, and a convoy of thirty trucks and tractors filled with Federal Police, officials from Funai and Ibama, and local cops—a show of force meant to head off any resistance. Marafon, the rancher, watched as prospectors flooded out, even in the dark, rather than risk arrest or confrontation. He ferried some across the Roosevelt River in his raft, but plenty of others simply swam. Most left dead-broke, lacking even seven *reais*—about $3.50—to pay for a ride on a flatbed truck back to Espigão. Those who did take the truck were stopped at a Federal Police checkpoint, where agents searched people for diamonds. Fifteen would-be smugglers were arrested; the wiser ones jumped off early and walked the thirty miles to town.

By the time government forces reached the mine, in March 2001, just about all the prospectors were gone. Unable to carry their equipment, they left most of it scattered across the wasteland of the Stream of the Blackflies: hundreds of pumps, diesel generators, jigs, and half-empty barrels of fuel, along with an estimated forty-six thousand feet of plastic tubing. Even tractors lay abandoned in the mud. Some prospectors buried their machines in hopes of digging them up later.

The Federal Police suspected Amorim—among many other members of the Rondônia establishment—of investing in the mine. As a politician, he was actually fighting for the same thing Pio was: to legalize prospecting inside Cinta Larga country. The difference was in who should be allowed to do it. "If they legalize the mine only for the Indians, it won't work," Celso Fantim, head of the prospectors union in Espigão, told a reporter. "The prospectors will probably invade. They feel they have a right to the mine as well. They were the ones who found it." Nor, Fantim added, would they allow an international mining corporation to take over: "The mine belongs to Brazilians. We're not going to work as servants here, knowing that we own a fortune, that everyone can provide a good life for their children, grandchildren, great-grandchildren. To have a company from outside come and take that? It won't happen."

All sorts of opportunists were homing in on Cinta Larga country. Perhaps the most eccentric was Jane Rezende, who called herself the national president of the Union of Prospectors and Miners of Brazil, an organization of dubious authenticity. She'd come to Espigão and started signing up prospectors, giving them union cards that, she claimed, would give them rightful access to the Stream of the Black-flies. She also sent letters to various politicians and government officials, including Brazil's president—letters that would inform Federal Police investigations, despite being almost entirely composed of wild rumors.

In a litany of run-on sentences, she laid out the baroque theory that Pio was at once the mine's supreme boss and a pawn of Funai, Ibama, and obscure foreign interests: "The CHIEF NACOÇA PIU [sic] CINTA LARGA and his warriors are said to be the only beneficiaries of the scheme, and the other Indians are forbidden from prospecting in the Indigenous areas. Despite being rich and powerful, enjoying his income from the scheme, living with his family in an enormous mansion in [Cacoal], having another mansion in the district of Riozinho, he is said to have bought a temple as a gift to a pastor at the evangelical church he frequents, owns a luxury vehicle, frequents the finest establishments, travels constantly, and is said to be buying an airplane in the [Pamaré] Association's name to serve the scheme, etc., [and] it is clear that NACOÇA PIU is above all a victim of the criminal organization that controls the riches in the Indigenous areas under his control, [and] his people are afraid, truly terrified, of the fury of NACOÇA PIU, who, dominated by the criminal organization that controls him, does not have many other options." Most fantastical of all, Rezende claimed that De Beers had secretly orchestrated the government takeover to clear the way for an operation of its own.

Many prospectors already took as an article of faith that, if not De Beers, the Cinta Larga themselves had engineered the crackdown, to get their hands on the machines. Roberto Carlos and Tataré now accompanied federal agents on patrols, giving the impression they'd switched sides. The warriors also detained wildcats all on their own, delivering them to federal checkpoints.

Some prospectors claimed to be owed hundreds of thousands of dollars by their Cinta Larga business partners, whether for machines lost or diamonds not accounted for. One told the slightly muddled joke that João Bravo resembled a "woman at a brothel. He can't help himself when he sees money, and then he doesn't fulfill the promise." Another said that Pio, likewise, "doesn't like to pay up," and called him "shameless." Oita, all agreed, was the worst. One white man was moved to leave a menacing voice message: "I might lose [my $10,000], but you're going to lose much more." True to form, Oita didn't allow himself to be intimidated. In town, he wore a pistol in his waistband. "You can't threaten another man's life, you fucking piece of shit son of a whore," he responded. "You better watch your step, too!"

Some disputes went beyond mere threats. Two armed men actually went to the home of a young chief named Marcelo, in town. Marcelo was away, so the men waited all night with his wife and children, keeping them hostage. Eventually they grew impatient and left, but not before telling his family that, if Marcelo didn't pay what he owed, they would be killed. Fearing for their lives, other chiefs signed over cars and properties purchased during the boom.

Despite all this, most prospectors still saw themselves as honest businessmen. Outraged to be treated like criminals, they received

Amorim's speech like a breath of fresh air. One machine owner told a reporter, "He looks out for us. He got lawyers for us. Prospectors are being massacred in this conspiracy that is using the police, Ibama, Funai, and the DNPM [National Department for Mineral Production]....A lot of us are desperate."

Ordinary pit workers and cooks, of course, were even more desperate. Women turned to prostitution. Some prospectors nurtured addictions, and in once-sleepy Espigão, strung-out men could now be seen wandering the streets in soiled clothes, sleeping in the very same square where Amorim was holding his rally.

"I'm the one in charge in this region," Amorim told them now. Go ahead and invade, he urged: "Whatever problem may arise with the police, I'll sort it out."

* * *

For Pio, it was shocking to see how fast his ambitions could fall apart, to be replaced by the same old stasis. Funai started sending shipments of food, but that didn't come close to making up for the lost income, and their cattle herd dwindled as chiefs sold off cows to get by. People could no longer turn to Pio when they wanted to send their kids to school or when they needed money for medicine, new clothes, a night at a hotel in Cacoal. One government anthropologist complained of their "immediatist perspective," a pseudo-academic way of saying they wanted Funai to fulfill its promises now, as if they hadn't spent years waiting. The "sustainable development projects"—to collect Brazil nuts, for one—never got off the ground.

The crackdown created new problems, too. With checkpoints on the roads into Cinta Larga country, the Federal Police intercepted any fuel that might be used at the mine, even if it deprived villages of their only energy source. This was especially hard for Roosevelt Village, which was so mosquito-infested that, in a Western-style shack where you couldn't keep a fire without burning it down, you needed a fan to get any sleep. Panderê once tried to bring in some diesel for a village meeting, but the agents, unmoved by his explanation, poured it on the ground.

The abuses extended to women. At one point Maria Beleza was riding in a car with a cousin and her cousin's husband. The police stopped them, and a female officer patted the two women down, even palpating their genitals, asking, "Where are the diamonds?" When the officer found nothing, Maria and her cousin were let go. In Brazil, police treated poor people like this all the time. But the Cinta Larga still didn't feel like poor people. The future Pio hoped to avoid, the future of the Xavante, still hadn't arrived—not yet. The Cinta Larga still clung to their independence, their age-old rejection to being ruled over, even if this made the humiliations more profound.

People were also embarrassed by their newfound fame as deadbeats. It wasn't only prospectors who claimed to be owed but ordinary white business owners, especially the car dealers who'd sold so many brand-new trucks to the chiefs. Debt wasn't entirely foreign to the Cinta Larga, with their culture of *wepíka*. What was mystifying was how fast a debt could grow, thanks to the magic of compound interest. A Public Ministry official would later find that they collectively owed hundreds of thousands, if not millions, of dollars. He'd also uncover abusive loan terms that doubled or even tripled the original amounts, as well as lawsuits in which creditors sought repayment for suspiciously unsigned invoices. On the hook for $75,000, Pio had most of his Funai salary garnished to pay it down. Oita, despite his status as a high-class *doutor*, had his ranch taken away along with all the cattle. The anthropologist João Dal Poz objected to the idea that the chiefs had ever been "rich" at all. "They don't accumulate wealth," he told a reporter. "The money gushes through their hands."

Little wonder that some chiefs tried to get around the shutdown. Despite the federal checkpoints and patrols, the mine was far too large to effectively police, stretching as it did for seven miles along the Stream of the Blackflies, in the middle of a Belgium-size rainforest. It wasn't hard to sneak in a few white men who hid during the day only to run the machines at night. They hardly needed to bring in fresh supplies, because the previous wave of prospectors, in their haste to flee the police, had also left behind stashes of fuel, food, and water.

In his desperation, Pio convinced himself he wouldn't get in trouble for a small operation if he was transparent about it. "I respectfully communicate," he wrote to Funai, the Federal Police, and Ibama in June 2001, "that the [Pamaré] association is having serious difficulties with its people in terms of health care, nutrition, and other areas.... Therefore we are putting 3 (three) pairs of machines to work...with labor performed by our association members (Cinta Larga Indians) under the orientation of two white men for each team." In a nod to the government's insistence that outsiders stay out, he added, "To be clear, as soon as the Indians have totally mastered how to operate the equipment, the white men will be dismissed from their employment and sent away from the Indigenous area....We state for the record that all of the revenue will be spent to benefit the Cinta Larga Indigenous People. Certain that once again the authorities will understand us, we thank you in advance."

João Bravo's approach was less subtle. His nickname, which literally means Wild João or Angry João, was born during this period. According to one popular story, a Federal Police agent was lying in a hammock at a checkpoint when João wordlessly approached and slashed one of the cords, dropping the agent to the ground. On another occasion, state cops stopped a truck transporting diesel engines and fuel to the mine, and the driver called up João to intervene. As one of the cops later reported, "Around 2100 hours, the now famous chief João Bravo showed up at the checkpoint accompanied by a few Indians armed with revolvers, and started threatening us." In the "gruff dialogue" that ensued, João "imposed conditions for the checkpoint to continue in place, among them that we permit prospectors to enter the reserve." A few hours later, "the Indians returned armed with twelve-gauge repeater shotguns and set up camp near the checkpoint." The next time prospectors approached, the cops saw no choice but to let them through. Shortly afterward, the checkpoint was dismantled entirely.

João Bravo's greatest claim to fame involved a high-ranking Federal Police inspector, Mauro Sposito. Something of a cowboy, Sposito was known as Mauro Bomba—the Bomb—because of the way he demolished clandestine airstrips across the Amazon. At the Stream of the Blackflies, the Cinta Larga accused him of dropping explosives from a helicopter to destroy a backhoe, not noticing, or not caring, that a Cinta Larga family was digging for diamonds there. (He denied this, and in any case, they weren't harmed.) Afterward, João invited Sposito to a meeting at his village. When the inspector arrived with a few other agents, warriors took their satellite phone and the keys to their truck, "detaining" Sposito so that, as João explained it, "he would understand how [the Cinta Larga] have suffered thanks to the police's actions." Each time it was told, the story grew more fanciful—one version held that the warriors painted Sposito red and beat him with the flat part of a machete. Sposito himself tried to downplay the episode, claiming they merely demanded he stay for a barbecue. He did say that Oita, ever eager to dominate, pointed an arrow at him.

"You think you're an authority?" Oita asked him. "You're an authority in town. Here, we are the authorities."

"Aren't you supposed to be a pastor?" Sposito asked.

"My arrow isn't a pastor."

Oita liked to seem dangerous, but he knew not to take it too far. The next day Pio came and negotiated the inspector's release, declaring for the benefit of the other Cinta Larga that the feds "should stop humiliating the Indians" and "never again threaten the Indians or violate their rights."

* * *

Tensions worsened after the discovery of the first bodies. Prospectors were already talking about how conditions had changed now that they were outnumbered. One team was working for a Cinta Larga named Canário when, as they later described it to the police, agents from Funai and Ibama showed up and started shooting. One of the prospectors ran for the trees, but the agents caught up with him and beat him until he handed over his best stone. Afterward he was allowed to stay and "teach the Indians" to run the machines; the rest of the prospectors were arrested and taken away.

It's hard to say how many of these stories were fabricated to make Funai, the prospectors' number one enemy, look bad. At one point Old Luca resurfaced to make wild allegations of his own, telling reporters that people in Funai uniforms, "heavily armed" and driving an official vehicle, were themselves mining for diamonds and "ambushing" prospectors to steal their haul.

A number of Funai agents truly were on the take. Some didn't bother to hide it, even visiting Noturnos, the brothel frequented by Cinta Larga chiefs. An agent named Valdir was described by the owner as "the one who caused the most trouble, always armed with a .38 caliber revolver, intimidating [her], saying he would close down the establishment and send [her] to jail." Claiming to be Federal Police, he never paid his bill. Sometimes, a brothel worker said, he was "accompanied by Indians, some of whom he called 'chief,' and they would drink together, and…[the agent] would talk about diamonds." Valdir apparently even showed the women at the brothel a small stone.

Life was harder for Funai agents who stayed clean. The federal takeover put them in the position of enforcing the law of the white man even though their ostensible job was to assist the people on the other side of that law. In one incident, Cinta Larga men shot their guns in the air to intimidate a Funai patrol. Pio intervened, admonishing them that Funai was there to help—the same message he and Roberto Carlos used to spread to those who were still "wild," back in the time of contact, though it felt thinner by the day.

Some of the most effective Funai agents followed the pragmatic tradition of Apoena Meirelles. To help Pio regain control of the mine, José Nazareno Torres de Moraes, for instance, helped to draft a select list of white machine owners to be allowed in. As Pio would remember it, "I trusted him…to make sure we didn't get taken advantage of." Apoena himself actually visited around this time, coming away convinced that the solution—like with the hardwood trade—was to end the prohibition, legalize the mine, and regulate it. The visit got many Cinta Larga's hopes up, but Apoena never had much influence outside Funai. "I feel great exhaustion," he admitted, "after years of writing the same reports." In the Amazon region, real power had always belonged to men like Ernandes Amorim, the prospector turned politician.

Even before Amorim's rally in Espigão, wildcats never stopped trying their luck at the Stream of the Blackflies. In August 2001, one small group sneaked in only to flee a day later in mortal fear. It was they who encountered the bodies. The first two lay sprawled in the muck near a sign that read ENTRY PROHIBITED—OITA. They saw another a couple of miles farther along. One of the wildcats would tell police he "smelled a strong bad smell" and saw vultures hovering, suggesting there were more. But he "didn't have the courage to go check."

Pio, in his usual role as go-between, accompanied the police on a mission to retrieve the corpses, and a fourth turned up. The skin was already dark from putrefaction, but they all belonged to white men. Oita himself turned out not to be involved; it was simply a quiet stretch of forest, convenient for dumping bodies. A witness, the underage white girlfriend of a Cinta Larga named Cesar, told the police she'd seen three of the victims when she and Cesar were driving to the mine; the white men had jumped in the back of another truck full of Indians, never to be heard from again.

When news of the deaths reached the press, the uproar was immediate: INDIANS SUSPECTED IN MASSACRE, read one headline. Already restless, underemployed, angry, prospectors said they were prepared to *matar ou morrer*—to kill the Indians or die trying. Jane Rezende, the rumormongering head of the Union of Prospectors and Miners of Brazil, fanned the flames by claiming there were dozens more bodies still to be found. As usual, these rumors were often false: once the local press reported that a cook's teenage daughter had been killed, only for the daughter to reappear unharmed. Pio complained that the prospectors themselves were never suspects, even though homicides were commonplace in mines *outside* Indigenous areas. "They kill one another to steal the minerals," Pio wrote to the authorities. "[Then] they quickly say that it was the Cinta Larga who killed them."

Open conflict was averted only when Pio and João Bravo, fed up by the government's failure to address their problems, reopened the mine in October 2001. Finding rare agreement, they tried to keep things organized, with just seventeen pairs of machines running at a toll of $10,000 each. That would have meant fewer than a hundred white workers at the mine; within weeks, two thousand had entered. At its peak, the number would hit five thousand, truly dwarfing the Cinta Larga's own population.

Before the year was over, Pio was already negotiating another shutdown with the Public Ministry. But the Federal Police had had enough. The Indians were mocking their authority, making them look bad. As one inspector wrote in an internal memo, "We believe that, if the local Indigenous community were unanimous about paralyzing the mine inside its territory, the Federal Police would already have achieved success in stamping out the clandestine activity." Forget the Belgians, the Israelis, the Koreans, the rich businessmen and politicians from across the region, the prospectors unions openly advocating for illegal invasions. "If someone is to blame for the current difficulty in removing prospectors from the Roosevelt reserve," the memo concluded, "this blame falls on the Indians."

CHAPTER 23

INVESTIGATIONS

At the moment of his arrest, Pio was at the Porto Velho branch of Youth with a Mission, an American Evangelical Christian organization. He was trying to get out—to quit the mine, to quit the Pamaré Association, and even, in a sense, to quit his own people. In the past he'd never been particularly religious. Going back to the 1980s, missionaries sometimes visited his home in Riozinho, hoping to convert him. His wife, Rute, was already a practicing Christian, and he accompanied her to services at a Methodist church. None of it resonated until the mine spun out of control, and he began to feel *perseguido*—persecuted, hunted, oppressed. In January 2002, he'd set aside his differences to join up with João Bravo for another lobbying attempt. The Federal Police had detained and searched them at the airport in Brasília, even frisking one of João's wives. They didn't find any diamonds, but it was another humiliation—and should have confirmed to Pio that the feds were after him.

In those days, Pio still spoke freely on his cell phone about goings-on at the Stream of the Blackflies. Listening in on his calls, federal agents heard him discussing the water supply, authorizations for prospectors, difficulties in exchanging dollars for Brazilian *reais* on the black market. They heard him asking prospectors for advances as small as $1,500, to be deposited in his daughter's bank account. Eavesdropping on his white associates, they also heard about payments to alias Barrigudo, or Potbelly, as large as $500,000. It didn't take long to figure out that was Pio. Internally, he was known as "the main instigator [who] controls all the illegal mining activity inside the Roosevelt Indigenous Reserve."

The feds were also gathering evidence on a few other survivors of contact—all born into a world without money, and now enmeshed in a truly global market. They heard talk of an even larger payment, totaling $900,000, to João Bravo. Marcos Glikas, an Orthodox Jew from São Paulo, was found to have flown to João's airstrip on behalf of a dealer from New York City's Diamond District, Marco Kalisch, who would himself be caught bringing Cinta Larga diamonds into the United States. Glikas also did business with Pio, fronting for Israeli and Belgian buyers who were never identified, and with Oita (whom he accused of stiffing him on mining equipment). Oita was further linked to a Sierra Leonean Arab who in turn had links to Hezbollah. Even Maria Beleza was targeted, arrested in a truck full of mining equipment, though her associates were lower-profile—low enough that they hardly seemed worth pursuing, unless the goal was just to produce numbers, to show that the Federal Police was doing its job.

Funai agents, unsurprisingly, came under investigation, too. One local cop was suspected of running his own machines, and there were surely others. Despite a reputation for incorruptibility, the Federal Police would even file charges against one of their own, an agent who gave a Cinta Larga a Glock nine-millimeter in return for precious stones. The highest-profile case involved no one less than Rondônia's governor, Ivo Cassol (who denied everything). Still, the focus remained on the Cinta Larga "diamond barons." At one point Pio was declared a fugitive simply because he was, in the words of an official memo, "ensconced in the Cinta Larga reserve, hiding from his creditors...[or] fearing a supposed kidnapping."

Pio had reason to be fearful. A twenty-eight-year-old Cinta Larga named Carlito had recently identified a group of loggers to Federal Police and prosecutors. Having received death threats, he asked for government protection, but none was forthcoming. At around 9:00 p.m. on December 19, 2001, as he arrived at his residence in town with his wife and daughter, gunmen approached their vehicle and shot him dead. Pio, too, received threats, and while he didn't necessarily fear for his own life, he did worry about "our children in school." One Cinta Larga boy was actually accosted by a prospector brandishing a revolver. "If you have money," Pio lamented, "everyone comes after you. You're pursued by the police, you're pursued by politicians, you're pursued by criminals....Diamonds are worse than cocaine."

Pio's old friend Roberto Carlos, well past his phase as the Rich Little Roberto of the hardwood boom, was quicker to arrive at the conclusion that the money wasn't worth the trouble. He'd already balked at running machines at the site of his people's single greatest tragedy. Now he saw how individualism was taking hold among the new generation of chiefs—how, in his words, "money ruins people." In the old days, when someone died, their belongings—what few they had—would be destroyed. He could never quite grasp the Western concept of capital as something exempt from death. The way he saw it, "You can never even say it's yours. At that moment you might have it in your hands, but later it's someone else's."

Pio, for his part, was already coming to regret his experiment with diamond mining. Two years in, what did he have to show for it? He was embarrassed to bring outsiders to Roosevelt Village, which reminded him of an urban favela. The wooden houses were overcrowded, run-down. Pio's wife, Rute, took immaculate care of their own dwellings, but most Cinta Larga never learned to deal with what Westerners saw as clutter, instead leaving things strewn at random around their homes: dusty plastic bottles saved to be used as containers, fishing hooks and nylon fishing line, spare flip-flops, lighters. Outside, so much trash littered the ground—candy wrappers, diapers, old car parts—it almost seemed purposely distributed, like a trash garden. In the absence of proper sanitation, kitchen sinks drained straight into the mud, leaving slimy pools where mosquitoes bred. Mangy fearful dogs curled up in whatever shade they could find. The residents themselves were growing overweight, even obese in some cases, just like that congressman had said. Hooked on deliveries of beef, white rice, soda, and processed foods, they'd not only given up on hunting but largely abandoned their fields, making them more sedentary than ever before. Whenever shipments faltered, they made their discontent known.

"Whatever little problem there was in our area, I was the one who solved it," Pio would complain. "Everything the Indians wanted, they would pass on to me, and I would pass it on to the government." Still they resented him: for continuing to receive a salary from Funai when they had no income at all, for driving his own truck while they hitched rides to Espigão, for living in a proper house while they had packed-dirt floors—and then for spending too much time in town, distant from their problems, rather than at Roosevelt Village.

Pio had long felt caught in some unreconcilable place between white society and his father's world. Now he found himself in another: at once an alleged kingpin, overseeing a multimillion-dollar mining operation, and a legitimate leader of his people, fighting for better education and health care and the integrity of their lands. While one arm of the Public Ministry was planning to prosecute him, another was negotiating with him to support the next shutdown. At one point the feds intercepted a call in which he lamented, "I should have stayed in the forest. At least we didn't worry there. There were no clothes, no money, nothing....There were no guns, no weekdays, no Sunday, no Saturday....To do anything [at the mine], you need money. You have to buy tools. You have to buy gasoline. You have to buy oil....The white man's things make us lazy. The machines moving [the earth], cleaning [the gravel]. Chainsaws! All of this stuff has a cost."

As these feelings swirled inside him, Pio was accompanying Rute to church as usual when, one day, he felt the Holy Spirit enter him. And it changed his life. In the natural wonders of the rainforest, he came to see God's artistry. He took to praying before meals with his family, asking everyone to close their eyes, lock hands, and thank the Lord for the rice and salty beans and beef on their plates. Rute was always telling him to take a step back from his role as tribal leader. Now, when she suggested they join a missionary training course—the Discipleship Training School, run by Youth with a Mission in Porto Velho, three hundred miles from Cinta Larga country—he agreed. He'd leave the other chiefs to fight over the mine, to fight with the government, to fight with prospectors. Over the weeks and months that followed, he even spent time at missionary workshops in Rio de Janeiro and São Paulo, where the Amazon was so distant as to seem almost imaginary. In his words, "I disconnected myself from everything."

* * *

Each year on April 19, Brazil celebrated the Day of the Indian, a paradoxical homage. Back in the nineteenth century, even as rubber barons killed "wild Indians" as if they were animals, Brazilian writers had made Indigenous people into romantic heroes, mascots for a new national identity—not unlike James Fenimore Cooper's *The Last of the Mohicans* in the United States. The holiday was born during a colonization effort known as the March to the West, in the 1940s. Each year, Indigenous groups would paint their bodies, don bright feathers and dried straw, and march to show off their cultures—a double performance, as Brazilian society also made a show of welcoming them, at least for that one day.

In more recent times, the Day of the Indian had also brought protests, as many Indigenous people, newly politicized, rejected the niceties of white domination. In other years, Tataré would join them. But in 2002, he was occupied with worldlier matters, on his way to the diamond hub of Juína. He'd just nodded off when the driver of his car hissed, "Police! Police!" It was a checkpoint.

A cop explained that they were looking for the suspect of a murder in a nearby brothel. "I'm no *bandido*," Tataré said, handing over his Funai employee ID. But when he consented to a search, the cop found a .38 Taurus revolver in his backpack and placed him under arrest. He was handed over to Márcio Valério de Sousa, a federal agent who'd once complained to a reporter, "The chiefs have cars and houses that I, after twenty-five years in the Federal Police, can't even dream of." Now he told Tataré, "We know you have ten prospectors at the mine." There was already a warrant out for him—and also for Pio, João Bravo, Oita, and Roberto Carlos.

Tataré rode in the back of Sousa's vehicle for the long drive to Porto Velho. He thought about somehow cutting Sousa's throat. But then he remembered his children, and imagined how they'd suffer if he went to prison. *At the very least I'm going to mess with him*, Tataré thought. Having come from the forest, he hadn't bathed or changed clothes in two days. He removed his shoes and allowed the stench of his feet to fill the car.

Sousa showed up at the local branch of Youth with a Mission the next day. "We need you to come with us," he told Pio. "Tataré is dead." It's unclear why he felt the ruse was necessary, but if he'd done his homework, he would have known that Pio, with his preternatural calm, wasn't the type to resist. What *was* true was that Tataré had been locked in a hot room at Federal Police headquarters, and had a kind of episode. As one of the first Cinta Larga to adopt a Western diet, he was also one of the first to acquire type 2 diabetes and high blood pressure, and the stress of the arrest had caused a spike. After being seen by a doctor, he was promptly returned to the makeshift cell.

The Federal Police building in Porto Velho, though just a few blocks from the wide, brown Rio Madeira, recalled none of the natural beauty of the forest that had once flourished there. Tucked behind a low concrete wall, it was a single story, also of concrete, with a corrugated metal roof. The only hint of the soaring architectural wonder of Brasília was the blue plastic shelter of a pay phone known as an *orelhão*, or "big ear," for its distinctive shape. Pio was taken to the same little room as Tataré, where there was nothing to do but watch TV. They were soon joined by João Bravo and a man named Amaral, who'd survived the measles outbreak with Pio and Tataré in 1971. (Who could have imagined, back then, that they would find themselves in a place like this?)

It might have been awkward for Pio and João to share this cramped space, after all their conflicts. Tataré, for his part, was one of many Cinta Larga whose relatives had been killed by João in some decades-old intrigue. But Tataré never let his bitterness come to the surface. Whatever their grudges, the survivors of contact shared a bond. They made one another feel less alone, as Tataré once said about Oita. It wasn't the same even with other Cinta Larga. Anytime men like Pio and João got together, they inevitably complained about the youths who spoke Tupi-Mondé all wrong, who lacked the coolheaded skill to hit a *curujpúú* snake with an arrow, who would lose themselves in a minute in unspoiled forest. Not to mention the new generation of "chiefs," whose disdain for the old way of the *zapiway* was so naked.

Pio's rivalry with João was more of a cold war. Outwardly respectful, they would take turns speaking at government meetings—even if Pio suspected that João never fully understood what was going on, as his oratory didn't necessarily match up with the topic being discussed. Beyond his personal feelings, Pio saw the usefulness in making a show of unity. João commanded respect far beyond his own village, and Pio couldn't hope to get the mine under control without him. At Federal Police headquarters now, Pio didn't actually find the detention too unpleasant. Rute brought a fan to cool them off. In Pio's mind, at least it was "a new experience."

*   *   *

In justifying the arrests, Inspector Sousa cited allegations that included not only illegal diamond extraction but "*evasão de divisas* [spiriting money abroad], tax evasion, receiving stolen goods, theft, larceny, extortion, false imprisonment, homicide, unlawful possession of a firearm, etc." Hiding the more personal resentment he'd hinted at in the press, he wrote of the Federal Police's ongoing embarrassment, the affronts that amounted to nothing less than the "demoralization of the State." He also adopted a pose of social concern, lamenting that the suspects were "benefiting in detriment to the Indigenous community, which is threatened by the growing number of prospectors in the region." And he added, "Indigenous rights do not authorize the committing of crimes."

In reality, a special jurisprudence existed for so-called *silvícolas*, or "jungle-dwellers": those deemed "isolated" or "integrating" were said to possess "incomplete mental development," and thus to merit attenuated sentences. On the one hand, this tradition was clearly racist, a legacy of the social Darwinism that relegated the Indigenous to an earlier stage of human evolution. On the other, it made sense: how could someone unaware of the existence of laws be punished for killing an invader?

The problem came in defining who fit into which category. To prove that Pio and the other chiefs were already "integrated and adapted to civilized society," Sousa took on the role of anthropologist, citing the fact that "they maintain their residences in cities near the area of their natural habitat [*sic*]; they possess voter registration, identification documents, [tax registration], driver's licenses, cellphones, and luxurious vehicles; they founded and preside over associations." He even read into their emotional state, claiming they were "taking a certain liking to life in society and the indulgences that money can provide."

To Sousa, as to many other white outsiders, assimilation was almost mathematical: if an Indian used a cell phone, then she understood the law; if she lived in Brazilian society, then she was effectively a white person. He didn't consider the opposite scenario: that a white person could become an Indian simply by donning a feather headdress (to cite a comparison the Cinta Larga never tired of). Nor did he presumably believe that a true German, say, had to wear leather breeches.

Pio, meanwhile, couldn't resolve these questions even for himself, and he wasn't alone. Tataré would state the dilemma out loud: "I don't know if I'm white, if I'm Indian....I don't know what I am." As much as they yearned to possess the white man's things, they never felt at home in the white man's cities, never felt at ease like when they bathed in the River of Rapids—the Roosevelt. As much as they did business with white men, they never quite understood how white men's minds worked—how a life could be an individual timeline in which the future grew logically from one's own actions, missteps, investments, divorced from the fate of one's family, one's tribe. Learning about money, similarly, was like learning the white man's language: the grammar never quite felt natural. It was no different for learning about the state or its laws, which to whites were a given, like the air they breathed.

Authorizing their arrests, the judge dispensed with this quandary in a couple of sentences. In his estimation, the mere fact the chiefs acquired mining equipment, hired prospectors, and sold diamonds was sufficient proof they were "perfectly integrated into so-called *'civilized'* society, being aware of the illegality of their acts." (He also tried some armchair anthropology of his own, speculating that their "thirst for *'easy profit'*" was "certainly acquired through proximity to the *'white man'* [*sic*].")

In a rare stab of good fortune, a Public Ministry lawyer named Raquel Dodge intervened. As she explained in a letter to the judge, she'd just persuaded Pio and João Bravo to help investigate the larger players at the mine—not just the usual local businessmen and low-ranking officials but big-time politicians and power brokers. Not only were the two chiefs "putting their own lives at risk," they'd also been led to believe they wouldn't be arrested if they backed a second shutdown. In return, all they expected was emergency aid. These negotiations, she said, were now "gravely compromised."

The judge was forced to reverse course, releasing the four men after less than a week. But the Federal Police appeared unchastened. Another inspector told a reporter, "The arrests are essentially didactic in nature, to show that anyone who commits infractions on Indigenous lands can be arrested, whether he is white, Black, or Indian. Now they'll think twice before getting involved in illegal activities."

For Pio, the episode was a kind of revelation: any attempt to escape his situation, to somehow start over, was futile. In a way it was like salt, which once burned his mouth but was now indispensable in any meal. No matter how he pined for the time before contact, when he was a boy dreaming of being a hunter—when the world was smaller, and his father was important to it—he knew there was no way to go back. Through the glass of his newfound religion, he could even see the mine as a gift from God: as destiny.

CHAPTER 24

THE CRAZY ONE

Woshyton Cinta Larga emerged from a shack at Roosevelt Village with a machete in hand. He slid the blade through the seat handle of a rusting Honda motorcycle, wedged the tip between exhaust pipe and chassis, and tied it in place with a plastic bag. "The bush gets thick where we're going," he explained. He was going to take a pair of journalists to the Stream of the Blackflies, a job he did for a small fee. He pushed his bike down a hill, leaping on the seat as he revved the engine—the only way to start it, because the battery was dead. Seventeen years old, he wore a child-size backpack over a black hoodie. The two journalists followed on a motorcycle of their own.

It was not yet dawn; clouds hung low in the dark blue sky. Woshyton's parents were old enough to remember a time before combustion engines, but now the high-pitched flap hardly made anyone stir. Crossing the Roosevelt River, the tires double-clacked the wooden bridge slats; then Woshyton hit a long straightaway of dirt and gunned it. As the canopy closed in, wheel ruts deepened into swamped-out gullies, puddles winking with fresh droplets of rain. The trick, the journalists saw, was actually to avoid the rain-slick hardpack in between. Rounding a bend, Woshyton's back tire slipped out from under him, but he pushed off the ground with one foot, like a dancer. Now and then he plunged into tight shortcuts through the trees where he paused to hack at fresh tendrils of green reaching across. The journalists, less agile, sometimes fell sideways into the mud.

Nearing the Stream of the Blackflies, the group came upon an old Toyota Land Cruiser with dusty plastic barrels of diesel in the flatbed; a man lay underneath as three others stood by. "Flat tire," one of them offered. He was older than the others, with pale skin and black hair that looked dyed. "Did you come from town?"

"We're going to the mine," Woshyton said, answering a question no one had asked. But the man didn't press for more. By now he had to know that any Cinta Larga kid could be the son of a chief. Woshyton was a nephew of Rondonzinho, which gave him a certain status—though he himself remained, according to the new ideas in circulation, poor.

Lacking a TV at home, Woshyton would often go to Rondonzinho's to watch soccer matches. Boys no longer dreamed of hunting jaguar or harpy eagle; they dreamed of being soccer stars, or at least owning the cars and phones shown in halftime ads. Cinta Larga country, they said, was boring; they wanted to go to "the city," where things happened. Now that they all lived in individual homes, elders no longer woke them in the predawn cold to dip in the stream and hear stories. Just about the only time they went into the forest to gather *açaí* straw or flute-bamboo or to strip the inner bark of the *wabép* tree to make the traditional belts, it was an activity sponsored by the state education department, dubbed "cultural rescue," with transport by motor vehicle. The department also hired a middle-aged Cinta Larga man as *sabedor de histórias*, literally the "story knower." But he couldn't always remember the details. Mostly he just hung out on the patio of the village school to make sure he got paid.

Thanks to TV, the outside world wasn't so foreign to this new generation. "Woshyton" was just Washington misspelled; one kid was actually named Wesley Snipes Cinta Larga. What remained a mystery was how to enter this other world. Pio was always talking about the importance of *educação*. The village school even started a class for young mothers. But the teachers, mostly white people from the Amazon frontier, couldn't always answer their questions: *Are there Indians in the United States? Have any graduated from college? Are there Indian doctors, Indian lawyers?* In a way, the new generation received an education similar to what existed before contact, when kids learned simply by observing adults. Now they saw that the way to acquire a phone or a car—to acquire anything of value in this new world of money—was by selling hardwood, selling diamonds. The older generations used to know a thousand footpaths marked only by broken twigs and twisted leaves; Woshyton's knew the crude roads carved by loggers and prospectors. The older generations used to live by rainy season and dry, monkeys and macaws, fruits and flowers; Woshyton's tracked the rhythms of outlaws and police. What had once seemed like upheaval came to feel routine.

*   *   *

By September 2003, the mine had fallen into an interminable cycle of shutdowns, threats, reopenings, investigations. Drawn back into the confusion, Pio finally rallied his people to attempt something new: "no corporations, no prospectors." Under the bill to allow mining on Indigenous lands, he'd realized they would receive an insultingly low royalty, just 2.5 percent. But he seized upon an idea from the white men who favored legalization.

While it remained illegal to bring in outsiders, the language of the 1988 constitution appeared to allow prospecting on Indigenous lands as long as it was only Indigenous people doing the work. In the interpretation of one expert, this covered only *faiscagem*—a word that refers to the sparks that fly when you strike metal with metal, which is to say, digging with a pickaxe. The Cinta Larga could, in theory, comb through the gravel already upturned by previous waves of prospectors—or at least tell the authorities that's what they were doing. As Pio put it in a letter to the Public Ministry, "We have decided not to work with white men anymore, but on our own, extracting what is necessary to sustain ourselves."

In protest, a hundred prospectors blocked Highway 364. In that same letter, Pio complained, "We are being monitored and threatened by criminals, [and] can't even leave the village when we need to buy food." Professional stickup men staked out the roads. One crew stopped Roberto Carlos in his truck, ordered him out, and drove off with it. Another strung a cord across one of their roads, yanking Pio's eldest daughter off a motorcycle to rob her. For a while, though, the trouble seemed worth it—almost like a return to a past time of independence, when the idea of relying on outside assistance, much less being ruled by some distant foreign power, was inconceivable. "The Indians' self-esteem was running high," one Funai agent noted, "as despite the pressures from prospectors and investors, they were holding firm.... Dissension in the villages ended, and the true leaders reemerged."

In November, Pio and the other chiefs even invited sympathetic officials to visit what was termed the "defunct Lajes mine." All along the Stream of the Blackflies, fresh jungle was already surging into the spaces between pits, old shelters collapsing into the mud. It looked like a landscape at war with itself, nature reclaiming what had been lost to human enterprise, except that the humans hadn't made a full retreat. In previous incursions, the authorities had used tractors to haul dozens of jigs into a jumbled pile of scrap. In the Amazonian wet, the metal rusted fast, turning the same color as the earth. Yet many jigs remained upright, perched on pit edges, ready to receive the slurry pumped by two dozen pairs of machines. The Cinta Larga also ran the odd excavator, the bulldozer with a hydraulic backhoe. They didn't try to hide it, but claimed there were only two white men, "mechanics," at the whole operation. Most chiefs felt they simply couldn't do without their expertise. One Cinta Larga man had already died when a pit wall collapsed, burying him.

Despite all this activity, the mine was nothing like before, when gunfire could be heard at all hours, and the only way to stay safe was to be *velhaco*—wily. "The impression is of peace and order," one of the officials wrote.

The problem was the same one as always: invaders. In the shallow valley of the Stream of the Blackflies, water collected from rainfall and a multitude of springs, forming sub-tributaries too small to appear on any map, which cut little valleys of their own. As the main line of the stream had grown crowded, prospectors explored these waterways in hopes of finding new deposits. Some proved rich enough to gain a name, such as Grota Nova, the New Gully. Many others, nearly four years after Old Luca found the first stones, remained untapped. Just past the New Gully, over a hill thick with forest and into another mini-valley, was one such area. Its name would become infamous: Grota do Sossego, the Gully of Tranquility.

Even after all the uproar in the press, the government maintained just a handful of checkpoints, and they weren't always manned. For several weeks in late 2003, state cops were removed from the posts entirely, apparently due to budget shortfalls; then, in early 2004, the Federal Police went on strike. As it turned out, the only thing worse than heavy-handed enforcement was no enforcement, as wildcats found it ever easier to sneak in. The Cinta Larga started noticing that food was going missing from camp freezers, parts being stolen from under the hoods of cars.

It was March when wildcats stumbled upon the Gully of Tranquility, a name they picked because the Cinta Larga couldn't bother them there. Though just two miles from the heart of the mine, the site never exceeded a thousand feet from end to end—and to keep it secret, the prospectors used only shovels, pickaxes, and sieves. They couldn't risk the noise of the usual machines, but they hardly needed to, because the gully was so rich, you barely had to dig to find stones. Rumor had it blue diamonds even turned up there. As usual, one prospector gossiped to another. By the beginning of April, it looked to one of them like a "homeless encampment," with two hundred men and a handful of women sleeping under black plastic tarps.

Many at the gully had previously entered the mine with permission. Walter da Silva had been hired as a "mechanic," that euphemism for white prospectors. According to a statement he later gave to the police, he'd produced nearly two hundred diamonds, possibly worth as much as $250,000, for his Cinta Larga business partner. Before he could receive his cut, though, his partner vanished. Antonio Marcos de Almeida would tell the police how his own Cinta Larga partner had driven him from town to Vila Bradesco, just south of Marafon's ranch. To skirt the checkpoint, he'd hopped out early and entered the mine via the "back door." But his partner never showed up at the agreed-upon meeting spot.

Some friends and family would swear that, as far as they knew, the wildcats had gone to the Gully of Tranquility to work for the Indians. The girlfriend of a prospector nicknamed Sem Rede (No Hammock) claimed he'd been invited by Maria Beleza. It wouldn't have been the first time a Cinta Larga broke their own agreed-upon rules. But the prospectors may well have been lying to keep loved ones from worrying. Others admitted they were going of their own accord, despite the risks.

The gully didn't stay secret for long. Warriors on patrol found fresh human tracks in the area; they searched the surrounding forest but found nothing. It was early April when Pio joined a contingent of Funai agents and state cops on a sweep of their own, but they didn't find anything either. Ultimately it was one of the wildcats themselves, possibly hoping to curry favor with the chiefs, who revealed the gully's location. Arriving at the Stream of the Blackflies, he spoke of two hundred *rodados* "stealing" from the Indians there. They were led by a man known as Baiano Doido, the Crazy One from Bahia, whom the Cinta Larga already knew well.

* * *

As his nickname suggested, Francisco das Chagas Alves Saraiva hailed from Bahia, on Brazil's northeastern coast. He was around forty years old, stout, with dark skin, a long ponytail, and a full beard. Initially, like many other wildcats, he'd entered the mine with permission. But it hadn't gone well for him. In October 2003, he'd been invited to speak at an official inquiry by Rondônia's state assembly, in Espigão's oddly well-apportioned Municipal Hall, where beds of bright red flowers cradled palm trees, and an air conditioner sat above every window. "They're such liars," he said of the chiefs. "They charged me 35,000 *reais*"—around $17,500—"to enter with my machines....Then the mine closed again. The Federal Police were called in. We had to leave, and we left our machines buried there. To start working again, we had to pay another 15,000 *reais*, but when we got there our machines were gone. So I had to buy someone else's machines there...for 25,000 *reais*." Then, once more, Baiano was forced to leave. "And when I asked to take my machines with me, they"—the Cinta Larga—"refused to authorize it. So what happened? I lost everything yet again."

Baiano's words came out in a torrent, jumping from one bizarre accusation to another. He said he'd tried to alert the authorities to alleged killings by Cinta Larga warriors, but "the chiefs give orders to move the bodies of the prospectors who were massacred. You get there with the Federal Police and they think you're a liar." His syntax was tortuous; sometimes the meaning was difficult to decipher at all. He said something about prospectors' flesh being consumed by the bugs in the ground. "Everyone says it's a lie, but it's the pure truth. [The Indians'] feathers, their weapons made of wood—none of that exists anymore. Now it's all steel, it's all machine guns, it's AR-15s. Now they have three guns they bought for 400,000 *reais*, that shoot four hundred bullets per minute—for what? To wait for prospectors to come in, and it's Funai who is arming them, and there are people here in Espigão who carry boxes upon boxes of ammunition to them...."

One of the assemblymen interrupted to clarify where the Indians had acquired this heavy weaponry. "It came on João Bravo's plane," Baiano declared—needless to say, pure fantasy.

The inquiry was little more than a political show, an official forum for prospectors to air their grievances. That was the Amazon frontier, where politicians backed ranchers, rubber barons, loggers, never mind if they were breaking the law. The Municipal Hall itself was named for one of the Melhorança brothers, Espigão's founding fathers, who'd forged the titles to much of the land.

As for Baiano, he'd recently been charged with armed robbery in Cacoal. According to the accusation, while working at the Stream of the Blackflies, he would alert his crew when an unsuspecting prospector was heading back to sell diamonds. In February 2003, the crew had shot a man and fled in a panic without even taking his stones. Baiano was acquitted for lack of evidence, but he bragged to anyone who would listen about crimes he *had* committed. If Rondônia's state assembly had invited the Cinta Larga to give their point of view, they might have heard a statement like this one, later given anonymously to a pair of anthropologists: "Baiano Doido told me that he's a real man, a fearless killer—not a thief, a killer. That he killed more than twenty men at a gold prospect in Mato Grosso." Even one of Baiano's own friends said he smoked so much coca paste—a substance that is halfway to refined cocaine but still contains kerosene—that it fried his brain. He was said to have taken a shit in the back of a Cinta Larga's truck, just to show his disdain. Perhaps the best proof he deserved his nickname, the Crazy One, was that he threatened Cinta Larga men to their faces. Just recently, he'd shown up at Tataré's home, shouting—he was always shouting— "Where's my money?"

"What money?" Tataré asked. Little did he know, Baiano had been working on a pair of machines owned by Tataré's daughter, but never received his cut of around $400 from a recent sale.

"Didn't your daughter sell my diamonds?" Baiano demanded.

"I don't owe you anything," Tataré replied. "I'll tell my daughter to pay you."

"I'm not joking around," Baiano said. "I'll kill you."

Finally, Tataré handed over some cash, and Baiano went on his way. In some ways, his reputation resembled that of another prospector, Sapecado—Maria Beleza's tormentor—except worse. In the words of another Cinta Larga: "I heard Baiano say his dream was to do away with all the Indians at the mine."

*   *   *

There are many versions of what took place at the Gully of Tranquility in April 2004. Among prospectors, the usual rumormongering went into overdrive. Among Cinta Larga, questioning by outsiders was often met with misdirection. Still, between the two sides, along with statements from government officials in the vicinity, enough details line up to tell the story with relative confidence.

There's little question the Cinta Larga tried to avoid violence, at least at first. After they received word of Baiano's invasion, the chiefs sent three of their own white mine workers—Pula Pula (Jumpy), Pomada (Pomade), and Ceará (a Brazilian state)—to the Gully of Tranquility. They gave Baiano a message: "Leave now, or the Indians will remove you." But Baiano just scoffed: "The Indians aren't in charge anymore. We are." Brandishing a gun, he even ordered one of the messengers to his knees and threatened to kill him, before finally letting him go. "There were a lot of prospectors there," another wildcat would recall. "[Baiano] didn't think they could kill everyone."

Tataré, that keeper of Cinta Larga stories, again found himself in the middle of one. The chief of Roosevelt Village, Carlão, asked him to join a reconnaissance mission with six other warriors. Though only two miles away as the crow flies, it was a long slog up and down mucky hills, through dense forest, and over rivulets that, in the dry season, shrank to pools perfect for beating with the *dakáptapóa* vine, with its poison that asphyxiates fish. Tataré couldn't help remembering when he was a little kid and his parents took him to the feast in this very same valley: "It was beautiful to me, so many people dancing, playing those flutes, climbing trees. Everyone was happy, drinking *i*....And then my mother began to feel sick." Now, more than three decades later, here he was in the very same place where the white man's disease first spread, looking for prospectors—always prospectors, their hunger for wealth pulling Cinta Larga history in one direction or another.

Tataré didn't get to see the Gully of Tranquility with his own eyes. Going back to the time before contact, his people had always tried to tilt the field of battle in their favor—and once he got close enough to hear the clacking of pickaxes, he knew Baiano's incursion was a major one. Lacking the numbers to confront them, he and Carlão turned around. They were on their way back to the mine when they noticed a large group of white men tramping through the forest in their direction. One was carrying a sawn-off shotgun. Before they could react, Carlão shouted, "Put it down or we'll shoot!"

There were fifteen white men in the group, but the rest were unarmed, and they all surrendered without a fight. "Why are you going that way if the mine is this way?" one of the warriors asked. "Didn't you see the road?" Another warrior gently told them just to go to the mine next time, because if there was work to be done, the Cinta Larga would employ them. "Don't come back here," he added, "because something bad will happen if you do."

Most wildcats weren't crazy like Baiano Doido. By now they knew the routine. Despite the warriors' bloodthirsty fame, in the vast majority of cases, invaders would be handed over to the police, arrested, and hauled back to town. There was never enough evidence to hold them for long, so they could try their luck again in no time. This time looked no different. The warriors walked the white men to a pair of pickup trucks on the nearest road, then drove them to the checkpoint known as Onça Pintada, or Spotted Jaguar. One police officer noted that none of the wildcats had been tied up or harmed in any way.

Handing over their prisoners, the warriors warned in no uncertain terms that, if the authorities didn't remove the invaders, *they* would. The cops hastened to point out they weren't equipped for the job. For one thing, they lacked a four-wheel-drive vehicle. Mere state police, they would also need reinforcements. The Cinta Larga offered up their own trucks, and warriors, for the mission, but the officers said they couldn't act without an order from their superiors, in any case.

By now the sun was setting, plunging fast, as it does this close to the equator. The whole way back to the mine, Tataré and the others discussed what to do. It should have been clear that the cops had no interest in helping. Typically assigned for a monthlong stint with automatic hardship pay, they had little incentive to get involved beyond controlling who went in. They were scared of the jungle, scared of wildcats, scared of the Indians, too. Meanwhile, time was of the essence. Baiano had already claimed a piece of Cinta Larga country as his own. Now it seemed he was forming a kind of army, the better to defend his claim. How many fresh recruits were already on their way? How many more carried guns?

*   *   *

Pio kept his own shack at the Stream of the Blackflies. Mostly, as he lay in his hammock at night, he thought about business. But there were also times when, just like Tataré, he couldn't help remembering when he was small, and he used to come here with his father, Mankalu, and splash around with kids from nearby villages. The forest was a babel of smells then—pig musk, cherrywood—smells now overpowered by diesel. It was a babel of sounds—bassy roaring frogs, multimelodic birdsong—all drowned out now by flapping, whirring machines. Roberto Carlos had grown up here; how long it had been since he took little Pio under his wing! Now it was Roberto who couldn't bear to spend the night there, and Pio who took charge. Not to say that Pio didn't feel the same sadness. As a young man he used to play that song on his flute, *"Father, Daddy, where did you go?"* But he'd learned to put those feelings away, like diamonds jammed into a section of bamboo and sealed with tape.

The workday over, generators at the mine were shutting down, others at camp heaving to life. Light bulbs flicked on, pale echoes of the earliest stars. Under the usual roofs of plastic tarp, prospectors lined up to shovel rice and beans and stewed meat onto their plates. Cinta

Larga men liked to joke they had no time to eat: anytime was good. Some filled their plate at one tent only to refill at another. A kind of camaraderie had sprouted between the two groups, as both came to see the Federal Police as their antagonist. While they never fully overcame their distrust, some Cinta Larga actually adopted the prospectors' political views, decrying the environmentalists who, the theory went, wanted to secure the Amazon's riches for foreign powers.

As soon as Tataré returned with the others, there was little question what to do. Of all the traditions that had fallen into disuse, one never faltered: the village meeting. The mine, of course, wasn't exactly a village, but wooden benches had been set out for that purpose in a little clearing not far from the stream itself. So many people came that not everyone could sit. Even white mine workers were invited, though they understood little of what was said.

All these years after the first prospectors were sighted on the Roosevelt, the outlines of the debate had changed remarkably little. Despite their warrior tradition, there had always been Cinta Larga willing to give outsiders the benefit of the doubt, to offer the customary greeting, *pa ikinin pa mã*—"Let's have a look at one another." Now it was Pio who took up this banner, saying, "Let's work in peace."

Oita had always been a contradictory sort of loner, alienated from his people even as he claimed to be one of their leaders. Now he could feel his hard-won recognition slipping away. He'd just been released from jail pending trial for illegal mining, receiving stolen goods, and conspiracy. The courts were seizing his cars, threatening to take away his mansion. Despite his hotheaded temperament, he didn't want to provoke the authorities further. He knew what it felt like when the state put its thumb on you. Sometimes he had trouble breathing. He even went to a doctor for this, receiving some pills to "make my head more peaceful." He, too, called for calm.

As for João Bravo, no matter how much he venerated the old days, when only a great warrior could become *zapiway*, leadership, he understood, also meant knowing the limits of your power. Even when he'd detained Mauro the Bomb, the Federal Police inspector, the act had been largely symbolic. Despite his fame for being *bravo*—wild—he was, like Pio, a realist at heart. Violence was bad for business, and it was business that, in today's world, allowed a chief to fulfill his duties. It was better, he said, to wait for Funai and the police to do their jobs.

To a Western observer, it might look like the other Cinta Larga weren't paying attention—staring at the ground, fiddling with twigs or picking their fingernails. But they hung on every word. Even those who detested Oita didn't want white men deciding who could lead them. If their chiefs went to prison, who would provide the few comforts they now enjoyed? It's unclear if Maria Beleza spoke that day, but this was hardly the first such meeting. Every time there was an invasion, there were those who simply said, "Let's kill them," and Maria always took the other side. She'd spent whole days sweeping the forest for wildcats, trying to save their lives—reinventing, in this way, the meaning of being a warrior. Despite what her own people had put her through, she was proud to be Cinta Larga. She wanted to keep the warriors from "dirtying the Cinta Larga name."

There was an even larger danger, too. Right now, despite the investigations by the Federal Police, the Cinta Larga still had friends in the Public Ministry, in Congress, among big-city activists and the ranks of Funai itself. But if the state truly wanted—if its inertia was finally overwhelmed by the clamoring of settlers, businessmen, TV pundits, and politicians—the Army could take over tomorrow. At worst, the Cinta Larga might lose control of the territory they'd fought so hard to keep. At best, they would be deprived of this once-in-a-lifetime chance to turn their natural wealth into prosperity, in its Western form. Once they had been contacted, back in the 1960s, there was no way they could have avoided the diseases or the massacres. But Pio still believed they could avoid the fate of so many other once-proud warriors, now reduced to poor people.

The Cinta Larga would always be reluctant to name their own warriors—that old taboo revived—some out of fear of retaliation, others out of solidarity, not wanting to incriminate their group. What can be said is that, while most voices for peace came from Roosevelt Village, most of the others hailed from the east. Traditions remained more intact there—especially the warrior tradition that Pio's father had once followed, but Pio, now, clearly did not. These men weren't like Pio or Oita or Tataré or Roberto Carlos, who'd lived side by side with Brazilians since they were young, had even met those rare white people with good hearts, like Apoena and his late father, Chico. "Funai never settles anything," one of the warriors said. "The police never settle anything. They remove the prospectors and the prospectors just come back."

Another chimed in, "Every time Funai and the police came in for an operation to remove prospectors, I joined them as a driver. And we took the prospectors and delivered them to the police station. But the invaders were never put in jail. Nothing happened to them at all. The police would explain that they couldn't jail the prospectors because there was no *in flagrante*. That same day, those prospectors would come back in here again. And they would even threaten us and say, 'You're delivering us to the police. One day we'll get fed up. And we'll kill you Indians.'" The warriors had had enough—not only of the prospectors themselves, but of would-be leaders like Pio, who always tried to rein them in.

Then there was Baiano Doido himself. The warriors had already removed him before. Still he threatened violence. Not only that, as another man pointed out, he was making these affronts "inside our home." Yet another agreed: "You can't make threats on our land."

For a long time, the two sides went back and forth like this:

"Don't hurt them. Just let them work."

"And what if they kill us?"

"We're not scared of dying. Let's wait for Funai."

"If Baiano wants to come and kill us, the police won't be here to protect us."

As one participant later described it, "We couldn't arrive at the same thinking. And during the conversation, one person started remembering the past. Another started remembering. They remembered...all the deaths that took place at [the Stream of the Blackflies] and also before that. They remembered every white man who harmed us, the diseases. They told of the many killings carried out by rubber tappers, prospectors—all of our old relatives who died at the white men's hands. And they asked one person after another, 'What do you think?'"

More than a few worried that the invaders could carry out another Massacre of the Eleventh Parallel, just like in 1963. In some ways they felt almost as vulnerable as back then. After all the broken promises, all the barbarism of "development," they could hardly swallow the rhetoric about trusting the Brazilian state. One participant said, "My uncle, my aunt, father, mother, everyone died. At eight years old I was already being attacked by the white man." And another: "My family was massacred, too." According to the concept of *wepíka*, these deaths weren't isolated events, homicides committed by individuals with no connection to one another. Each death was added to a running tally with white men on one side and Cinta Larga on the other. There was no escaping your debt, because there was no escaping who you were.

When Pio called for calm, he spoke not with the empty morality of a bureaucrat seeking to impose the white man's law, but with the authority of someone who'd suffered the same tragedies. Funai had spread measles to Pio's own father; now here Pio was, asking the warriors to trust Funai. Oita, for his part, had led two prospectors back to his own village, only for their poison to kill his family. Now here he was, asking for mercy on prospectors: "I used to think all white men were evil. I used to be angry. Not anymore."

The warriors always came back to Baiano and his threats. "It's him or us," said one. "We have to do it before he does," said another.

Of course, consensus was needed only for *inaction*. Whether or not everyone agreed, the warriors couldn't be dissuaded: they would go to the Gully of Tranquility and remove Baiano and his crew. All Pio could do was remind them that the principle of *wepíka* wasn't exclusive to the Cinta Larga. Any bloodshed would be met with a response, whether from prospectors on the street or from the Brazilian state with its police, its courts, and its prisons. "All the warriors knew they weren't to hurt or kill anyone," one participant later recalled. "They were only to take the prospectors and deliver them to the checkpoint."

Pio, meanwhile, would head to Roosevelt Village to beg the authorities to intervene.

CHAPTER 25

APRIL 7

I t wasn't so long ago that, on the eve of battle, warriors would dance
all night, drinking *i* until they vomited, repeating this until it was
time to venture forth with a light, insomniac buzz. This time, when
morning came and people emerged from tents to sip sugary coffee
from plastic thermoses, the warriors just drove along the Stream of the
Blackflies in a few pickup trucks, asking able-bodied men to join the
mission. They recruited a few from other groups, such as the Apuriná,
connected to the Cinta Larga through Pio's marriage to Rute, and the
Zoró, those onetime enemies who had themselves once sought their
neighbors' help in removing invaders.

The most precise memories put the number of warriors at
fifty-three. Many were old veterans of battles past, from the eastern
part of Cinta Larga country, but a few from Roosevelt Village piled in.
They also gathered up teenagers, saying, "You're young, you don't know
how things are done, but we're going to show you." Then they painted
themselves with jaguar spots and sang songs, like in the old days. The
precise words have been lost, but the melodies were remembered from
the time before contact, some intoned with high-pitched voices, others deep in the throat, in call-and-response. The motifs, too, were the

same as always: the warriors were jaguars, apex predators, their enemies monkeys or tapirs—defenseless prey.

The war party drove to the point where they would have to abandon the road and walk. A few witnesses saw them on their way, noticing the black *wesuáá* dye painted on bare chests, the bows and arrows, axes, and heavy wooden clubs, also the twelve-gauge shotguns, Winchester rifles, and .380 caliber pistols. One prospector would claim he saw a Funai official driving one of the trucks, but this was almost certainly fiction, as it became almost a point of pride for the Cinta Larga to insist that no white men were involved. Another prospector would claim he himself was on his way to the gully when men from another Indigenous group, the Rikbaktsa, warned that the warriors were going to kill everyone there. But it's not clear how the Rikbaktsa would have known this.

As late as that morning, at least some of the war party believed the authorities might join the mission. According to one account, they actually waited on the road for a while, just in case Funai or the state police showed up. If they had, the outcome might have been different. But the warriors got tired of waiting, and plunged into the trees on their own. Even then, the debate hadn't concluded, as the men stopped multiple times along the way to discuss their plan. Recounting the events later to their fellow Cinta Larga, some would let on that they'd always intended, if nothing else, to kill Baiano. Others, unaware of this, still thought the goal was merely to "arrest" everyone. The teenagers carried only the featherless arrows known as *sala ip*, used for practicing on little birds. One small encounter also suggested that, at least at that point, the warriors could show restraint: they ran into two wildcats heading back to town to be treated for malaria, and let them continue on their way.

On the prospectors' side, the first sign of what was coming went unheeded. That morning, a wildcat nicknamed Brabinho (Feisty) was about to start work at the gully when he noticed two Indians in the trees, scouts observing the operation. But he didn't think much of it, and nobody else saw them. Unlike the Stream of the Blackflies, where all the trees had been knocked down, the horizon here was jungle-short, with an intact canopy that kept the gully dim. Most of the two hundred wildcats were working in one of eight narrow, shallow trenches dug without the aid of water jets. They sorted through their haul the hard way, like Old Luca had done, dumping the muddy gravel into sieves, dunking it in the rivulet, flicking and whirling until the odd glint shone through.

It was around 11:00 a.m. when the larger war party approached. Going back to the old days, the Cinta Larga had always favored ambushes, though there was more to it than that. Waiting for the moment to strike, some used to tie leaves into knots believed to deafen their targets, while also focusing the warriors' attention, keeping it from straying to matters of the home. Those were the days when warriors would boldly creep into their enemies' houses at night, to club them to death in their hammocks. Now the plan was to quietly surround the gully so that no one could escape. But it seems they'd abandoned the old magic or at the very least were out of practice. "Look at the Indians!" a wildcat shouted. And then another: "We've been found!"

The men in the trenches started chaotically clambering out until one of the warriors leaped inside and shouted, "Stop right there, prospectors! Get on the ground!" It's impossible to say whether the warriors started shooting once the wildcats attempted to flee, or whether the wildcats fled because the warriors started shooting. In any case, once the first shot was fired, the shooting became near-continuous. In the confusion, one wildcat mistakenly ran *toward* the warriors. Another was trying to escape up a hill when he knocked into a cook and fell to the ground. Yet another thought he heard the rapid-fire volleys of a machine gun. But there's no evidence the Cinta Larga ever possessed heavy weaponry of any kind, and the only person known to have been hit during the initial onslaught was a man known as Sarrapilha (Burlap), struck in the foot by a stray shotgun pellet. One group of wildcats was digging in a separate area perhaps a mile from the main gully, and thought at first that the shots might be Indians hunting monkeys. They kept working for the better part of an hour, until they heard the shots coming closer, along with screams of "Run! Run!"

Having previously worked at the Stream of the Blackflies, some wildcats would later claim to have recognized their attackers, even with their faces painted. Others would claim to have seen at least one white man among the Indians—or at least they assumed he was white from his mustache. They also described "white" voices shouting, "Put a bullet in these fuckers! Shoot!" Of course, even if any of this was true, these could have been Apurinã or the Cinta Larga sons of mixed marriages, who grew up speaking Portuguese. Prospectors also claimed to have seen Funai vests among their attackers, but they may have confused them with the official-looking Pamaré vests that read INSPECTOR.

For all the warriors' fear the wildcats might be armed, just one of theirs came away wounded: a teenager with a bullet lodged in his leg.

*　*　*

Baiano Doido didn't even try to run. Some believe he had an injured foot from an accident at the gully. One wildcat, before fleeing, heard him say he was going to negotiate. He shouted for the others to stay put, too. He was supposed to be their leader, but only a handful obeyed.

At this point, the only accounts come from the warriors themselves. Passed from one Cinta Larga to another, they became history in the old way, through collective retelling. On one fact there is full agreement: the warriors had no intention of negotiating. They demanded that Baiano surrender, but he insisted on standing his ground: "Let me work!"

One of the warriors pleaded, "Just go, man. I don't want to hurt you. For the love of God, just go. I'm ordering you. I'm ordering you *now*."

No other wildcat would have been foolish enough to persist at this point. But with each back-and-forth, Baiano only worked himself up more. Abandoning any pretense of dialogue, he sputtered insults: "You Indians don't know anything about prospecting. We do." He didn't realize, or didn't care, how serious all of this was—how, by laying claim to their territory, he was conjuring the ghosts of so many past invasions, so many past deaths. Like so many other outsiders going back five hundred years, he didn't see the Amazon's original inhabitants as people with a moral right to their territory, but as wild creatures to be purged so the land could be made productive, so he could make his fortune. He even said it to their face: *animals*. When a warrior asked why he was being so stubborn, he responded, "Because I have a family to feed. I'm Brazilian and I have to work for a living. You Indians have all this land and you don't work. You're lazy."

"He's no worker," one Cinta Larga scoffed. "All he does is dig holes like an armadillo."

Another spoke to Baiano directly: "Go now. I don't want to use my arrow."

Still Baiano was defiant. Living up to his fame as the Crazy One, he threatened to come back and kill them all. You didn't need an anthropologist to explain why this was such a provocation. In the Cinta Larga tradition, though, he was committing *akwésotá*, "bad talk." Traditionally, of course, this was an offense equivalent to physical violence, all but obliging the receiver of the insult to respond in kind. As one Cinta Larga put it, "He was asking to be killed." Another finally ended the conversation with a phrase in Tupi-Mondé: "That's enough mockery from you."

The first arrowhead poked from Baiano's back. The string of a Cinta Larga bow was left thrumming. Then came another, and another, the six-foot bamboo stalks almost seeming to sprout from his body, bright red and blue feathers briefly vibrating. Wildcats hiding in the trees later claimed to have heard him shouting in agony, "Oh! Don't do that to me. Just kill me now..." Among the Cinta Larga, though, the story goes that he kept laughing even as the arrows went through him, finally leaving a total of eleven inside his body.

Two other wildcats were standing next to him. One, never identified by name, was struck by four arrows. The other, known as Irmão (Brother), was shot with a gun. The warriors dug a shallow grave by a tree and dragged the bodies into it.

*   *   *

According to those wildcats who managed to flee, the shooting finally died out around 1:00 p.m. They waited a few more hours, completely silent, to make sure the warriors had left. Sarrapilha, who'd taken a shotgun pellet to the foot, limped back to the gully with several others to retrieve buried diamonds. They found their shelters smoldering. Following a trail of blood, they came upon Baiano's body in a pile with the two others, covered perfunctorily by some earth and branches. Some would claim to have seen additional bodies there, but if they existed, they were never found. There were also more fantastical rumors. A cook claimed to have seen bloody condoms on the ground—again, something no investigator saw.

One group of survivors made it back to Espigão that same day.

Arilton Carlos dos Santos worked as a contractor for the Pamaré Association, building village improvements and transporting diesel in his Mercedes-Benz truck. He was on his way to Espigão when, by the side of the road, he saw two white men, their clothes soiled with mud and sweat, frayed by so-called cat-scratch plants with their razor-sharp spines. Recognizing them from the mine, he opened up the passenger door and invited them into the cab. They were starting to tell him what they'd witnessed when another man emerged from the bush, followed by several more. Arilton's flatbed was empty, so he told them all to hop in.

Sarrapilha had tried to make his way back with the others in his group, but he was too slow, so they'd left him behind. Alone, he limped through the forest until around 3:00 p.m. the next day, when he ran into a cop on the road near the Onça Pintada checkpoint. Others, though unwounded, took even longer to reach safety. "We spent two days pretty much lost," one Waldemiro Marques later recalled. "Even though we knew the forest well, we were very afraid, seeing Indians where maybe there weren't any, imagining that we were surrounded, hearing noises. All of this made us walk very slowly, because we were so scared that we would be found if we tried to leave right away. On the second day we even ended up back where we started, at the Gully of Tranquility....On the fifth day we started to see machete marks we'd previously left on trees, and finally I managed to figure out where I was and make my way to a trail I knew near the Rio Anta. We walked on this trail for six hours until we reached the Roosevelt River around 11:30 p.m. We stopped there to rest for a while, and at 1:30 a.m. we swam across the river and went to the Bradesco school."

Local whites would come to believe the true number of dead was a staggering *two hundred*. The Indians, the theory went, used the mine's backhoes to bury them in mass graves. While it's impossible to disprove this, the truth is that some survivors simply decided not to go to the police, perhaps out of fear that old warrants would catch up with them, perhaps out of fear that the warriors would find out and finish the job. Polaco (Polish), for instance, had hidden himself in a pile of refuse at the gully, and stopped at Marafon's ranch on his way out. His name would appear on a list of the missing, but he wasn't dead; he'd just moved on.

* * *

What none of the survivors knew—yet—was what had happened to those who remained at the gully. There were at least twenty-six of them. Perhaps imagining that, like so often happened, they would be brought to a checkpoint, arrested, and promptly released, they didn't put up a fight when the warriors tied their hands behind their backs with woody vines and started leading them back toward the Stream of the Blackflies. Other warriors stayed to burn the tents, leaving nothing standing, as their fathers and grandfathers had always done.

The jungle here was unusually dense, the forest architecture long ago disrupted by logging, with vines and bamboo and spindly, fast-growing stalks taking the place of the old giants. Later, when federal agents came by helicopter, they would notice from above how the vegetation looked trampled from some intense commotion. According to some Cinta Larga accounts, one of the warriors overheard a wildcat saying the Indians were small and could be overpowered. According to others, the wildcat was talking about buying firearms in town and returning to kill the Indians. Still others say the warriors simply wanted to eliminate the witnesses. Whatever the truth, the warriors stopped for a brief meeting in Tupi-Mondé, and some kind of consensus was reached.

Hands bound, the wildcats could hardly defend themselves.

Twenty-three apparently accepted their fate, lining up to be killed right then and there. Forensic examiners would actually raise the hypothesis (never substantiated) that the warriors used poison to subdue them. Some were shot with arrows, some beaten with clubs; sometimes the job was finished with a gun. Three victims tried to run, hands still bound. One took a bullet in the brain in a clearing about sixty-five feet away. One was killed with an axe blow to the head a hundred feet farther along. The last one made it another hundred and sixty feet before he was struck by an arrow. Following tradition, the warriors pulled their arrows from the bodies before moving on; only two arrowheads would later be found, broken off inside. Two of the bodies were missing their eyeballs, giving rise to rumors that the warriors had covered the victims' eyes with honey to attract ants and bees. One body was found castrated, the wound reaching all the way to the lower intestine, suggesting a blow of extreme violence. But all of this could have been the work of forest scavengers, which left clear marks on others.

In this forest that Cândido Rondon had once called "monstrously fecund," it didn't take long for the bodies to decompose, to be reused by the Amazon's teeming, voracious life. Speaking to the police, wives and girlfriends would provide intimate details to identify them. A prospector named Ari had a bridge on his lower teeth and a second toe much longer than all the others. Parazinho had a broken front left tooth and wavy graying hair and wore a wedding ring. Cabeça (Head) was missing his incisors and had a faded tattoo on one arm and didn't wear a wedding ring. Cabelo (Hair) had prosthetic incisors, wore a black necklace with a heart-shaped crystal, and had a small scar on the left side of his nose. Antonio had broad shoulders and used to complain of pain in the meniscus of his knee. Pedro was missing the second and third upper molars on both sides of his mouth, and his left knee was always swollen. Maranhão had black skin and a deformed foot and a scar from a bullet wound in his back. Odair had a tattoo of a bee on his left arm. Dourival had the deep mark of a bullet wound in his scalp. Baiano Doido had a faded tattoo of an eye and a sword on his right ankle.

Twelve of the bodies, never identified at all, would be buried in a row of anonymous graves in Espigão. They may have belonged to men who'd already gone missing at some other prospect, elsewhere in the Amazon.

*   *   *

Sometime before lunch on April 7, two Funai officials showed up at Roosevelt Village to discuss Pio's criminal cases. Pio had already made his appeal for help, radioing the Funai base in Cacoal; the agents had promised to intervene but said they couldn't right away. It was the end of the rainy season, and like the cops at the checkpoint, they lacked a suitable vehicle. At that point, an intervention might still have been possible. But the authorities had become inured to the crises of Cinta Larga country. They'd missed the chance to provide the protection promised ever since Chico and Apoena set up their attraction posts. They'd missed the chance to provide a way to make a living—to somehow acquire the things the Cinta Larga had been taught to want—without breaking the law or ravaging the forest. And now it was too late to prevent the bloodbath so many had seen coming. After the officials left that evening, one of the warriors showed up at Roosevelt Village, went to Pio, and said simply, "We fucked up."

"Fucked up how?" Pio asked, a sensation of cold unspooling in his chest. Even as he waited for an answer, word of the killings was spreading in Espigão. Donivaldo would soon be tied up and beaten. When the news reached the national press, Pio—of all people—would become the public face of a gruesome atrocity, rather than the survivor of one. He would later think back to this moment, which, bizarrely mirroring the fateful feast of 1969, forever divided their history into a before—when Pio felt somehow innocent, naive, bumbling through life's ordeals, trying to make the best of a terrible, fascinating new world—and an after, when he saw himself as the Brazilian state now did, as an adult who could be made to pay for his mistakes. He'd wanted to believe there was no contradiction between his quest to save his people and his quest to make his fortune—and in any case, he didn't know a better way. Now he felt the full weight of open-eyed regret, a kind of regret his father could never have imagined, because his world was so much smaller.

But in that moment before everything changed, with the truth still suspended in the air, Roosevelt Village carried on as usual. A pastor fired up a diesel generator to amplify the nightly church service. A few people lay in hammocks, swatting at the mosquitoes that began to feed at this hour, as the plunging sun stained the horizon briefly blood-red. Down by the river, women squatted in the sand to wash pots and pans, the suds spiraling before they dissipated in the flow. In the rushed Amazonian dusk, the Roosevelt River was almost turning black as kids of all ages gathered at the bridge. Laughing and joking in Tupi-Mondé, they kept their clothes on as they leaped into the faintly white-tipped waters, fifteen feet below. It took a second or two for their heads to bob up a short distance downstream. They swam against the rushing current and grabbed at reeds to pull themselves out. Then they scampered back up, leaving wet footprints on the bridge's faded wood, and did it all over again.

EPILOGUE

The first time I traveled to Cinta Larga country, it was raining so hard that, even with the windshield wipers slamming back and forth, the dirt road ahead was a rust-colored blur. I could barely make out the sign that read PROTECTED LAND, pocked by rusting bullet holes; nobody stood guard at the old Federal Police checkpoint. Eventually, though, the rain let up. We crested a hill, and I saw how the landscape had changed. Behind was pale pastureland where ribby cattle huddled from the wet. Ahead was a deep green sea, the forest canopy.

I was tagging along with a Public Ministry official named Reginaldo Trindade, a balding man with a gentle demeanor who was assigned to the Cinta Larga after the 2004 massacre. Pulling into Roosevelt Village, we passed the soccer field and entered a warren of wooden shacks, now interspersed with houses of cement with red-tile roofs. I myself would sleep in a spare room at the village clinic, which, surreally, now had air-conditioning. Electricity, albeit patchy, had finally arrived, with power lines hanging between incongruous streetlamps. The problem, Trindade told me, was that people racked up energy bills they couldn't pay. The government had started issuing monthly welfare checks, but to cash them, people had to spend much of the money on trips to town. Funai sent occasional shipments of rice and beans, but hunting had declined so much that meat now felt like a blessing. Pio's old friend Barroca, once a respected warrior, was one of many who sometimes went hungry. Over the days that followed, he often hinted that he wouldn't mind if I shared my canned sardines with him, so I did.

In the center of the village was a thatch-roof structure everyone called the *maloca*, or hut, though it was nothing like a traditional longhouse. It followed the straight lines of Western constructions, only with the sides left open, lined by benches where some twenty people waited to meet with Trindade. Most wore the standard uniform of the Brazilian poor—flip-flops, faded T-shirts. But then I saw Oita approaching in an immaculate button-up. He was carrying an umbrella, the only umbrella I ever saw in the Amazon. Just one person stuck out more: an elderly man dressed more or less in traditional fashion, naked except for athletic shorts and a slew of necklaces, who clutched a bow and a bundle of arrows.

Trindade had come to introduce his replacement, as he was being reassigned. When it was Oita's turn to speak, he didn't hesitate to complain that this other official had failed to return his calls. "If I offend you, excuse me," he added. "I was born in the jungle."

Oita noticed me, too. Once the meeting was over, he approached and said, "Hey, you. Where are you from?" Eager to tell his story, he invited me to his home in the village for the first of what would turn out to be many conversations. Despite his polished look, he was no longer the high-class *doutor* of the boom times. He'd lost his ranch, his mansion, his fleet of cars, and even his white wife, Alba, who'd finally sensed his interest in her waning and took the opportunity to leave once and for all. With nowhere else to go, he'd returned to Roosevelt Village and shacked up with a Cinta Larga woman. Oita's hair was graying, his head nearly bald, but he remained the same Rapscallion. Eventually his new companion got fed up with him, too, and he was forced to move in with his half-white son Ezequiel.

After the massacre, the government hardly needed to shut down the mine, as Pio had feared. Instead, production began to decline on its own, as if "cursed," in the words of one Cinta Larga who stubbornly persisted there. In concrete terms, prospectors had already dug up all the diamonds that were easy to find—and without a large-scale industrial operation, there was no way to reach the underlying kimberlite. You could still find the odd gem, but you were likely to go into debt just running your machines, and you had to sell before the next crackdown, when federal agents choppered in to blow up your equipment.

Oita, entertaining me on his porch, suddenly leaped from his chair. Furious that a skinny village dog was sniffing for scraps, he stomped his feet and growled, grabbed a broomstick, and made like he was going to beat it, until the dog scampered off. Over the years, I often saw displays like this. But he was a captivating storyteller, with that infectious laugh, and until I heard other people's versions, I had no reason to disbelieve what he said. Early on I even agreed to bring him a Samsung smartphone from abroad, where the price was cheaper; he promised to repay me, but never did. Phones were a prized item at Roosevelt Village, usually cheap Chinese brands. A few families had installed Wi-Fi they charged a small fee for others to use. No one seemed embarrassed to ask how much my iPhone had cost me. People also asked how much my plane tickets cost, how much my New York rent was, their eyes always widening at the answer.

Once when I arrived for a fresh stint at the village, Oita showed me a comic book featuring muscular, white-looking Indians in the jungle. In my absence, he claimed, the author had offered him $40,000 for his story, but he'd refused because he was already committed to giving *me* his story. I was left to speculate why he might have come up with this tale. He never asked me for money, though others did, including the chief of Roosevelt Village at the time. It struck me that Oita simply wanted to increase his value in my eyes. When he wasn't around, I noticed how others snickered at his name. Now he saw a chance to rewrite history, to make himself the hero of the Cinta Larga story, to finally receive the recognition he felt he deserved.

On a later visit, Oita claimed that others in the village wanted to throw me out, but he'd defended me. I assumed it was one of his embellishments until I discovered that I had, in fact, become the subject of rumors. One held that my portable voice recorder was actually a device for detecting precious metals and stones, the better to inform the US government about the riches of Cinta Larga country. There were also whispers that I was making "millions" from this book, a hilariously inflated sum—but one that accurately reflected the gulf between my standard of living back home and theirs at Roosevelt Village. It also reflected the very real sense that I was yet another white person extracting something of value from their lands—not diamonds or rubber or gold, but stories.

At first none of this concerned me too much. But more pointed rumors surfaced. Loggers and prospectors were an everyday presence, and they didn't want a journalist nosing around. Apparently one swore he'd seen me, face hidden by a hood, in a federal crackdown on the hardwood trade. Then I learned of yet another rumor: that I was actually an informant for the Federal Police. I considered abandoning my reporting altogether, fearing what might come of all this.

Despite the understandable suspicions about my motives, I found that most Cinta Larga wanted to tell their stories. They wanted the world to know what they'd lived through, and didn't necessarily expect anything in return. Some even invited me to eat boiled turtle or monkey brains, an honor that was all the greater in light of how little they had. They called me *oyatu*, or "tall man." I made them laugh by learning phrases in Tupi-Mondé.

With few exceptions, they didn't try to whitewash their past. When it was Pio's turn to speak that day at the *maloca*, he spoke of his regret he'd quit school to save for a car, a motif he came back to over and over again. "Why do we keep doing the wrong things?" he asked, and didn't need to explain what he meant. He wore a necklace of palm-fruit beads, a spotted jaguar-skin headdress, and wire-rimmed glasses. "We do these things to survive, but it's a lack of knowledge, a lack of comprehension. What opens a human being's mind is to study."

*   *   *

All these years later, Pio remained the government's number one target. Shortly after the massacre, he'd given a disastrous interview to TV Globo. Asked if the warriors had truly killed the prospectors, he answered with his usual forthrightness: "Yes…because they were tired of always sending them away." He could have made it clear that he himself had opposed the violence. Instead, to discourage future invasions, he added what sounded like a threat: "Don't let your son come here anymore, don't let your husband come here anymore, don't let your sister come here anymore. Know that this can happen, because I can't keep everyone under control."

It's hard to overstate the panic that gripped the region in those days. After Donivaldo was tied up and beaten in Espigão's central square, a fifteen-year-old Cinta Larga named Moisés was riding on the back of a white friend's motorcycle when three masked men ambushed them, shooting the kid to death. For months or even years afterward, many Cinta Larga didn't dare leave the Indigenous area except when absolutely necessary. When they did, prospectors spat out threats in broad daylight: "Five years might pass—ten, twenty, thirty years—but we will have our revenge." They even spoke of poisoning the village water supply. Local columnists stoked the outrage; in a blog post titled "Civilized Cannibals," one lamented that, unless the Cinta Larga were punished for the killings, they effectively enjoyed the right to impose the death penalty on their lands. As the story went national and then international, members of Congress joined the chorus. In Brasília, one decried the "impunity of murderous Indians who massacre Brazilians searching for a place to work." Meanwhile, onetime allies distanced themselves.

Funai called on Apoena Meirelles, still seen by many Cinta Larga as "our father," to reestablish calm. Pragmatic as ever, he took up Pio's quest to legalize the mine—but he was barely getting started when, in October 2004, he was gunned down in Porto Velho. The Cinta Larga were sure it was an assassination. Many white activists believed this, too. But it appears to have been a simple mugging gone wrong. Whatever the truth, his death signaled the end of something. A century after the founding of the Indian Protection Service, the old mold of the swashbuckling Indian agent—the mold of Apoena's father, Chico, and their hero Cândido Rondon—is going extinct. Within Funai, many almost sound like a young Apoena arguing with his father, criticizing the old insistence on assimilation. Pio himself now regrets his own role in Funai's contact efforts, saying, "Leave them alone. Otherwise they'll never have peace."

Thanks to *sertanistas* like Sydney Possuelo, this has actually become official policy: to allow the "uncontacted" to remain as they are. Thus the demarcation of the Javari Valley, an area three times the size of Cinta Larga country, on Brazil's border with Peru. With nineteen distinct groups identified, it is the Amazon's—and the world's—largest concentration of Indigenous people in what is termed voluntary isolation. If they want to make contact, that's now up to them. In the meantime, there's little question that this approach will keep lives from being lost to disease, societies from being shattered, warriors from being turned into poor people. Funai, though, is as badly funded as ever, little match for the unrelenting pressure of the Amazon frontier. Agents who get in the way are often murdered; investigations rarely go anywhere.

* * *

At the time of my first visit, the new "general chief" was a young, mixed-race man named Marcelo, who wore a goatee no full-blooded Cinta Larga could hope to grow. Addressing the meeting at the *maloca*, he lamented, "Any day now, our leaders could go to prison." Lacking evidence to place Pio at the scene of the massacre, the Federal Police had again resorted to armchair anthropology, quizzing suspects on the role of the chief to prove he was somehow responsible for the warriors' actions. The interrogations weren't recorded, but from the paraphrased transcripts, it seems the investigators simply ignored responses such as Tataré's that the warriors "are not subordinated to the chiefs." Other Cinta Larga resorted to wry misdirection, with one responding "that the warriors live 'in the jungle'; that he cannot explain how the warriors, given that they do not have contact with anyone, possess firearms; that [he] has only seen Indians in war paint on television."

Some, though, refused to feign ignorance. According to the transcripts, seven men—two from Roosevelt Village, the rest from the east—admitted having gone to the gully, though they claimed not to have carried out the killings. Faced with the reality of prison time, they would later recant these statements—the best evidence against any of them. But the sentiments truly seemed to be theirs. One was paraphrased saying "that they did not wait for Funai because the land is theirs and it is the Indians' duty to protect it and defend it from invaders." Another said "that the prospectors invaded the Indigenous Area and stole from the Indians, and thus the Indians who 'did the job' were within their rights."

Pio, for his part, insisted that "if [he] had been present, [he]...would not have allowed the events to take place." At least one police officer had heard his appeals for intervention via radio, and two government officials placed Pio at Roosevelt Village before lunchtime on the day in question. Just the same, the Federal Police accused him of "leading" and "instigating" the massacre along with a few others. Tataré was indicted, too, as were Oita and Roberto Carlos, though the latter two had their charges thrown out for lack of even the thinnest of evidence. All in all, twenty-two Cinta Larga men were accused of homicide; João Bravo, notably, was spared. (A white Funai agent was also among the accused, seemingly for no other reason than to placate the pundits and politicians who blamed Funai for the massacre.)

As with Inspector Sousa's 2002 arrests, the case raised unanswerable questions about the defendants' "integration" into Brazilian society. This time, the state was obliged to consult with a pair of anthropologists. It was a strange ritual, pitting the moral relativism of academia against the absolutism of Western criminal law—and the result, though useful for the defense, seemed to reduce the Cinta Larga, once again, to something far simpler than what they were. Elaine Amorim and Kênia Alves had no specific expertise on the group, but after two weeks in the field, they picked up on the old "warrior ethos" and the seemingly existential threat posed by Baiano Doido. What they missed was that other tradition: giving strangers the benefit of the doubt. Even if the group was adopting Western norms, they argued, it would have gone against the Cinta Larga "way of being" not to move against Baiano. "Inside Cinta Larga territory," they concluded, "it is the group's culture that prevails, and the simple fact of being there means to be subject to their morality."

Needless to say, this wasn't the place for intellectual debate. The report was just a box to be ticked, and prosecutors waved it away with a simple argument: "Corrupted by the mine," the accused were motivated by "business interests...to secure exclusivity over the illegal extraction of diamonds." The prosecutors didn't seem to realize this contradicted their own case—if you wanted to keep the money flowing, it was far better to *avoid* spectacular violence. After the massacre, interest from international investors had all but dried up, and with the brief exception of the Bolsonaro years, no one in government would even discuss legalization. In Pio's words, "The doors closed."

The bigger problem was that the case relied heavily on hearsay, much of it from prospectors, hardly disinterested parties. To support the notion that Pio and his fellow chiefs had planned the massacre—a major claim—the accusation cited a prospector known as Black Osmar. The day before, he told the police, João Bravo had warned him to leave the Stream of the Blackflies because Pio and Panderê were planning "something dangerous." Even if this was true, though—a big if—João Bravo was frequently hard to understand, and his words could have meant any number of things.

Brazil's justice system has always been notoriously slow. For once this played to the Cinta Larga's benefit. The anthropologists issued their report in 2009; the prosecutors filed their *denúncia* in 2014. Still the case dragged on, passing from one judge to another. As I finished writing, it had yet to go to trial, and I came to suspect that no one apart from the victims' families—people without the resources to keep up public pressure—had any real interest in a verdict. Beyond the quality of the prosecutors' case, beyond the defendants' fitness to stand trial, how could the state punish the Indigenous warriors behind the massacre of 2004 when it had never punished the white tycoons behind the Massacre of the Eleventh Parallel? How could the state claim the authority of blind, objective justice when its own agents had cultivated the chiefs' supposed motive: greed for wealth and Western goods? It was easier to let old tragedies stay in the past, to avoid a resolution that would only enrage one side or the other, not to mention the bad international press.

Of course, the real reason may just have been the usual incompetence, the usual failure of the state to do its job. Two decades after the feds started investigating the "diamond barons," almost all the charges had passed the statute of limitations, expiring without a verdict—though new charges occasionally popped up.

But then, toward the end of 2023, the Gully of Tranquility case heaved back to life, as that pink-shirted judge, Rafael Slomp, held a hearing in Vilhena to decide whether it would go to a jury of their "peers" (almost certainly not their fellow Cinta Larga). Letting such an important case go, it seems, would be too embarrassing even for the dysfunctional Brazilian state. As of this writing, the outcome remains unclear, but there's the prospect of a kind of Western *wepika*: that Pio will be made to pay for acts he didn't commit and even, in a sense, for a past he left behind.

*　*　*

Maria Beleza wasn't at Roosevelt Village on my first visit. She hardly came at all anymore, ever since the day she and Oita's sister Alzira had tried to enter the mine and were confronted by warriors—some of the same ones who'd killed Baiano and his crew, apparently. The two women had always tried to keep them from spilling prospectors' blood; now the warriors drew their bows and pointed arrows at *them*. "You two are fake Indians," one said. "You live in town, and anyone who lives in town can't work here anymore."

Maria protested, "But I was born here!"

"My father built his village here," Alzira chimed in. "You all are from Mato Grosso"—from the east. "You only came because of the diamonds."

Never mind that more than a few chiefs—male chiefs—lived outside the Indigenous area. Never mind that Maria had come to feel she was now a kind of chief, too. With diamonds scarcer than ever, turf was highly contested, and the warriors couldn't be moved. Left without any other income, she and Alzira turned to selling traditional handicrafts to white people in town. Their only good fortune was that they'd refrained from taking on debts, buying cars, so at least they kept their homes in Riozinho. Over the years that followed, I often visited to buy monkey-teeth bracelets or necklaces of armadillo shells. Alzira's hair, like her brother's, was graying, but Maria's was still perfectly black. She had an easy smile and an effortless charisma that helped me understand why her beauty was so renowned.

The two women took solace in their children, now adults, but seemed lonely. Maria told me how, after she'd left her Pacaa Nova husband, she'd made a new "friend" who was not an Indian and not exactly a white man either. She described him as *bem pretinho*, very Black. A prospector, he couldn't resist the temptation to try his luck at the Stream of the Black-flies, and he ended up paying for it with his life. In Maria's mind, it was the warriors' way of "humiliating" her once again. She ended up with another Indian, a Parintintin, but it was a loveless marriage, encouraged by her pastor, who didn't want her to live in sin.

After I finished my reporting, Maria Beleza would sometimes send me audio messages on WhatsApp, always addressing me with mock formality as "Alex, the American journalist." She never let on that she'd been diagnosed with cancer. In April 2023, she was admitted to the hospital; she died shortly after.

*   *   *

Over the time I spent working on this book, Pio's health declined, too. His limp evolved to the point he had difficulty walking, and he had a severe case of diabetes that damaged the retina of his remaining good eye. He no longer traveled to Brasília. He no longer contested elections for "general chief." Still, he exercised a kind of symbolic leadership. "From now on I want to do everything right," he told me. "No more of the mistakes we made—enough headaches, enough problems. I want to fix things, to have peace." He threw his weight behind a cooperative that gathered *maam*, the nut from which Pio's lineage was said to have emerged. Not that Pio believed in preserving the forest for its own sake. He simply saw that a Brazil nut tree, left standing, could provide a reliable income instead of a one-time profit.

Two American entrepreneurs proposed selling carbon credits, financial products designed to "offset" emissions by preventing deforestation. But they seemed to be the same kind of adventurers who'd always chased fortunes there—carbon cowboys. Personally, I wondered why, in this age of climate crisis, rich countries couldn't simply pay the Indigenous groups now preserving the Amazon for free, easing the pressure on them to resort to logging and mining. Just in Brazil, this would cover land equivalent to Texas and California combined, vast areas of rainforest that benefit the whole world. As a bonus, the payments could serve as reparations for the crimes of contact, which, after all, were partly financed by the World Bank and USAID. Pio, for his part, didn't care how it was put together so long as they got paid.

I spent a lot of time at Pio's home in Cacoal. He would lie in a hammock by a cacao tree, telling stories while he petted a little green bird called Flor. When it came to the new generation, he wrestled with contradictory feelings. If he lamented what had become of his first protégés, Panderê and Rondonzinho, he felt even more alienated by the youths coming up now. I saw the shift firsthand at Roosevelt Village. A few boys still played at archery, but most preferred a smartphone game called Free Fire. Girls spent hours upon hours on Facebook, posting photos in which they filtered their faces lighter. "That's not our culture," Pio grumbled. "Our culture is to dance, to learn to hunt and tend our gardens." Granted, this was almost the same argument used by white people who claimed the Cinta Larga were no longer real Indians. Granted, Pio himself hardly ever did these things either. But he knew where he came from: the world of the forest. That was the culture that had shaped him.

For an outsider like myself, it was tempting to think the Cinta Larga had already lost their identity, becoming indistinguishable from poor Brazilians anywhere. Instead of holding feasts, they watched soccer games. Having abandoned the communal longhouse, they gathered at church. Pio himself worried that, if the government realized just how far they'd strayed, it might decide to use their land for something else. And yet, the more time I spent there, the more I saw that Roosevelt Village remained unlike any Western kind of town. It was a community in the most literal sense, in which, for better or worse, there was no possibility of an individual existence. Everyone knew everyone else's business; they also knew they could turn to anyone there for help. On the rare occasions when a man went hunting, he still shared the surplus meat with his neighbors. Children, always roaming free, were treated as a collective responsibility—and still grew up speaking Tupi-Mondé. Those who grew up in town—including Pio's own children—never really learned at all: yet another failure he blamed himself for.

At the same time, of course, Pio still wanted Cinta Larga children to receive the Western education he never had. Despite his worries that they would forget their traditions, he actually believed it was the only way to keep their land. He knew that the hardwood would run out one day, just like the diamonds. Without a way to make a living in Cinta Larga country, young people would have little choice but to become laborers elsewhere on the frontier, to become "slaves to white people," like Apoena had feared. It was a question of maintaining their independence, their self-sufficiency, those age-old Cinta Larga virtues. If the new generation took the best from each world—white and Indigenous—they could become doctors, lawyers, agronomists, administrators, and then come back and build a new kind of Cinta Larga society. In a way he was intuiting the philosophy of the Brazilian poet Oswald de Andrade, who turned Indigenous cannibalism into a metaphor for national strength through cultural borrowing. "Don't think the Indian will go back to the way things were," Pio told me. "From now on we want to evolve just like everyone else."

Pio's sons, drawn to the diamond trade, never fulfilled this dream. His daughters, though, took the path he'd always dreamed of, receiving an education at schools in town. For all that he missed his father's world, Pio was willing to imagine a new world in which—like Maria Beleza believed of her grandmother—a woman could do whatever a man could. Pio's eldest, Luana, became a schoolteacher at Roosevelt Village. Naiá, one of his daughters with Rute, was the first Cinta Larga ever to graduate from college—and when I met her, she'd just become a nurse for the Indigenous health service, providing vaccines and diabetes shots and all manner of care in Cinta Larga country. These young women had no idea how to prepare *i*, how to skin a monkey, how to speak Tupi-Mondé. But they were, Pio could see, his people's future.

ACKNOWLEDGMENTS

I owe my greatest debt to the Cinta Larga who let me into their homes and their lives, especially Pio (along with his wife, Rute), Tataré and his son Diogo (both of whom also helped with the reporting), Maria Beleza, Roberto Carlos, and Oita. They told me about the most difficult days of their lives, but never lost the ability to laugh—truly astonishing examples of resilience.

I'm also indebted to Inês Hargreaves, a walking encyclopedia of Tupi-Mondé history, culture, and language. In addition to vital insights along the way, she gave the manuscript a thorough read and offered corrections. João Dal Poz also shared his decades of expertise in multiple conversations, as well as important materials, and he and Nadja Marin both gave generous feedback on the manuscript. Needless to say, any errors that remain are mine alone.

The reporting would have been a lot more difficult without Maisa Garcia and Geraldo Bueno, who invited me to share countless meals at their temporary home in Roosevelt Village, and Marafon, who always welcomed me at his ranch and his house in Espigão. Reginaldo Trindade arranged for my first visit to Cinta Larga country, and gave me essential documents. João Castellano, whose beautiful photo is on the cover, encouraged me to stay longer than I'd planned on that first visit. I'm also grateful to Neide Oliveira, who dug up hard-to-find documents and contacts.

My agent, Howard Yoon, saw the potential in this story even before I did, worked his customary magic with the proposal, and gave crucial feedback on the manuscript. My editor, Maddie Caldwell, understood my ambitions from the start, patiently waited through multiple extensions, and was unfailingly insightful in her edits. Susan Southard helped me navigate the chaos of way too much research and reporting. My friends Ted Alcorn and Noah Shannon also gave thoughtful feedback. The Alicia Patterson Foundation and the Fund for Investigative Journalism financed the reporting with generous grants.

My wife, Isobel, has been hearing about the Cinta Larga for the last six years, and has always been my first reader. More importantly, she cared for me after a serious rock climbing accident, in the hospital and through a long rehabilitation. My parents flew all the way to Nairobi to help out—just one example of the support they've always given me, which is why I dedicate this book to them.

NOTES ON SOURCES

This is a work of nonfiction, based on my own interviews and reporting, scholarly papers, official documents, court cases, and press reports. My most important sources were the three dozen Cinta Larga I interviewed, some many times, for many hours, in addition to just hanging out, chatting, and observing. The vast majority of these conversations were in Portuguese, which I speak fluently, but Tataré and his son Diogo translated a few from Tupi-Mondé. Starting with my first trip in 2017, I visited Rondônia ten times, usually for two or three weeks, splitting my time between the frontier towns and Roosevelt Village, in addition to shorter stints at other villages and two visits to the mine at the Stream of the Blackflies. For details of Cinta Larga culture and history, I relied in part on the Cinta Larga themselves—through my own interviews and Pichuvy's 1988 book—and in part on the brave and difficult work of João Dal Poz, Inês Hargreaves, and Carmen Junqueira. Cinta Larga music is beautifully described in the work of Priscilla Ermel, and Nadja Marin's interviews with João Bravo were essential. I also spoke to loggers, prospectors, settlers, and government officials.

Memories are often unreliable, especially decades later, but whenever possible, I corroborated them with written accounts. To this end, my most important source was Funai, which provided thousands of documents going back to its founding. The Museu do Índio did the same for Indian Protection Service documents, and I obtained the records of Funai's intelligence wing during the military dictatorship, ASI-Funai, from the Arquivo Nacional. Lilian Newlands's 2007 book was enormously helpful for the sections involving Apoena. For visual descriptions and various other details, I drew on the photos taken by Jesco von Puttkamer in the 1970s, as well as on his diaries, which are held at the Instituto Goiano de Pre-História e Antropologia at the Pontifícia Universidade Católica de Goiás. Dal Poz shared a collection of press reports going back to the 1950s; I also trawled the press archives of the Instituto Socioambiental and the Biblioteca Nacional. For events at the Stream of the Blackflies, I pored through thousands of pages of court files, and Reginaldo Trindade provided a trove of documents from the Public Ministry. I converted most amounts in Brazilian *reais* to dollars at a rate of two to one.

Along the way, I often had to tease out fact from rumor. Different versions didn't always line up perfectly, and in many cases I made my own judgment calls on which was closest to the truth. When I felt it was necessary, I noted the conflicts in the text.

A few additional notes and a bibliography follow.

PROLOGUE
4 "diamond baron": "Os caciques do diamante," *O Globo*, May 5, 2002. See also the notes for Chapters 21 and 23.

CHAPTER 1: A NEW KIND OF YEARNING
10 "*He has traveled here*": Ermel 1988.
11 "Men would look and see who had a large vulva": Marin 2017.
13 "between one and two thousand": Dal Poz 1991.
13 "experts with the bow": Tressmann 1993.
15 "The bodies are cut into pieces": Mário Arruda, "Jesco e os acervos indígenas: os Cinta-Larga," Moura 2017.
17 "to everyone's surprise": Ramis Bucair, SPI report, May 25, 1966.
17 "The house that [the Nambikwara] had built": Afonso José de Azevedo Junior, SPI report, April 26, 1960.

CHAPTER 2: THE INDIAN PROTECTION SERVICE

20 bouts of malaria: Possidônio Bastos, "Foi malária que fez a vítima," *O Globo*, August 31, 1970.

20 "after two months in the bush": Apoena Meirelles, resignation letter to General Ismarth de Araújo Oliveira, February 7, 1972. Unless otherwise noted, the rest of Apoena's quotes are from Newlands 2007. Other details of his and his father's lives come from Freire 2005 and Milanez 2015.

21 as many as twenty million people: Juan Forero, "Scientists find evidence discrediting theory Amazon was virtually unlivable," *Washington Post*, September 5, 2010; see also Mann 2005.

22 "boar or deer": Hemming 2008, citing Padre Antonio Vieira.

23 "I don't go so far as to think": "Theodore Roosevelt Timeline," American Museum of Natural History website. The quote continues: "and I shouldn't like to inquire too closely into the case of the tenth."

23 "Die if you must": Rohter 2019. Most details of Rondon's life come from this excellent biography. Details of his journey with Roosevelt also come from Millard 2005, Rondon 1916, and Roosevelt 1914. It remains unclear which tribe was shadowing the Rondon-Roosevelt expedition. Both the Cinta Larga and the Zoró make arrowheads out of bamboo, and although the area where Lobo was killed is now well within Cinta Larga territory, it was, according to the anthropologist Gílio Brunelli and a Cinta Larga source interviewed by Dal Poz, long disputed by the Zoró. In 1927, the self-styled explorer George Miller Dyott retraced the expedition and met a group of Indigenous people who, from Hargreaves's review of the images, appear to have been Zoró. Dyott described their attempt to communicate with sign language: "They laid their shaggy heads on their hands and closed their eyes as if asleep; then, pointing to the opposite bank of the river they shook their fists energetically from side to side. This was followed by an imitation of chopping off a hand or foot, and of eating food. In plain English, they warned us not to sleep on the opposite bank of the river, because the people who lived there cut off the hands and feet of strangers and ate them." These people may have been the Cinta Larga.

In 1992, Theodore Roosevelt's grandson Tweed retraced the expedition once more, and reported hearing richly detailed Cinta Larga stories about the encounter with Rondon and Lobo. Two journalists, Larry Rohter and Candice Millard, would come away with similar stories in the 2000s. It's possible the Cinta Larga they interviewed were conflating their fathers' and grandfathers' stories of other old conflicts, such as the one with Rondon's Lieutenant Marques de Souza, who navigated a parallel river in 1915, or those at Rondon's telegraph line, decades later. It's also possible that the Cinta Larga were simply making things up; it wouldn't have been the first time playful Indigenous misdirection influenced outside accounts, including those of renowned anthropologists. (For more on this quandary, see King 2019's discussion of Owen Dorsey and his Omaha "informant" Two Crows.) Oita would always tell me Theodore Roosevelt had raked the forest with a machine gun as he went—obviously apocryphal. He also claimed he'd told this story to Tweed's face, but Tweed, supposedly embarrassed, stayed silent.

In any case, the two people who have dug deepest into Cinta Larga history, Dal Poz and Hargreaves, never heard the Lobo story from the Cinta Larga themselves. Roberto Carlos was on Tweed's expedition, but he reminded me that, in those days, the Cinta Larga kept their villages far from major waterways, instead preferring *igarapés* like the Stream of the Blackflies, so it's unlikely they were involved. Still, given how little information there is about that time, it can't be ruled out.

25 "always the feeling that someone would fire a bullet": Newlands 2007, citing Aguinaldo Araújo Ramos.

25 a prospector known as Amiguinho: "Diamantes das desilusões," *Gente de Opinião*, June 11, 2011.

26 "Vulture Indians": Hargreaves (personal information) and an SPI report, both cited in Dal Poz 1991. The attack was also reported in "Os índios assaram e comeram os garimpeiros," *A Manhã*, July 23, 1952.

26 "The victim's body had the flesh cut from its bones": Azevedo Junior, SPI report, cited above.

26 "great appreciators of human flesh": Armando Leite, comments before Congress, March 11, 1965.

26 Operation Cinta Larga: Various Funai reports but especially Francisco Meirelles's dated December 31, 1968.

27 the largest Amazonian tribe that didn't yet know "civilization": This and the population estimate are in "Cintas-largas se aproximam e trocam presentes com os brancos," *Jornal do Brasil*, May 11, 1969.

28 The story was similar with just about every other group: Hemming 2003.

28 "A bad deal is better than a good fight": "Meireles [sic] acha que um mau acordo é melhor do que uma boa briga para os índios," *Jornal do Brasil*, November 14, 1972.

29 "It looks like they're up for civilization": "Silêncio da expedição cinta-larga não preocupa," *O Globo*, October 22, 1968.

30 The Massacre of the Eleventh Parallel: "50 contos por um Cinta Larga morto," *O Globo*, February 14, 1966; "Genocide" by Norman Lewis, *Sunday Times Magazine*, February 23, 1969; and Dal Poz 1991.

30 SPI agents were exposed: Comissão Nacional da Verdade, 2014, citing the 1967 report by public prosecutor Jader de Figueiredo Correia.

30 Serviço de Prostituição de Índias: "Fala o Fundador da Funai," *Porantim*, September 1989.

31 targeted with dynamite: According to Dal Poz, who later interviewed many Cinta Larga in that area, this detail is almost certainly apocryphal.

31 "I've never worked on a front like this one": "Sertanistas penetram na selva para pacificar os cinta-larga," *Jornal do Brasil*, August 21, 1968.

31 "constitution": Hemming 2008.

31 "We have no problems with Indians": João Américo Peret, Funai report, October 17, 1968.

CHAPTER 3: WHAT THE ELDERS COULDN'T EXPLAIN

34 Women had a particular way of sitting: Richard Chapelle, *Les hommes a la ceinture d'écorce* (film), 1979. Chapelle visited a village yet to be subsumed by Funai.

34 "*Let's go find firewood*": Ermel 1988.

36 "Giant hawk that purrs like a jaguar": Arruda (cited above), again quoting João Bravo.

CHAPTER 4: RAUL'S MEN

42 "Any little thing I heard": Marin 2017.

45 "It was around noon on Sunday": "Adiantada a pacificação dos cintas-largas por Meireles" [sic], *O Globo*, March 14, 1969.

46 "carpenter": immigration card, August 27, 1954. Other details are from Raul's widow, Maria Graça, and "Diamantes das desilusões," cited above.

46 According to one fellow prospector: José Lucas do Bonfim, personal interview.

47 an eighty-three-carat stone: Kanfner 1993.

48 kids would run after the plane: "Avião estacionado no Bairro Urupá em Ji-Paraná na década de 70," *Portal Rul*, February 19, 2021.

48 thirty-ounce bottles: Serviço Geológico do Brasil, "Aspectos da geologia dos polos diamantíferos de Rondônia e Mato Grosso," 2010.

48 "first class adventurer": Puttkamer, diary entry, December 16, 1969.

50 "This teaches the way of life": "Diamantes das desilusões."

50 "You might earn nothing for six months": Gaúcho (nickname), personal interview.

CHAPTER 5: IDEALISTS

52 A group of prospectors showed up: Francisco Meirelles, Funai telegrams, July 1969.

52 "I must say, in all honesty: I was afraid": Newlands 2007, citing Ramos.

53 He was thrilled by what he observed: "Cinta-larga quer brinde mas ainda teme o branco," *O Globo*, August 26, 1970; "Só uma palavra separa branco do cinta-larga," *O Globo*, September 3, 1970.

54 "to live like us": Ramos, "Chico Meirelles, pai e mestre," Newlands 2007.

54 "You know [the Indians] are naive": "Na primeira visita aos suruís a decisão do novo pacificador," *O Globo*, December 9, 1971.

55 publicly advocated arming Indians: Newlands 2007.

55 "strong suspicions": Isnard de Albuquerque Câmara, ASI-Funai report, undated. This and the following quotes are included in an ASI-Funai dossier on Apoena.

55 "I'm not going back to Brasília": "Na primeira visita," cited above.

56 "Interpret my decision how you please": "As cartas de Possidônio: 'Se necessário morro pelos índios,'" *O Globo*, December 7, 1971.

CHAPTER 6: THE FEAST

58 "*I want a lover*": Ermel 1988.

60 "*When the pig runs*": Dal Poz 1991, citing a Cinta Larga called Capitão Maam.

62 the settlement of Pimenta Bueno: Oita and Roberto told me this story themselves, but it's possible that their visit was also reported by Puttkamer in a December 14, 1969, diary entry. His language is vague, but he mentions Didi in the context of "three Wide Belt Indians, who came to Pimenta Bueno at the end of September."

64 wiped out the Omagua people: Hemming 2008.

64 killed nine out of ten Hopi: Mann 2005.

65 documented cases of flu: Jean Chiappino, "The Brazilian Indigenous Problem and Policy: The Aripuanã Park," International Work Group for Indigenous Affairs, 1975.

65 memories mingled with rumors: It's not only the Cinta Larga who conflate

the Massacre of the Eleventh Parallel with other atrocities. In 2014, an official truth commission released a report detailing human rights violations in Brazil from the 1940s to the 1980s, with one volume dedicated to crimes against Indigenous people. The report cites a Cinta Larga death toll of five thousand—impossibly high, given Dal Poz's estimate that the group numbered between one and two thousand before contact. The report may have based the death toll on the population figure reported in the press in the 1960s, which encompassed not only the Cinta Larga but other neighboring groups, and was, even so, likely far too high. The report also lists causes of death—"food mixed with arsenic; airplanes that dropped toys contaminated with flu, measles, and smallpox viruses," and dynamite attacks—that seem to come from rumors in the press prior to contact, rather than interviews with Cinta Larga. (As far as I can tell, no field research was carried out.) Dal Poz, based on his own interviews with the survivors of disease outbreaks and attacks by settlers, believes these rumors to be apocryphal, though they certainly aren't impossible. In any case, as this information trickled into popular accounts, the Massacre of the Eleventh Parallel has become—a bit like it is for the Cinta Larga—a catchall for a series of atrocities both real and imagined, and much closer to international law definitions of genocide. It may seem strange to quibble with these inaccuracies, but the point isn't to diminish the Cinta Larga's suffering. The atrocities that definitely did happen are terrible enough without exaggeration.

CHAPTER 7: GRAVEDIGGER

68 Raul the Spaniard found two hundred: Raul Moreda, "Declaração," May 31, 1968 (among SPI documents held by the Museu do Índio).

69 the camp had changed hands: The fateful feast likely took place late in the dry season of 1969; Manoelzinho Cinta Larga recalls that a particular fruit was ripening and waterways were low. Didi's disappearance was noted in November, and Posto Roosevelt started in December. Pio and his father's first visit almost certainly took place after that (likely between May and October 1970), because they apparently went two dry seasons in a row, and Pio moved to Posto Roosevelt shortly before Possidônio was killed in November 1971.

69 invited Didi to return to their village: Puttkamer, diary, December 14, 1969.

70 "Emergency call": "Cintas-largas deixam sertanista à míngua," *O Estado de S. Paulo*, January 14, 1970.

70 "the food was contaminated": Jerônimo Santana, comments before Congress, June 26, 1972.

71 the only agent on duty was Pedro: Betty Mindlin, "Aula Magna de Pedro Arara Karo," *Estudos Avançados*, vol. 30, no. 87, May–August 2016. This is also the source for the dialogue at the end of the section.

73 "I don't want to be the Indians' gravedigger": Valente 2017, which also details Indigenous epidemics under Funai during the military dictatorship.

CHAPTER 8: REVENGE AND FORGIVENESS

74 "temperamental": undated ASI-Funai report in Apoena's dossier.

74 After just a few months on the job: According to "Luta pelos índios tem novo mártir," *DI—Jornal Nacional*, December 19, 1971, Possidônio arrived in May; according to Funai records, he was officially hired on August 1.

74 trading clothes for sex: "Funai garante que índios mataram repórter e acaba com especulação," *Jornal do Brasil*, December 17, 1971.

74 "chubby, beautiful": "Missão enfrenta perigo da selva rumo aos Cinta Larga," *O Globo*, June 9, 1970.

74 "The first time he met me, he gave me three chocolates": Newlands 2007, "Morte de reporter é desvendada após 10 anos," *Jornal do Brasil*, December 31, 1981.

75 "incoherent": Funai memo, June 22, 1971.

76 "Indians, like children": "As cartas de Possidônio," cited above.

77 One little boy survived by foraging: Arruda, "Jesco," cited above.

82 "This could have happened to me": Funai memo, December 6, 1971.

82 "The Indians have already seen guns": Funai memo, undated.

83 "Who ever heard a monkey whistle": *Jornal do Brasil*, December 9, 1971.

84 "He was very abrupt": Newlands 2007, citing Ramos.

84 "never liked": "Na terra dos tupi," Newlands 2007.

86 "like flying sardine tins": Newlands 2007.

CHAPTER 9: A KIDNAPPING

88 "It will be too difficult for me": "Sertanista transferido para a serra do Cachimbo," *Folha de S.Paulo*, March 12, 1972.

88 "enfant terrible": Newlands 2007, citing Apoena.

90 "very primitive cultural stage": "Sertanista foge com índia," *O Globo*, October 9, 1973.

90 wanted for nine homicides: Francisco ("Chicão") Assis da Silva, personal interview.

92 "I report a new marriage": Dal Poz 1991, citing a Funai report by Ubirajara Fagundes.

CHAPTER 10: INTO THE WORLD

95 more tractors than cars: Roberto Rodrigues dos Santos, personal interview. I also reviewed his photos from the time.

CHAPTER 11: CHIEFS

106 "must be the wards of the nation": Roosevelt 1914, describing a conversation with Rondon.

107 loan from the World Bank: Robert H. Wade, "Boulevard of Broken Dreams: The Inside Story of the World Bank's Polonoroeste Road Project in Brazil's Amazon," Grantham Research Institute on Climate Change and the Environment working paper, August 2011.

107 USAID financed bridges: Davis 1977.

107 the Brazilian government endlessly subsidized: Branford 1985.

108 "in peaceful contact with civilized people": Itaporanga map, January 15, 1972, included in ASI-Funai's dossier on Apoena.

109 thirty-nine families: Carmen Junqueira and Mauro de Mello Leonel Jr., "Observações recolhidas nas últimas viagens," Fundação Instituto de Pesquisas Econômicas (on Polonoroeste program), March 1984.

109 "I don't know whether to shoot you": Funai agent Izanoel Sodré, personal interview.

109 his own road through Cinta Larga country: Junqueira and Mindlin, "The Aripuanã Park and the Polonoroeste Programme," International Work Group for Indigenous Affairs, July 1987. When I interviewed Rodrigues dos Santos, he denied having had any conflict with the Cinta Larga, saying, "I always got along with the Indians."

110 "I would prefer to die fighting": from "Sertanista transferido para a serra do Cachimbo," cited above.

110 "I never intended": Newlands 2007.

111 Funai supposedly "imported" some: José Lucas Filho (and several other ranchers), letter, January 28, 1986. The conflict is detailed in dossiers kept by Funai and ASI-Funai.

111 "guerrilla warfare": Lucas Filho et al. letter, cited above.

112 a hundred thousand acres: "Questão indígena—invasão na área do posto indígena Roosevelt/RO—índios Cinta Larga," ASI-Funai, April 1986.

112 beef wasn't suitable: Tressmann, personal interview.

113 "a serious fight": Newlands 2007, citing Ramos.

CHAPTER 12: POOR PEOPLE

115 recently turned up dead: "Matador de índia gravida é morto com 3 flechadas," *Jornal do Brasil*, August 14, 1984 (and personal interviews).

116 "defamatory campaign": "Sertanista foge," cited above.

117 "I'd like to see Funai remove me": Hargreaves, personal interview.

117 "repay" his sister's torture: personal interview.

118 poorly paid hardship posts: Junqueira and Mindlin, "The Aripuanã Park," cited above.

122 "wear civilized clothes": Treuer 2019.

122 tapirs, for instance, didn't always run: Funai agent Francisco "Chiquinho" Nôbrega da Silva Filho, personal interview.

CHAPTER 13: ENCOUNTERS WITH THE BUREAUCRACY

124 "the historic responsibility": interview by Sérgio Meirelles, Newlands 2007.

125 Pio and Pichuvy to dream about: "Plano de aplicação para a tribo indígena Cinta-Larga," Funai, October 25, 1984.

126 Funai's own president was accused: "Funai prepara novas acusações contra Jurandy," *Folha de S.Paulo*, October 6, 1984.

126 One Funai agent who refused: Sodré, personal interview.

126 "Don't give us the runaround": Edivio Battistelli and Gerson da Silva Alves, Funai report, November 7, 1984.

126 "The Indians demand payment": Funai telegram, October 31, 1984.

126 Comexmad again won the bidding: Augusto Silva, Funai memo, October 25, 1984.

126 a new Funai president said: "Índios negociam na base de juros," *Jornal de Brasília*, November 10, 1984.

129 "central station for lobbies": "Ilusões da natureza," *IstoÉ*, March 26, 1986.

130 a moneymaking opportunity: "Da Funai à Lava Jato, Romero Jucá coleciona escândalos e já perdeu ministério antes," *El País*, May 24, 2016.

130 *rentabilização*: Dal Poz 2004, citing an official Funai statement by Jucá.

CHAPTER 14: UNITY AND BETRAYAL

131 "stole" women: Junqueira and Cinta Larga sources, personal interviews.

132 "We report [that] Indian Oita Matina": Láercio (last name omitted), Funai telegram, May 17, 1976.

135 part of the Summer Institute of Linguistics: Clive Sandberg, letter to Funai's president, April 17, 1972.

136 "father of the civilized ones": Pichuvy 1988.

136 "If there was no nurse": José Nazareno Torres de Moraes, personal interview.

136 "Many thought it was impossible": Dal Poz, personal interview. His 2004 work was vital for describing the Cinta Larga hardwood trade.

137 "to make money": In Portuguese, the expression is *ganhar dinheiro*, which can literally be translated as "to win money," and brings its own semantic baggage.

138 loggers offered up their own daughters: Hargreaves, personal interview.

138 "prestige item": from a 2009 report by anthropologists Elaine Amorim and Kênia Alves for the Gully of Tranquility case.

140 "the law of the Indian": Olide Marafon, personal interview. He abandoned the hardwood trade to become a farmer.

140 NGOs, sawmill owners: The NGOs include COIAB (Coordenação das Organizações Indígenas da Amazônia Brasileira), APIR (Articulação dos Povos Indígenas de RO e Norte do MT), and CIMI (Conselho Indigenista Missionário), which compiled a joint 1992 report on logging in Indigenous areas. Marafon recalled that when loggers sold him hardwood, they sometimes asked for their payments to be given directly to Oita. Oita also talked business with his logger while I was at his home in Roosevelt Village, and I personally witnessed the patrol described later in this section.

141 $45 million: Shawn Blore, "Rough Justice," *The Walrus*, November 12, 2004, citing Ibama.

142 an illegal settlement: this conflict, including Oita's involvement, is detailed in multiple ASI-Funai documents.

142 under the guidance of an Indigenous intellectual: Chicoepab Suruí, "Reflorestamento da terra indígena Sete de Setembro," Universidade de Brasília, master's dissertation, 2013; and Hargreaves, personal interview.

142 "Our war now": Hargreaves, personal interview.

143 "Funai won't remove the settlers": "Ocorrências na AI Zoró," ASI-Funai, September 21, 1988. See also, e.g., "Confronto se agrava na área indígena," *Jornal do Brasil*, October 24, 1988.

144 "revolution": Antônio Rodrigues da Silva, personal interview.

CHAPTER 15: "WHO WANTS TO BE CIVILIZED?"

147 threatened to confiscate: Cynthia Peter, "Índio dá dinheiro," *Senhor*, October 20, 1987.

147 signing away hardwood: "Documentos da década de 1980 ligam Romero Jucá à maior maldição dos índios brasileiros," *Vice*, July 12, 2016.

148 "research": Diogo Cinta Larga, personal interview.

149 a sawmill of its own: Ministério Público Federal, "Ofício/PR/MT/No. 404/92—Ação Civil Pública," October 26, 1992.

149 "Now everything is going to work out": Hargreaves, personal interview.

149 "*Father, Daddy*": Ermel 1988.

150 they remained muscular: Dal Poz 1991 (photos).

CHAPTER 16: OLD LUCA

155 a hundred white people surrounded the car: Federal Police depositions; Hargreaves, letter to Ministério Público Federal, April 11, 2004; and press reports including "Garimpeiros fazem índio refém após chacina em RO," *Folha de S.Paulo*, April 11, 2004.

156 "These are family men": "Funai quer punir garimpeiros em RO," *Agência Folha*, April 12, 2004.

156 "eliminate the evidence": "Índio é amarrado em praça pública e ameaçado de linchamento," *Folha de Rondônia*, April 12, 2004.

159 "Do you know who your father is?": personal interview. I interviewed Old Luca at age 103; he died in 2023.

159 "supernatural powers": Airton Nogueira de Oliveira, former head of the National Department of Mineral Production office in Porto Velho, as cited by a federal judge in an administrative case against him, 2018.

162 he wanted to be rich: personal interviews and Rohter, "Diamonds' Glitter Fades for a Brazilian Tribe," *New York Times*, December 29, 2006.

CHAPTER 17: THE STREAM OF THE BLACKFLIES

166 De Beers had become a global monopoly: Kanfner 1993.

167 chose not to explore them: Serviço Geológico, "Aspectos da geologia," cited above. De Beers's Brazilian subsidiary was called Sopemi.

169 turned up but one *chibiu*: Washington Cordeiro, personal interview.

171 Funai blamed him: Antenor Vaz et al., "Isolados Urueu-Wau-Wau," January 4, 1991.

CHAPTER 18: A SMALL OPERATION

174 "Pio wanted something that would be exclusively theirs": Nazareno, personal interview.

174 suspected of moonlighting: Federal Police memo, March 14, 2001.

175 "pair of machines": Bete and Diogo Cinta Larga, personal interviews. Among other sources on the mechanics of prospecting at the Stream of the Blackflies, I also interviewed a prospector who identified himself only as O Renegado (The Renegade).

179 "Let's spread the word!": Chiquinho, personal interview.

180 *diamante xixi*: diamond buyers Eudack Colombi and Marcos Glikas, personal interviews.

181 a marketing operation: Edward Jay Epstein, "Have You Ever Tried to Sell a Diamond?" *The Atlantic*, February 1, 1982.

181 De Beers invited the Soviets: Kanfner 1993.

181 a sixty-five-year-old Israeli-Belgian: "Um crime brilhante," *Valor Econômico*, October 16, 2015.

CHAPTER 19: THE RUSH

185 the records of a diamond buyer: Federal Police memo on Ancelmo Peron, October 20, 2001.

190 "abandoned": "Índias ligam chacina a estupro e prostituição," *Folha de S.Paulo*, May 10, 2004.

192 a sprawling home: Federal Police memo, February 27, 2004, in addition to personal interviews. I also drove by with Alba.

CHAPTER 20: LOSING CONTROL

195 In November 2000: Francisco Marinho, Public Ministry memo, November 22, 2000; anonymous deposition, November 21, 2000; and Valdir de Jesus Gonçalves, Funai report, January 23, 2001.

196 Antonio Marcos de Almeida: Federal Police deposition, April 12, 2004.

196 a kilo of sausage: "Autorização para garimpo era [illegible] em código por associação indígena," *Diário da Amazônia*, February 22, 2002.

202 "I don't like wearing clothes": Marin 2017.

202 "Why didn't you bring me any money?": personal interview.

204 "Pio was overruled": Nazareno, personal interview.

204 "Cinta Larga leaders have once again": Geneval Rosa, Funai memo, January 18, 2001.

205 An official at Funai's base: Laerte Mendes Ferraz, Funai report, January 22, 2001.

CHAPTER 21: NEGOTIATIONS

206 "Indians today are synonymous with obesity": Alberto Fraga, comments before Congress, April 28, 2004.

206 "How can the people": conversation with Governor Ivo Cassol in September 2003, which I obtained video of.

207 "flying rivers": Alex Cuadros, "Has the Amazon Reached Its 'Tipping Point'?" *New York Times Magazine*, January 4, 2023.

208 "not doing well financially": Funai agent Osny Ferreira, deposition, February 28, 2003.

208 *pobre coitado*: Airton Oliveira, personal interview.

209 "pilot": Hargreaves, letter included in Public Ministry documents, January 21, 2002; and Max Salustiano, personal interview.

209 letter to Funai's president: January 10, 2002; the editorial is by Cláudio Weber Abramo, *Folha da Manhã*, September 13, 1994.

211 "suffocate agribusiness": "Bolsonaro diz que OAB só defende bandido e reserva indígena é um crime," *Campo Grande News*, April 22, 2015, cited by Survival International.

211 according to a former mining official: Oliveira, personal interview.

211 $6 million: "A nova maldição," cited above.

212 "two-story chalet": "Índios se associam a garimpeiros para explorar diamantes em reserva," November 11, 2007.

213 "one of the priciest neighborhoods": "Os caciques do diamante," cited above.

213 One journalist marveled: "Arco e flecha, só para pose diante das câmeras," *O Estado de S. Paulo*, April 23, 2004.

213 Other articles: e.g., "A nova maldição," *IstoÉ*, December 4, 2002.

213 he openly admitted: "Garimpeiros encontram mais diamantes em reserva indígena," *Diário da Amazônia*, February 20, 2001.

214 "family men": "PF tem dificuldade para retirar garimpeiros de reserva," January 15, 2001.

214 "People say I have bank accounts": conversation with Cassol, cited above.

215 "a preventive effort": Federal Police report, January 8, 2001.

215 A later video: I obtained this from a Federal Police agent who asked not to be named.

215 "steel box": Polícia Civil report, January 31, 2001.

215 Luca himself had informed them: Federal Police report, January 30, 2001.

216 a spectacular raid: personal interviews and untitled news item, *Jornal do Brasil*, May 24, 1999.

216 "Countless machines": Oliveira, letter to the Public Ministry, January 2, 2001.

216 "The Cinta Larga people are feared by all": Federal Police memo, undated but apparently from January 2001.

216 "the sincerity that is peculiar": Walter Blós, email to Public Ministry official, January 16, 2003.

217 "It was the white man who brought": Funai minutes, meeting with Cinta Larga leaders, August 23, 2004.

217 "It was Funai that taught us": November 17, 2017, meeting with Reginaldo Trindade.

217 "Why didn't you leave me": Funai minutes, cited above.

217 "sustainable development projects": "Policial diz que pode haver confronto," Agência Folha, February 16, 2001.

CHAPTER 22: BODIES

218 "Indian lands are there to be invaded!": "Amorim confirma invasão de reserva," *O Estadão do Norte*, April 26, 2002.

218 "record-holder for crimes in the state": "Amorim governará Rondônia do presídio 'Urso Branco,'" *O Estadão do Norte*, April 28, 2002.

218 cocaine trafficking: "Senado investigará suspeito de tráfico," *Jornal do Brasil*, February 16, 1995.

218 stripped of his seat: "TSE cassa o senador Ernandes Amorim," *Folha de S.Paulo*, August 25, 2000.

219 "If they legalize the mine only for the Indians": *PBS Frontline*, January 24, 2006.

220 "The CHIEF NACOÇA PIU": Jane Maria Rezende, letter to Public Ministry in Cacoal, October 15, 2001.

221 "woman at a brothel": Paulo Fermiano da Silva, Funai report, December 26, 2001.

221 "I might lose": I personally heard these messages.

222 "He looks out for us": "Empresário desmente denúncias contra Amorim," *Diário da Amazônia*, April 30, 2002.

222 "immediatist perspective": Edmundo Alves Gomes Filho, field diary, Procuradoria da República de Rondônia, March 2002.

223 A Public Ministry official would later find: Reginaldo Trindade, Procedimento Administrativo no. 1.31.000.000258/2004-16.

223 "They don't accumulate wealth": "Contato mudou vida dos cinta-larga," *Diário de Cuiabá*, July 14, 2002.

224 "I respectfully communicate": "Documento informativo aos seguintes órgãos e autoridades: FUNAI, Polícia Federal e Ibama," June 11, 2001.

225 "Around 2100 hours": Relatório de serviço da PMRO na Operação Roosevelt no período de 23/12/2001 a 30/12/2001.

225 He denied this: personal interview.

225 "he would understand how": testimony included with Public Ministry documents, undated.

226 "teach the Indians": deposition by José Esteves da Silva, May 21, 2001, case number 2001.41.00.001960-9, Porto Velho federal court.

226 "heavily armed": "Garimpeiros denunciam mais tocaias à justiça," *O Estadão do Norte*, August 31, 2001.

226 "the one who caused the most trouble": Sandra Martins de Araújo, deposition included in Funai internal investigation, case number 8620-1886/2001.

227 "I trusted him": testimony in Porto Velho federal court, April 13, 2004. case number 2331-67.2004.4.01.4100.

227 "I feel great exhaustion": Newlands 2007.

227 "smelled a strong bad smell": Samuel Ferreira de Souza, Federal Police deposition, August 23, 2001.

228 "Indians Suspected in Massacre": "Índios são suspeitos em chacina," *Diário da Amazônia*, August 28, 2001.

228 "cook's teenage daughter": Jean-Pierre Leroy, "Relatório Provisório da missão realizada junto ao povo Cinta Larga do 16 ao 18 de novembro de 2003."

228 "They kill one another": Pamaré Association document cited by Leroy.

229 "We believe": Federal Police inspector Marcos Aurélio Pereira de Moura, "Ofício no. 101/02-GAB/SR/DPF/RO," April 17, 2002.

CHAPTER 23: INVESTIGATIONS

231 "the main instigator": "Cadastro de envolvido," IPL no. 248/02-SR/DPF/RO. The court cases I drew on are mostly located at the federal courts in Ji-Paraná, Porto Velho, and Vilhena, and include case numbers 5532-91.2009.4.01.4100, 3584-82.2007.4.01.4101, 1925-04.2008.4.01.4101, 6477-88.2003.4.01.4100, 4613-20.2014.4.01.4103, 3618-57.2007.4.01.4101, 2112-12.2008.4.01.4101, 1364-43.2009.4.01.4101, 2405-79.2008.4.01.4101, 1893-94.2011.4.01.4100, and 4613-20.2014.4.01.4103, in addition to cases already cited above.

231 Marco Kalisch: "United States of America vs. Approximately 1,170 Carats of Rough Diamonds Seized at John F. Kennedy International Airport on January 13, 2002." See also "A New York Operator's Trail of Blood, Bankruptcy, and Brazilian Diamonds," *The Village Voice*, March 9, 2010.

231 links to Hezbollah: "Brasil vai ser investigado pelo tráfico de diamantes do garimpo Roosevelt," *Estado de Minas*, May 16, 2005.

232 "Diamonds are worse than cocaine": "Líder cinta-larga afirma que diamante é pior que cocaína," *Folha de S.Paulo*, Nov. 15, 2004.

232 "ensconced": "Cadastro de envolvido," cited above.

233 the feds intercepted a call: cited by Federal Prosecutor Daniel Azevedo Lobo, accusation in case 4613 (cited above), January 8, 2016.

234 *The Last of the Mohicans*: I owe the comparison to Skidmore 2005.

237 *"evasão de divisas"*: Federal Prosecutor Carlos Roberto Diogo Garcia et al., April 9, 2002, and Sousa, "Ofício no. 210/2002-Operação Resgate/SR/DPF/RO," April 21, 2002.

239 "perfectly integrated": Federal Judge Selmar Saraiva da Silva Filho, April 12, 2002.

CHAPTER 24: THE CRAZY ONE

240 a pair of journalists: myself and the photographer João Castellano. Woshyton now calls himself Washington.

242 "no corporations, no prospectors": "Índios Cinta-Larga realizam assembléia e querem autonomia em relação ao garimpo," Instituto Socioambiental website, citing João Dal Poz, June 19, 2002.

242 an idea from the white men: Oliveira, personal interview.

243 "We have decided not to work": letter dated April 19, 2003.

243 "The Indians' self-esteem": Walter Nicanor Fontoura Blos, "Memo no. 537/Grupo Tarefa/Portaria no. 1166/2002," December 8, 2003.

243 "defunct Lajes mine": Leroy, cited above.

245 "homeless encampment": Almir Rogerio Cancian, Federal Police deposition, April 22, 2004.

246 "They're such liars": Testimony before the Comissão Parlamentar de Inquérito "com a finalidade de apurar denúncias de irregularidades no garimpo denominado Roosevelt," October 30, 2003.

248 "Baiano Doido told me that he's a real man": Elaine Amorim and Kênia Alves, report for the Gully of Tranquility case (case no. 790-04.2015.4.01.4103 at the federal court in Vilhena).

248 one of Baiano's own friends: Max Salustiano, personal interview.

249 "Leave now, or the Indians will remove you": Hargreaves, personal interview, and Divaldo Pinheiro Moraes, Polícia Civil deposition, April 8, 2004.

249 "There were a lot of prospectors there": unidentified prospector, *Fantástico* (TV Globo), April 25, 2004.

250 One police officer noted: Sergeant Agnaldo Lube, Federal Police deposition, May 25, 2004.

253 It was better, he said: Hargreaves, letter to the Public Ministry, April 10, 2004.

254 "Funai never settles anything": Amorim and Alves, cited above.

CHAPTER 25: APRIL 7

258 A few witnesses saw them: among others, Antonio Marcos de Almeida, Federal Police deposition, April 12, 2004.

261 "Just go, man": Amorim and Alves, cited above.

262 Some would claim to have seen additional bodies: among others, Waldemiro Marques, Federal Police deposition, April 15, 2004.

262 A cook claimed to have seen: Orilza Cardoso Cruz, Federal Police deposition, April 11, 2004.

263 Arilton Carlos dos Santos: personal interview.

264 Polaco...had hidden himself: Marafon, personal interview.

265 rumors that the warriors had covered: Maria Gertrudes Veras da Silva, Federal Police deposition, April 12, 2004.

266 two Funai officials showed up: Walter Blós and Daniel Farah, testimony in federal court in Vilhena, November 23, 2023.

EPILOGUE

272 "Yes...because they were tired": *Fantástico*, cited above.

273 "Five years might pass": Pio, personal interview.

273 "Civilized Cannibals": "Cinta Larga: os canibais civilizados de Rondônia," *Rondoniagora*, April 19, 2004.

273 "impunity of murderous Indians": Alberto Fraga's comments before Congress on April 26, 2004.

273 nineteen distinct groups: Instituto Socioambiental.

274 "are not subordinated": Federal Police deposition, June 15, 2004.

274 "that the warriors live 'in the jungle'": Zezinho Cinta Larga, Federal Police deposition, June 29, 2004.

274 "that they did not wait": Isaac Cinta Larga, Federal Police deposition, July 26, 2004.

275 "that the prospectors invaded": Gabriel Cinta Larga, Federal Police deposition, July 27, 2004.

275 "if [he] had been present": Federal Police deposition, June 16, 2004.

SELECTED BIBLIOGRAPHY

Branford, Sue, and Oriel Glock. *The Last Frontier: Fighting over Land in the Amazon.* London: Zed Books, 1985.

Chapelle, Richard. *Os índios Cintas-Largas.* Belo Horizonte: Livraria Itatiaia Editora, 1982.

Cinta Larga, Pichuvy. *Histórias de maloca antigamente.* Edited by Ana Leonel Queiroz, Ivete Lara Camargos, and Leda Lima Leonel. Belo Horizonte: SEGRAC-CIMI, 1988.

Dal Poz, João. *No país dos Cinta Larga: uma etnografia do ritual.* Universidade de São Paulo, master's dissertation, 1991.

———. *Dádivas e dívidas na Amazônia: parentesco, economia e ritual nos Cinta-Larga.* Universidade de Campinas, doctoral thesis, 2004.

Davis, Shelton H. *Victims of the Miracle: Development and the Indians of Brazil.* New York: Cambridge University Press, 1977.

Ermel, Priscilla. *O sentido místico do som: ressonâncias estéticas da música tribal dos índios Cinta-Larga.* Pontifícia Universidade Católica de São Paulo, master's dissertation, 1988.

Freire, Carlos Augusto da Rocha. *Sagas sertanistas: práticas e representações no campo indigenista no século XX.* Universidade Federal do Rio de Janeiro, doctoral thesis, 2005.

Hemming, John. *Die If You Must: Brazilian Indians in the Twentieth Century.* London: Pan Macmillan, 2003.

———. *Tree of Rivers: The Story of the Amazon.* London: Thames and Hudson, 2008.

Junqueira, Carmen. *Sexo e desigualdade: entre os Kamaiurá e os Cinta Larga.* São Paulo: Olho d'Água, 2002.

Kanfner, Stefan. *The Last Empire: De Beers, Diamonds, and the World*. New York: Farrar Straus & Giroux, 1993.

King, Charles. *Gods of the Upper Air: How a Circle of Renegade Anthropologists Reinvented Race, Sex, and Gender in the Twentieth Century*. New York: Doubleday, 2019.

Levi-Strauss, Claude. *Tristes Tropiques*. London: Hutchison, 1961.

Mann, Charles. *1491: New Revelations of the Americas before Columbus*. New York: Knopf, 2005.

Marin, Nadja. *Memória, violência e território: de zapiway a cacique e a constituição do Povo Cinta Larga*. Universidade de São Paulo, doctoral thesis, 2017.

Milanez, Felipe, ed. *Memórias sertanistas: cem anos de indigenismo no Brasil*. São Paulo: SESC, 2015.

Millard, Candice. *River of Doubt: Theodore Roosevelt's Darkest Journey*. New York: Doubleday, 2005.

Moura, Marlene C. Ossami, ed. *Memória das imagens: olhares multiculturais sobre o Acervo Jesco Puttkamer*. Goiânia: Editora Acadêmica, 2017.

Newlands, Lilian. *Apoena: o homem que enxerga longe*. Goiânia: Editora da UCG, 2007.

Rohter, Larry. *Rondon: uma biografia*. Rio de Janeiro: Objetiva, 2019.

Rondon, Cândido Mariano da Silva. *Conferências realizadas nos dias 5, 7 e 9 de Outubro no Theatro Phenix do Rio de Janeiro e referentes a trabalhos executados sob sua chefia pela Expedição Scientifica Roosevelt-Rondon e pela Comissão Telegráfica*. Rio de Janeiro: Jornal do Commercio, 1916.

Roosevelt, Theodore. *Through the Brazilian Wilderness*. New York: C. Scribner's Sons, 1914.

Sahlins, Marshall. *Stone Age Economics*. Chicago: Aldine Atherton, 1972.

Silva, Amizael Gomes da. *No rastro dos pioneiros: um pouco da história rondoniana.* Porto Velho: SEDUC, 1984.

Skidmore, Thomas. *Black into White: Race and Nationality in Brazilian Thought.* Durham: Duke University Press, 2005.

Tressmann, Ismael. *Panderej: os peritos no arco.* São Leopoldo: Conselho de Missão entre Povos Indígenas, 1993.

Treuer, David. *The Heartbeat of Wounded Knee: Native America from 1890 to the Present.* New York: Penguin, 2019.

Valente, Rubens. *Os fuzis e as flechas: história de sangue e resistência indígena na ditadura.* São Paulo: Companhia das Letras, 2017.

Wallace, Scott. *The Unconquered: In Search of the Amazon's Last Uncontacted Tribes.* New York: Crown, 2011.

ABOUT THE AUTHOR

Alex Cuadros is the author of *Brazillionaires: Wealth, Power, Decadence, and Hope in an American Country*, which was long-listed for the *Financial Times* Business Book of the Year award. A former Bloomberg staff reporter, he's also written for the *New York Times Magazine*, the *New Yorker*, *Harper's*, *The Atlantic*, and the *Washington Post*, and his article on the Amazon's ecological tipping point was chosen for 2024's *Best American Science and Nature Writing*. This book was supported by the Alicia Patterson Foundation and the Fund for Investigative Journalism. Cuadros has also received grants from the Pulitzer Center on Crisis Reporting. He spent six years based in Brazil and has been reporting from the Amazon since 2013. He now lives with his wife in San Francisco.